ROYAL HISTORICAL SOCIETY

STUDIES IN HISTORY 65

RELIGION AND URBAN CHANGE

RELIGION
AND
URBAN CHANGE

CROYDON
1840–1914

J. N. Morris

THE ROYAL HISTORICAL SOCIETY
THE BOYDELL PRESS

First published 1992

A Royal Historical Society publication
Published by The Boydell Press
an imprint of Boydell & Brewer Ltd
PO Box 9   Woodbridge   Suffolk IP12 3DF   UK
and of Boydell & Brewer Inc.
PO Box 41026   Rochester   NY 14604   USA

ISBN 0 86193 222 6

ISSN 0269-2244

British Library Cataloguing-in-Publication Data
Morris, J. N.
    Religion   and   Urban   Change: Croydon,
    1840–1914. – (Royal Historical Society Studies
    in History, ISSN 0269-2244; No. 65)
    I. Title   II. Series
    942.19108
    ISBN 0-86193-222-6

Library of Congress Cataloging-in-Publication Data applied for

The paper used in this publication meets the minimum requirements
of American National Standard for Information Sciences –
Permanence of Paper for Printed Library Materials, ANSI Z39.48–1984

Printed in Great Britain by
St Edmundsbury Press Ltd, Bury St Edmunds, Suffolk

Contents

The Society records its gratitude to the following whose generosity made possible the initiation of this series: The British Academy; The Pilgrim Trust; The Twenty-Seven Foundation; The United States Embassy's Bicentennial funds; The Wolfson Trust; several private donors.

Publication of this volume was aided by a further generous grant from the Twenty-Seven Foundation.

Acknowledgements

My first thanks must go to the staff of the Croydon Public and Reference Library, and especially to Deborah Garrett, Martin Hayes, Howard Taylor and Steve Roud for their constant patience and thoughtfulness over the years it has taken to complete this study. They are probably aware that Croydon possesses an unusually rich and largely unresearched local archive; their readiness to make the treasures of this collection available to me (despite the incomplete and somewhat antiquated catalogue) has made my work much easier than it would otherwise have been. I have benefited from the work of a number of local historians who have raided this archive; in particular, as will be evident from the footnotes, I have been able to draw on that of Dr R. C. W. Cox, and on his enthusiasm and encouragement. I must also thank the staff of Lambeth Palace Library, Surrey County Record Office, the Greater London Record Office and the Public Record Office.

This book began life as an Oxford DPhil thesis. I owe a great debt to my supervisor, Colin Matthew, who consistently supported my research, offered frank and constructive criticism, and gave up much of his valuable time to helping me. Others who have read parts of this work over the years, offered encouragement and comment, and whom I would like to thank are: Dr A. H. Halsey, Professor F. M. L. Thompson, Dr John Davis, Dr J. D. Walsh, Dr W. S. F. Pickering, Canon P. B. Hinchliff (under whose aegis I studied the special subject out of which my interest in this thesis first arose), and Mr J. M. Prest. Also I want to thank, for their support and for their conversations on this research, Chris Zealley, Graham Wright, Ying Chang, Hazel Mills, Chris Williams, and Jonathan Devlin. Latterly I want to thank in particular my editor, Christine Linehan, for her patience in seeing this book through to its production.

There are many local people I ought to thank: Mrs Gladys Osmotherley, Miss Nina Foster, Miss Helen and Miss Mary Smorthwaite, Mr L. W. Hoare, Mr D. O. Rawling and Mr W. D. Tonkyn, who all shared with me their memories of pre-1914 Croydon; those clergy of the archdeaconry of Croydon and ministers of the Free Churches who helped in locating church records and made them available to me; and many members of the Croydon Natural History and Scientific Society who shared their local interest with me. I would also like to mention my gratitude to the following: the Rev David Curwen, the Rev David Tonkinson, the Rev Philip Hendry and the congregation of St Andrew's Church, the Rev Canon John Cox, the Rev Steven Williams, and all the members of my adult education classes. Thanks too to the Rev Alun Glyn-Jones and Mr Kenneth James, headmaster and deputy-headmaster of my old school, who have always been a source of support, and to Mr Albert Ashmore of the Salvation Army, Mr Henry Ecroyd, Clerk of the Croydon Friends, and Mr Mark Hayler, Quaker, pacifist and temperance historian.

I owe a special debt to my family for the tolerance with which they have met my enthusiasms and for the support they have always given, and to Alex, my wife, for her unfailing encouragement and attention.

J. N. Morris
Cambridge 1992

Abbreviations

C Ad	*The Croydon Advertiser*
G Guardian	*The Croydon Guardian*
C Chron.	*The Croydon Chronicle*
C Ref Lib	Croydon Public and Reference Library
C Review	*The Croydon Review*
LBH	Croydon Local Board of Health
Proc CHNSS	Proceedings of the Croydon Natural History and Scientific Society

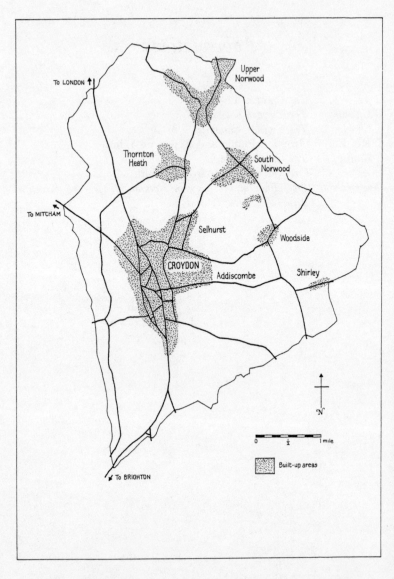

Map 1: Principal roads and settlements of Croydon Parish, c.1868
(Based on the parish engineer Baldwin Latham's map of the
parish, dated March 1868; visible at Croydon Public Library)

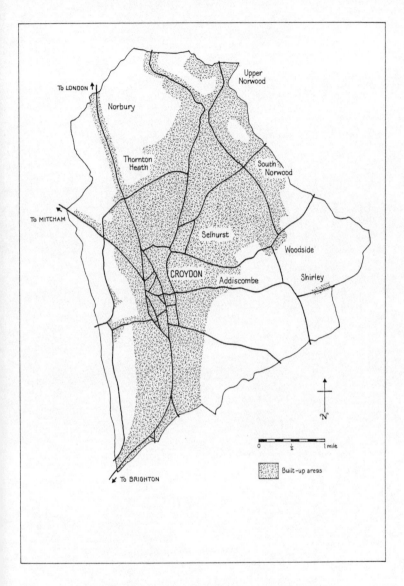

Map 2: Built-up areas of Croydon Borough, c.1914
(Based on Ordnance Survey One-Inch Series,
revised c.1910–1911)

1

Introduction

The subject of this book is the impact of urban expansion and the processes of social change which accompanied it upon the development of Victorian and Edwardian organised religion, that is to say the religion of churches and their associated agencies. The area chosen for investigation, the borough of Croydon, underwent massive urban expansion in the period under study, a process the physical and geographical outlines of which have been described in some considerable detail elsewhere by R. C. W. Cox.[1] The general contours of Victorian suburban growth in London and its environs have been mapped out by the work of H. J. Dyos[2], F. M. L. Thompson[3], D. J. Olsen[4], and Cox himself and others, and it is not with these geographical and physical aspects of urbanisation as it impinged upon the churches that this book is directly concerned, but with the social and cultural conditions of Victorian urban areas, the changes brought about in this superstructure by urban expansion, and above all the impact of this kind of growth, with its cultural and social implications, on organised religion.

The particular problems in the historiography of nineteenth- and early twentieth-century religion which I have sought to confront are those which bear directly upon what has (often misleadingly) been called the decline of religion in England, though it could be argued that the changes in church and local life identified did not always imply actual shrinkage in terms of numbers of members and attenders and of financial resources, since they could subsist within a context of modest growth. The problems which the churches faced in the period were not exclusive to urban areas – as Obelkevich's study has demonstrated[5] – but they derived peculiar force from the increasing concentration of the population in towns and cities; the whole pattern of English cultural and social life was increasingly

[1] R. C. W. Cox, 'The Urban Development of Croydon 1870–1940', unpubl. MA thesis, Leicester 1967; 'The Urban Development and Redevelopment of Croydon 1835–1940', unpubl. PhD thesis, Leicester 1970.
[2] H. J. Dyos, *Camberwell: the growth of a suburb* (Leicester 1961).
[3] F. M. L. Thompson, *Hampstead: building a borough* (London 1974).
[4] D. J. Olsen, *The Growth of Victorian London* (London 1976).
[5] J. Obelkevich, *Religion and Rural Society in South Lindsey 1825–1875* (Oxford 1976).

ordered and directed by urban expansion and by the particular cluster of values and conditions the Victorians came to associate with the city. It is generally accepted by historians that urban development carried enormous significance for the churches, but the nature of the linkages is more contentious.

Contrary to the impression given by many clergymen and ministers of religion in the nineteenth century, who had their anxieties too closely pinned to working class districts, urban growth was not a monolithic process which necessarily spelt long-term disaster for the churches. It could present opportunities for religious organisations, especially because in the particular economic context in which it occurred it involved a growth in the numbers and wealth of those social classes – the middle and lower middle classes – on which the churches above all relied. Attention has been drawn by Geoffrey Crossick to the expansion of these groups (particularly white collar, clerical workers and their families) against a background of growth in an imperialist, international economy in the late nineteenth century (which boosted the financial and commercial importance of London), by the growth of an internal service sector of the economy, and by the commercialisation and bureaucratisation of the 'secondary sector'.[6] All of these general economic trends took place in a specific context of suburban growth as the increased labour force demanded more housing; an important but secondary process was the associated growth of retailing and other services. It is appropriate, then, to study the religious practices and habits of the suburban middle and lower middle classes as they affected religious organisations, and in the process to move away from the concentration upon the study of working class responses to religion and the performance of churches in industrial centres which hitherto has tended to mark the local study of organised religion in nineteenth century Britain.

The general social effects of urban expansion and industrialisation in the nineteenth century can be characterised as falling under four headings: first, social differentiation, particularly the separation and specialisation of work and leisure which was both a product and a cause of the differentiation of social groups; second, the social segregation of residential patterns of the different social classes. There was, thirdly, the routinisation of work and leisure, a process which implied the subjection of work and leisure to more rigid, formal procedures and written regulations. Finally, there was the dissolution of pre-existing social and economic ties and their replacement by alternative social bonds. These effects had certain implications for

[6] G. Crossick, 'The emergence of the lower middle class in Britain. A discussion' in *idem*. (ed.), *The Lower Middle Class in Britain* (London 1977).

voluntary organisations, perhaps the most immediate of which were the problems they faced in trying to maintain numbers and appeal and to resist the temptation to make themselves secure by drawing on ever more specialised categories of membership, and the problems of maintaining, extending and consolidating their financial and institutional structures.[7] The Victorian churches were affected by the process of urban change perhaps to a greater extent in that, given the character of salvationist religions, they tended to lay even greater stress on the importance of expansion than other kinds of organisations. Religion was perceived by religious groups themselves in the nineteenth century as an essential component of social life, and not as a specialised interest or as one alternative form of commitment amongst many available to the urban population; however they may have defined membership – and the definitions were naturally subject to social perceptions – most churches continued to see their ultimate aim as drawing in the largest possible numbers to their exclusive kinds of religious activity.

Fears about declining influence were just as acute, if not more so, amongst churchmen at the end of the nineteenth century as they were amongst activists in strictly non-religious movements in the same period. The belief that the churches were passing through a crisis was widespread, and the local evidence is reviewed in detail later in this book. However the decline was not universal, and – from a late twentieth century standpoint – was as yet slight. The issue of decline poses two distinct if related problems: first, the question why organised religion by the late nineteenth century appeared to be failing to keep pace with the growing population and in some areas was facing positive decline (and thus what were the origins of the sense of crisis to which many churchmen in the period gave expression); and second, the question as to whether any changes (and if so, of what kind) in the status and role of the churches were taking place, and what was the significance of these changes for the future of organised religion in England.

The decline of religion in England has been the subject of lively historiographical interest in recent years. Three particular kinds of approach to the problem have helped to influence the research on which this book is based, as much by the ways in which they fall short

---

[7] One of the 'bones' of Stephen Yeo's argument was that 'Many religious organisations circa 1890 in Reading were, alongside many other voluntary organisations, trying to attract numbers unlimited into their doors. By a variety of provisions *for* people, they were trying to render themselves *of* unlimited numbers of the people to the deepest extent possible.'[italics original]: C. S. Yeo, *Religion and Voluntary Organisations in Crisis* (London 1976), p. 2.

of a total explanation as by the very real contributions they make to the subject. One of these approaches is characterised by a concentration upon intellectual and high political changes, implying that the weaknesses of the churches in late Victorian society were largely conditioned by the political controversies surrounding church reform, by sectarian rivalry in politics, and by the convergence of various strands of intellectual criticism of religion. Exponents of this approach have tended to devote their attention principally to the activities of leading religious intellectuals and politicians of the period. Owen Chadwick, for example, argued of the 'unsettlement of faith' of the mid-century that: 'Three forces were driving Christianity to restate doctrine: natural science, historical criticism, moral feeling. Natural science shattered assumptions about Genesis and about miracles. Criticism questioned whether all history in the Bible was true. Moral feeling found the love of God hard to reconcile with hellfire or scapegoat-atonement.'[8] Although in *The Secularization of the European Mind in the Nineteenth Century* Chadwick laid stress on 'unsettlement in society', it was examined chiefly through the medium of the writings of influential politicians and writers, and even then equal weight was accorded to 'unsettlement in minds, rising out of a heap of new knowledge in science and in history, and out of the consequent argument'.[9] Marsh's account of the archiepiscopacy of Tait illustrates a related tendency, namely to accord a key role to influential ecclesiastics.[10]

The cogency of such an approach at the national level begins to disintegrate however the more carefully evidence is sifted at the local level. K. S. Inglis drew attention to the extreme difficulty churchmen of all denominations experienced, whatever the strategies they adopted and however influential they were in themselves, in countervailing a tide of apparent indifference in working class areas.[11] Religious and political controversies clearly had an impact on local religious life, even if in a filtered-down form; nevertheless there is little hard evidence to support such a contention. The absence of systematic, reliable evidence of clerical and lay reading habits at the local level means that it is almost impossible to gauge the real impact of intellectual changes in the period.

---

[8] W. O. Chadwick, *The Victorian Church* (London 1966–70). i, 551.

[9] *Idem, The Secularisation of the European Mind in the Nineteenth Century* (Cambridge 1975), p. 250.

[10] P. T. Marsh, *The Victorian Church in Decline: Archbishop Tait and the Church of England, 1868–1882* (London 1969).

[11] K. S. Inglis, *Churches and the Working Classes in Victorian England* (London 1963), pp. 333–6.

A second approach to the study of organised religion in the Victorian and Edwardian period offers not so much an explanation of change as a description of it: it is the attempt various authors have made to characterise the development of the churches according to some variant of the church-denomination-sect typologies developed by sociologists of religion, and generally arguing for a convergence on 'denominational' features in the period. Bryan Wilson characterised the denomination as voluntary but not exclusive, ready to admit new members without exacting tests of merit, disclaiming exclusive monopoly of truth (and hence prepared to work with other religious organisations), prepared to accept a measure of religious specialisation (i.e. a professional ministry and full-time executive agencies), evolving a bureaucracy (even though, Wilson asserted, the denomination may carry over an emphasis on lay participation from a sectarian past), and, finally, compromised with the world in the sense of accepting generally the values of the wider society, making only formal demands for different and higher standards from its own members, and no longer emphasising its hostility to the world.[12] All of these characteristics would ally the 'denomination' as described by Wilson (and others) to the model of an 'associational' kind of organisation derived from the work of Ferdinand Tönnies[13], its leading characteristics being its voluntary nature, its formal organisation, its rational administrative methods, its relatively low required commitment, and its specialised constituency. The problems posed by this kind of analysis are important for an analysis of urban religion because the assumption apparently made by such writers as Wilson, and explicitly emphasised in A. D. Gilbert's *Religion and Society in Industrial England*, is that the effect of long-run industrial and social change in the nineteenth century, particularly in the context of urbanisation, was to produce a situation in which most churches and religious groups were forced more or less to approximate to a denominational type of religion in order to survive:

First non-Anglican religious institutions, once forced to adopt the sectarian position of withdrawal from a rejection of the dominant culture, were able increasingly to choose the denominational alternative of accommodation to one of the cultural components of the pluralistic society. Secondly, the church type organisation was placed in an increasingly untenable position as the unitary culture fragmented. Thus, while the early nineteenth century saw

[12] B. R. Wilson, *Religion in Secular Society* (London 1966), p. 70.
[13] F. Tönnies, *Community and Association* (1888, trans. London 1955).

previously sect type Nonconformist organisations evolving towards denominationalism, it also witnessed the religious Establishment being forced inexorably towards *de facto* denominational
status.[14]

An initial objection to the denomination-association characterisation
of religious organisations in the late nineteenth century, apart from
the more obvious problems of maintenance of a certain Establishment
status on the part of the Anglican church, is that originally suggested
by R. S. Moore with regard to Methodism in Durham mining
communities,[15] but applicable in some degree to urban churches,
namely that in many important respects the church or chapel
functioned as a centre of communal attention, providing, for
example, a focus of community leisure and culture and a forum for
inter-marriage, and stressing church membership as membership of a
community; the implication of this is that whilst a church may
ostensibly conform to the denominational type by making relatively
low demands of its membership in terms of commitment and
articulated standards of behaviour, the informal or non-theological
pressures towards common modes of behaviour amongst its membership may in fact be very strong. Although in organisation and
administration a religious group in modern urban society may
approximate to Wilson's 'type' of a denomination, in operation, and
in terms of the relationship it tends to encourage amongst its
members, its character may be much more akin to communal kinds
of organisation. This presumably is a very strong factor behind the
relative stability of endogenous growth in the churches in the
nineteenth century noted by Currie, Gilbert and Horsley,[16] the
importance accorded to the maintenance of pre-existing membership
once revivalistic cycles had passed, and the relative instability of
exogenous growth; after all, although the formal demands of the
organisation may not have been very high, the demands made upon
an individual convert in terms of lifestyles, personal contacts, and so
on, could mark a sharp break with his previous pattern of life.

This leads on to a second and, from the point of view of religious
reactions to urban growth, a more important criticism of the
conventional denominational typology, which is that despite the

[14] A. D. Gilbert, *Religion and Society in Industrial England* (London 1976), p. 140.
[15] R. S. Moore, *Pitmen, Preachers and Politics: Methodism in a Durham mining community*
(Cambridge 1974), p. 27.
[16] R. Currie, A. D. Gilbert and A. Horsley, *Churches and Churchgoers: patterns of church
growth in the British Isles since 1700* (Oxford 1977), pp. 79–84.

abandonment of exclusive religious claims, religious organisations which have eschewed quietism and a predestinarian theology by their very nature cannot renounce supra-group aspirations; their emphasis on offering to those ready to believe in their message the prospect of salvation exerts a strong pressure within the organisation towards the constant expansion of the organisation's membership. In this sense, religious organisations are not simply voluntary organisations. The extent to which they seek to express these implicit, missionary impulses will be dependent upon other sets of variables, the most immediately operative for the churches being the recognition that sections of the population are 'untouched' by religion or touched by the wrong kind of religion, the belief that missionary activity is possible given the resources the churches are able to draw upon and the kinds of conditions in which they will have to work, and so in turn the perception that previous, similar kinds of evangelising have exhibited a degree of success which will make further effort worthwhile. Also operative are the standards of commitment and behaviour a religious group requires of its members. In the nineteenth century population expansion and urban concentration created for the religious a particularly strong incentive to increase missionary activity, and this combined with the salvationist claims made by the churches to intensify sectarian rivalry wherever the urban context made available to the competing churches a pool of the 'spiritually destitute' as potential members. Operating inexorably inside the churches themselves, forcing constant revaluation of tactics and resources, was the logic of their own expansion: this included the need to finance buildings and pay ministers, and to fund and man the various ancillary bodies which, clustered around church or chapel by the end of the century, the churches themselves had come to see as necessary adjuncts to the missionary enterprise.

A third argument employed to explain the vicissitudes of the churches in nineteenth- and twentieth-century society has centred around a close analysis of the social basis of religious support, and has tended to suggest that the character of organised religion and the responses to it were conditioned principally by the life styles of the different social classes. The most ambitious attempt to relate religious behaviour to social class in the Victorian city which has appeared so far is Hugh McLeod's *Class and Religion in the late Victorian City*. McLeod's work is quite consciously an exercise in the study of religious behaviour as it was affected by social class, and not a history of religious groups and religious organisations. Middle class attitudes and ways of life, and in particular the series of moral values implied in adherence to notions of respectability, made the middle class, McLeod argues, especially receptive to organised religion in the late

Victorian city.[17] Upper class families tended to retain strong links with the Anglican Church, but McLeod queries the qualitative strength of their attachment, implying that the social and political overtones of religious belief were ultimately for most of the upper class more important than its spiritual and than religious experience – the truly religious were exceptional.[18] The working class, by reason of their necessary preoccupation with material problems relating to food and survival, their suspicion of the political and social associations of religious organisations, and the hedonistic 'here today, gone tomorrow' attitude towards leisure that tended to accompany a pattern of life in which surplus income for 'luxury' spending was comparatively irregular and unpredictable, were generally impervious to the activity of religious organisations:[19] families who did join a church tended, by virtue of their changed pattern of life as well as because of their neighbours' reactions, to become separated in outlook from the rest of the working class, and eventually to rise in the social scale.[20] Obviously there are important patterns of differentiation within the middle and working classes as a whole. McLeod's work has been supplemented by subsequent commentators, directly or indirectly, at various points. Crossick's study of the labour aristocracy in Kentish London reinforces McLeod's picture of lower middle class status anxieties, and supplements the overall picture of late Victorian society in the city by delineating the relationships of the artisan elite, conscious of its separation from the lifestyles of the unskilled working classes and less susceptible to the same kind of self-consciousness about social position as the lower middle class, to other social groups, stressing the independent and self-help elements of artisan ideology that subsequently emerged, and how this tended to make them receptive to moral crusades with religious overtones such as the temperance movement, but less inclined than their lower middle class partners towards active participation in religious organisations.[21] Gray has drawn attention to similar features in the social structure of Victorian white-collar workers.[22] The explanation sought for the religious behaviour of the social classes in these works tends to be framed in terms of the receptivity of groups to organised religion, that is to say it is depicted largely as a passive process. Gray, it is true, admits elsewhere that in

[17] D. H. McLeod, *Class and Religion in the Late Victorian City* (London 1974), pp. 139–43.
[18] *Ibid.*, pp. 200–3.
[19] *Ibid.*, pp. 43–60.
[20] A point also noted by Inglis, *Churches and the Working Classes*, pp. 334–5.
[21] G. Crossick, *An Artisan Elite in Kentish London* (London 1977).
[22] R. Q. Gray, *The Labour Aristocracy in Victorian Edinburgh* (London 1978).

some respects the absorption and adaptation of upper class hege-
monic values by the 'middling strata' gave these social groups some
part in shaping urban culture, but his analysis does not make clear
what specific role religious organisations played in this process,
whether they became 'projections' of middle strata ideology, whether
they were impositions upon middle class cultures, or whether they
held a purely instrumental value.[23] The 'McLeod' perspective has
been outlined in some detail here because I see no reason seriously to
question the description of the mores, lifestyle and attitudes of
different social classes in the Victorian city to which this group of
writers has drawn attention, although I note, in McLeod's more
recent work, a greater emphasis on the persistence of religious
awareness in the working class for most of the nineteenth century.[24]

There are, however, from the point of view of an explanation of the
changes churches underwent in the Victorian and Edwardian period,
certain problems in the kind of analysis McLeod and others have
presented. Since they are describing norms of behaviour and
underlying structures of motivation, the ways in which religious
organisations actually engaged with the society in which they were
situated, and the dynamic reasons for their expansion, stagnation or
decline, tend to be obscured. A religious message could be
understood by social groups in terms of their collective attitudes,
traditions and expectations, yet within this scale of values their
response to churches could still be interpreted in terms of ulterior,
ultra-religious ambitions, whereby churches became the subject of
attention from certain social groups because they could be valuable
instruments for achieving desired ends, of rejection by others who
were unable for various reasons to use the churches in the same way,
and of bitter in-fighting amongst others because the churches were
held to be so important in shaping the pattern of local life. A second
point follows on from this: if the churches could become valuable as
perceived means to certain specific ends (ends which could be
practical as well as ideological) rather than simply ends in themselves,
then there is a sense in which they would have become particularly
useful to minority groups or elite groups, precisely those who would
tend to be eliminated from an analysis of class-based religious
behaviour which delineated class typologies or norms of behaviour.
McLeod's configuration of late Victorian urban culture in terms of
overlapping circles of community-consciousness leads him to omit

---

[23] *Idem*, 'Religion, culture and social class in late nineteenth and early twentieth
century Edinburgh', in Crossick, *The Lower Middle Class*, p. 151.
[24] See especially D. H. McLeod, 'New perspectives on Victorian class religion: the
oral evidence', *Oral History*, xiv (1986).

from discussion that social group whose influence in shaping the pattern and success of church activities would have been of the greatest importance: the 'petty capitalists', whom he describes as retailers and small employers who shared both a working class localism and a middle class taste for organisation, and who held to a definition of community less narrow than that of the working class.[25] These 'petty capitalists' were certainly, as McLeod admits, a class apart from the rest in the local context: they were a local elite, active in local government, running local newspapers and taking up important posts on local charities, leisure societies and churches, and their role in the development of religious organisations at local level was enormous. Their distinct community sense was reflected in the plethora of local registers, newspapers and municipal histories published by local printers in the late nineteenth century, and typical as much of market towns rapidly growing into metropolitan suburbs, such as Croydon itself, as of rural market towns. Furthermore, although in economic terms a separate class, they were reinforced from below by small independent artisans and tradesmen who 'made it good' as businessmen and from above by professional men who could, despite the wider national sense implicit in higher education and training, be just as dependent upon local business and remain rooted to local boundaries as the petty capitalists – this is particularly so with doctors, teachers and, of course, clergymen. Asa Briggs, with the examples of Birmingham and Manchester in mind, criticised 'continental sociologists' for regarding urban relationships as impersonal;[26] even in rapidly expanding Victorian cities facing mass problems of housing, poverty and working conditions the urban elite was nevertheless compact, highly motivated by an interest in local affairs, and reliant upon personal contacts within the elite to control their cities. Religion was often inseparable from local politics: it is Briggs again who has suggested that Nonconformist ministers were a significant influence behind the 'civic gospel' which emerged in some mid-nineteenth century cities,[27] and for Anglicans the connections would always have existed.

Having considered at some length three of the most influential modes of explaining the history of organised religion in Victorian and Edwardian England, it is necessary briefly to outline a fourth which has appeared too recently to influence the research on which this book is based. In his *Competing Convictions*, Robin Gill has advanced a theory that the origins of church decline in Britain are to be sought in

[25] McLeod, *Class and Religion*, pp. 14–15.
[26] A. Briggs, *Victorian Cities* (London 1963), p. 102.
[27] *Ibid.*, p. 195.

inter-church rivalry in the last century, because this led to a situation in which denominations built more accommodation than was needed in practice, and so in time their 'over-provision' would appear to have discouraged would-be attenders. Gill's argument is based in part on data on church attendance and accommodation drawn from a series of rural, north-eastern parishes in which the picture of 'over-provision' was sharply accentuated by population decline, though he asserts that it has wider implications, not only for rural society but also, tentatively, for urban society since urban church decline followed as a 'second stage' the decline perceptible in rural areas from the mid to late nineteenth century. I find this argument a puzzling one. Gill charts two quite separate, observable trends – over-provision of church accommodation, and a decline in per capita church attendance – and simply assumes a link between them. He attempts to amplify the nature of this link, which is crucial to his argument, at one point only: 'Over-building must have contributed to empty churches and empty churches contributed to the closing of churches and the closing of churches may have contributed (along with persisting empty churches) to a percentage decline in church-going.'[28] That speculative 'may have' demonstrates how weak, in practice, the assumption of a link really is: it depends upon an assumed pattern on the part of would-be churchgoers for which Gill provides no substantial evidence. There does not seem to be any reason why, *a priori*, inter-church rivalry should be seen as deterring churchgoers, nor does there seem to be any reason, necessarily, why would-be churchgoers should be deterred by less than full buildings. The argument, then, does not appear to work satisfactorily as an explanation for the data presented by Gill himself; even less so can it work as an explanation for areas where the population was expanding rapidly, where church accommodation remained well below the level of population, and yet where per capita decline was already occurring in the last decades of the nineteenth century.

This book seeks to build upon these criticisms of previous types of explanation of changes within the Victorian and Edwardian churches and of their changing role within society in several ways. First, it is a deliberate examination of localised tensions, conflicts and relationships. A realisation of the need to locate religious developments in terms of their local as well as national social and political contexts is implicit in Yeo's work; it is arguably one of the most neglected areas of the study of nineteenth century religion generally. This is not to say that local religious studies in themselves are too thin on the ground, but rather that those local studies which have appeared have

---

[28] R. Gill, *Competing Convictions* (London 1989), pp. 91–2.

11

in the main concentrated on the congruences between church growth and social change without examining where the linkages occurred in terms of church policy, local religious activity, and the local aspects of national developments. Attention to local issues does not neutralise generalisations about church growth, because it is possible still to construct general arguments and typologies of development on the assumption that despite the infinite variation in local circumstances from one area to another, underlying structural developments in the British economy and society conditioned the emergence of certain common strands in social relationships. Such a realisation underlies W. R. Ward's study of local issues such as the struggle over church rates in Rochdale and Manchester and that over church building in Manchester and its surrounding environs to illuminate the weakness of Anglican central authority, the use of issues such as church rate to stoke up heat in arguments between Anglicans and Dissenters, and the problems of order and the inflexibilities of the parochial system.[29]

Secondly, since organised religion has been taken as the principal focus of analysis, the book tends to concentrate on the religious beliefs and above all practices of the middle classes. The pressures the churches faced towards the expansion of their organisations and scale of activities in a society undergoing urban growth meant that they tended to become reliant for finance, active, voluntary, lay support and ultimately recruitment to ministry and membership on the middle and lower middle classes. This trend was rarely absolute: dilution was still possible by older, 'aristocratic' or 'establishment' values at one end, and by working class influence at the other end. Religion thus became moulded after the middle class fashion: religion itself became one vital facet of middle class culture in Victorian towns and cities, and although the churches constantly aimed to expand to embrace all social groups, the methods by which they hoped to do so began to acquire specifically middle class forms. Even revivalism tended to become assimilated to urban middle class norms, with the abandonment of the spontaneous emotional excesses of earlier revivalistic movements for more restrained, orderly and planned occasions relying for their impact upon preaching by trained professional preachers and organised singing, as John Kent's studies have shown.[30] The corollary of this was that the churches also became a means by which middle class values and aspirations could be expressed, so that they became important participants in local issues and in local power struggles between rival political and social groups;

[29] W. R. Ward, *Religion and Society in England 1790–1850* (London 1972).
[30] J. H. S. Kent, *Holding the Fort: studies in Victorian revivalism* (London 1978).

the shape of religion in urban centres was affected by the course and result of these power struggles.

Having stated that organised religion was a middle class phenomenon in the main, two important qualifications need to be made here. The first is that there were a number of areas of overlap between working class culture and middle class religion which enabled the churches to sustain some degree of activity amongst the urban poor and working class: first there was a degree of popular religiosity and interest in religious matters very different in kind from the religion of the churches and very difficult to measure in extent and depth, but which nevertheless at times represented a possible point of convergence with the churches, although the working class generally showed considerable reluctance to make regular attendance and commitment which the churches generally demanded of its members;[31] secondly, and more particularly, the rites of passage retained religious content for the working class, and in this respect above all tended to favour the Church of England;[32] thirdly, perhaps most significantly, the working class was itself differentiated, with the very top groups (the labour aristocracy) showing in some respects a greater degree of religiosity than the 'solid' working class, evidenced in a greater propensity towards church attendance (particularly Nonconformist) and influenced by the ideology of ethical self-restraint and work which tended to sustain their social status; and finally, wherever the immigrant labouring Irish settled their national identity and sense of social isolation was preserved by adherence to Roman Catholicism. The second qualification is that the cultural values of the urban churches were not monolithic: the churches showed some flexibility in their reactions to working class culture, a flexibility that is most noticeable in the instances of priests and ministers who consciously cultivated close associations with working men, and some of whom tried to radicalise the churches' social and religious messages; these men were in a minority in their churches, but they were often an influential minority. Consequently there was no sharp division between middle class religion and working class culture, but rather a tendency towards polarisation combatted at certain points with varying degrees of success by members of both social strata.

The third direction in which this book has developed follows on closely from the second: if religion in its institutionalised form was mainly practiced by the middle class and therefore related directly to

---

[31] D. H. McLeod, *Religion and the Working Class in Nineteenth-Century Britain* (London 1984), pp. 63–4; and *Religion and the People of Western Europe, 1789–1970* (Oxford 1981), p. 124.
[32] *Ibid.*, p. 125.

the power conflicts, relationships and aspirations of the middle class, then there is considerable importance to be attached to the activities and divisions of the urban elites, their political affiliations and, from the point of view of this study, the extent to which they participated actively in the affairs of the churches. The power struggles between the different groups reinforced and were themselves intensified by other forms of conflict and competition over religion, particularly inter-denominational competition. Again the perspective returns to a local one, since the origins of the sectarian disputes in the Victorian period are as much to be sought in the reactions of the churches to local issues, to the ways in which these issues were to be fought out, and hence the whole pattern and structure of local church organisations and support, as in apparently national issues such as church reform and parliamentary education bills.

Finally, it follows on from the previous three points that this book is concerned as much with the structure and development of local political and social life as they affected the churches as with the churches themselves; it seeks to analyse the changing role of the churches in local society by relating directly what was happening in the churches to change in the society at large, particularly through the points of contact which were the strongest, including action in welfare and politics, elite action in politics and the churches, and church efforts to reach out to the urban population. It does not seek to exclude the explanations put forward by other historians on a national scale – intellectual, political and social – but it does start from the assumption that churches, rooted in particular time and place, are necessarily and directly affected by issues of power and control at the local level, and that no analysis which seeks to separate them from this local context can be complete. Although, like Jeffrey Cox's study,[33] the general context of political development in which church activity was set has been characterised here as a move away from voluntarist and permissive initiatives to collective ones, unlike his study this book does not assume a correspondence between central State initiatives and church life, but instead locates some key developments in the reform and organisation of local government.

[33] J. Cox, *The Churches in a Secular Society: Lambeth 1870–1930* (Oxford 1982).

2

Social Structure

Though it became well known in the late nineteenth and early twentieth centuries as a typical example of one of the outer metropolitan 'dormitory suburbs', there were in fact peculiar features of Croydon's growth in the period which were of considerable significance for the efforts of the churches. It is the intention of this chapter to indicate how this was so, by analysing briefly the content and processes of development and by indicating how particular aspects of development affected the activity of organised religion in the area. Croydon's relative isolation from London before the First World War makes it a good area in which to analyse the performance of churches facing problems associated with urbanisation similar to those experienced in the metropolitan suburbs. At the same time, Croydon's development socially was sufficiently mixed, sufficiently 'typical' of suburban experience to warrant wider-than-local conclusions being drawn. Due to its size, its location and the pattern of its urban growth, Croydon was a city in all but name, deprived of the name only by its proximity to London. Its rapid growth and the independence of its civic life serve to illustrate particularly clearly, therefore, the important relationship at the level of local elite and middle class behaviour between the development of civic management and the changing role of organised religion which lies behind the main thrust of the argument of this book.

Geography and urban growth

Croydon's situation directly favoured its development in the nineteenth century as a commuter suburb which at the same time could acquire an active, independent municipal tradition. The *Surrey Magazine* in 1844 described the parish of Croydon as one of the largest in the Kingdom, thirty-six miles in circumference, containing over 10,000 acres and, in addition to the town itself, eight hamlets. Similar in shape to other parishes lying on the edge of the Thames basin and North Downs between Croydon and Guildford, in 1800 it was twice the size in area and population as most of the others.[1] Situated therefore in north-east Surrey at the southernmost point of the inexorable expansion of the metropolis, throughout the nineteenth century the parish was caught between the differing and sometimes conflicting demands of urban and rural networks. Only in the last decade of the nineteenth and the early years of the twentieth centuries, with the rapid development of large settlements of predominantly lower middle and working class housing to the north of the town centre around the 'hamlets' of Thornton Heath, Norbury and Selhurst, could an unbroken chain of 'city' be said to stretch from the centre of Croydon to the City of London; by this period Croydon was sometimes being included by statisticians and social scientists for convenience's sake within the urban conglomorate known as 'Greater London', like other parishes and boroughs outside the London County Council such as Bromley, Ilford, Enfield and Isleworth.[2] Even in the 1900s, however, it would be wrong to think of Croydon as a homogeneous urban web for it still contained a number of rural communities to the south and south-east of the town centre.

It was to the north and north east of the town centre in the nineteenth century that urban development in the main occurred, though there were some considerable developments immediately south and east. Thornton Heath, lying on the London road just to the north of the town, was still principally a rural hamlet in the 1840s, though with development proceeding along the highway it could not remain so for long. South Norwood and the two patches of development which came together to form Upper Norwood were not marked as communities at the time of enclosure in 1801;[3] by the 1840s South Norwood had appeared, mainly it seems as a result of the opening of the Surrey Canal in 1809 and subsequently of the London, Brighton and South Coast railway: Upper Norwood came into being as a residential area from the very beginning.[4] Nor did the development which occurred in the late nineteenth century between Norwood and Croydon in the areas which came to be called Selhurst and Norbury take place around the 'core' of a hamlet, for only isolated farmsteads were marked there in the 1840s.[5]

Settlement had probably occurred originally because of the plentiful supply of water in the area. The town's other great natural

[1] Cited in Anon., *Old and New Croydon Illustrated* (Croydon 1894), p. 14.
[2] See, for example, R. Mudie Smith (ed.), *The Religious Life of London* (London 1904).
[3] See J. C. Anderson (ed.), *The Enclosure Award of 1801 for the Parish of Croydon* (Croydon 1889) and the accompanying map.
[4] K. Maggs and P. D'Athe, *South Norwood and the Croydon Canal* (Croydon 1984); A. Warwick, *The Phoenix Suburb: a south London suburb* (Richmond 1972).
[5] Tithe Commissioners Map of the Parish of Croydon, 1847.

resource until the early eighteenth century, surrounded as it was by thick woodland on the hills, was wood; it provided charcoal for London as well as timber for building purposes.[6] The rise of the coalmining industry, part-exhaustion of woodland supplies and the changeover to coal-fired processes in the iron industry undermined the importance of timber production, but by the time this occurred the town's location had become its great asset, for on a principal high road into London from eastern Surrey it had become established as an important market for agricultural goods within easy reach of the metropolis.

In another sense too the location of Croydon, given its size and importance as a market by the early nineteenth century, was of greater importance than its immediate natural resources, for it was able to function virtually as the capital of East Surrey. By the 1840s the only other towns in the county outside the metropolitan area which even began to approach it for size were Guildford in the west and Kingston. All three were the assize towns of the county, though the biennial duty of quartering the assize justices involved some expense and effort for the town authorities (who had to procure comfortable quarters for the judge and who never found a permanent, entirely satisfactory arrangement); defence of the effort involved often ran along the lines that the assizes made a vital contribution to the town's confidence and self-respect.[7] Hustings for the Eastern Division of the Parliamentary County of Surrey, formed in 1832, were held at the Town Hall,[8] and when Croydon Parish was thrown in with rural parishes for poor law administration in 1836, the area formed became known as the 'Croydon Union'; Croydon contributed seven to the board of twenty Guardians (Mitcham sent three, Merton two and all the other surrounding parishes one each), and the town became the effective headquarters of Poor Law operations in the area, with meetings of the Board held at the Town Hall and the Union Workhouse sited about a quarter of a mile south-west of the town centre.[9] Though it had sponsored its own police force

---

[6] J. C. Anderson, *A Short Chronicle Concerning the Parish of Croydon* (Croydon 1882), p. 170.

[7] See, for example, *C Chron*, 22 Dec. 1860; 19, 26 Jan. 1861.

[8] See *ibid.*, 7 May 1859.

[9] The ten parishes were: Addington, Coulsdon, Sanderstead, Woodmansterne, Beddington, Mitcham, Morden, Merton, Penge Ville and Wallington. All but Merton (Brixton Hundred) and Penge (Kent) were in the ancient Hundred of Wallington. Croydon, with a rateable value of £6,486, surpassed the total rateable value of the other ten parishes (£6,097), so either some concession was made to the principle of geographical representation, or the Poor Law Commissioners did not want to give Croydon a majority voice in setting rate levels: Poor Law Commissioners for England and Wales, Order for Croydon Union, 1836.

from 1829, in 1840 the parish was incorporated into the area covered by the metropolitan police, and 'W' division's main station built on the western side of North End;[10] by 1850 the division commanded about one hundred men, and covered an area including the Poor Law Union of Croydon (excluding Penge), and Carshalton, Sutton, Streatham and Warlingham – in other words, the whole of north-east Surrey.[11]

Besides trading and administrative links, there is evidence of other, more informal ways in which Croydon acted as the centre of non-metropolitan, north-east Surrey. The annual meeting and dinners of the East Surrey Agricultural Association were usually held in Croydon.[12] Major political meetings for East Surrey before Croydon was formed into a parliamentary constituency in its own right in 1884 were generally held in Croydon, where there was the best chance of attracting a large audience.[13] Primitive and Wesleyan Methodists formed circuits centred on Croydon which sent out local and travelling preachers to villages in some cases up to fifteen miles away.[14] The East Surrey Sunday School Union, a Nonconformist organisation formed in 1872, regularly held its meetings in Croydon, generally at the Public Hall or in the schoolroom of George Street Congregational Church.[15] All this is not to deny that Croydon showed considerable differences from contiguous rural parishes in its administration, social structure and general 'character', or that in some respects it remained or became isolated from rural communities as its connections with the metropolis increased, or that the importance to its economy of its contacts with rural Surrey declined as it became a prosperous, rapidly expanding commuter town.

There are two key distinguishing characteristics of the urbanisation of Croydon which need to be borne in mind in an analysis of church activity in the area and its relationship to municipal life. The first, noted by Dr Cox, is the striking degree to which development in the town and probably within the parish as a whole was self-contained, for in by far the majority of cases studied by Dr Cox and others building plots were purchased by Croydon men who employed

[10] D. C. H. Hobbs, 'The Croydon Police 1829–1840', *Proc CNHSS*, xvii (1983), 150.
[11] Cox, 'Urban Development and Redevelopment', p. 28.
[12] See, for example, *C Chron*, 1 Oct. 1859; 25 May 1864; 21 Oct. 1865; 1 Aug. 1874 – these represent dates noted only because the meetings contained material interesting on other grounds as well.
[13] See, for example (for the 1874 general election), reports of meetings in Croydon at the Town Hall and Public Halls in *C Ad*, 31 Jan. 1874 and *C Chron*, same date.
[14] Details of Wesleyan Circuit from *Ward's Croydon Directories*, 1876–1914; details of Primitive Methodist Circuit from circuit plans and Quarterly Meeting Minutes 1849 to 1914, at C Ref Lib.
[15] *C Chron*, 16 Mar. 1872; 10 Apr. 1875; 28 Apr. 1877.

Croydon builders to develop the land.[16] Urbanisation was a process which worked to the considerable advantage of many of the town's leading businessmen and political figures; what is later written in this book concerning the buoyancy of this urban elite cannot be separated from the possibility that their influence was in part sustained by their readiness to cash in on the very processes which in so many other ways were pulling the churches, charities and voluntary services in which they were also active in different directions.

The other striking characteristic of urban development in Croydon is that building did not proceed in such a way as to push the social segregation of housing patterns to an extreme. Development was on the whole socially mixed. In contrast to Edgbaston, to take a good comparison, where the extensive Calthorp estates were developed to near-uniform middle and upper middle class pattern,[17] middle class development in Croydon occurred in patches of modest size, interspersed often with housing aimed at lower social groups. The Waldrons, a middle class estate south-west of the town centre, for example, contained no more than about thirty-four houses.[18] Upper middle class development at Addiscombe, the Park Hill estate near the town centre, and Upper Norwood was on a larger scale than this, but still insufficient to stamp Croydon indelibly as an upper middle class area. More extensive and, in a sense, more typical of the area was the lower middle class housing which sprang up throughout the parish, yet even from these areas large patches of working class housing could not be excluded. Yet neither were the working class areas of Croydon large and highly concentrated; again patches of concentration existed, such as Old Town and the Barracks area north-west of Old Town, but much working class housing was scattered throughout the parish.[19] As a consequence few ecclesiastical districts were altogether devoid of the financial assistance and active support middle class churchgoers could provide, yet few escaped altogether the problems of non-churchgoing, the 'social evils' of drink, prostitution and gambling, and the poverty of working class areas.

[16] Cox, 'Urban Development'; *idem*, 'Urban Development and Redevelopment'; J. B. Gent (ed.), *Croydon, the story of a hundred years* (Croydon 1970); an exception to this, the role of the British Land Company in development at Addiscombe, was studied by D. C. H. Hobbs, 'Nineteenth Century Addiscombe', unpubl. diploma thesis, Portsmouth 1985.

[17] D. Cannadine, *Lords and Landlords: the aristocracy and the towns* (Leicester 1979), *passim*.

[18] *Ward's Croydon Directory*, 1876.

[19] *Ward's Croydon Directories*; Croydon Borough Council, *Report of the Poor Dwellings Committee*, 1883–4.

A brief consideration of the role of landowners and developers reinforces this picture of the mixed nature of development. By the beginning of the nineteenth century land ownership in the parish of Croydon was already highly fragmented: there were few large, consolidated estates, and those in and around the town itself and at Norwood were particularly prone to sub-division.[20] During the course of the century there was little evidence either of resistance from landowners to urban development or of planned, controlled development by landowners for financial advantage: development by sale of land for freehold was virtually universal in Croydon, Cox asserts.[21]

There were two significant exceptions to this overall picture and in both cases corporate owners were involved. The Ecclesiastical Commissioners held the most extensive estates of all owners in the parish, and were clearly concerned with the planned development of these sites: an extensive development on their land at Park Hill east of the town centre, using ninety-nine-year leases, brought them some of the highest rents in the Greater London area;[22] the large houses built for upper middle class families on their land at Upper Norwood signalled the same readiness to plan the course of urban growth and benefit either from high rents or from the increasing value of land held elsewhere in the vicinity.[23] The second largest landowner in the parish was also a corporate religious body, the Whitgift Charitable Foundation, founded by Archbishop Whitgift in the late sixteenth century and endowed with considerable property to maintain an alsmhouse and a poor school in Croydon. The Whitgift Foundation did not develop its estates systematically in the manner of the Ecclesiastical Commissioners, because in the main its land was not situated as favourably, and possibly because the long-running and often bitter disputes within the parish over the constitution of the governing body may have dampened the readiness of the successive governors to take risks in property development;[24] however the Foundation in the second half of the century was certainly capable of efficient management of its properties, and using twelve-year leases in many cases by the late nineteenth and early twentieth century had very much benefited from the rise in urban property rentals, whereas

[20] Principal sources for these assertions are: Anderson, *Enclosure Award*, and Anon., *The Domesday Book for the County of Surrey in the Year 1873* (Croydon 1876): a more detailed consideration of these sources can be found in J. N. Morris, 'Religion and Urban Change in Victorian England: a case study of the borough of Croydon 1840–1914', unpubl. DPhil thesis, Oxford 1985, pp. 46–8 and appendix 2, pp. 405–8
[21] Cox, 'Urban Development', p. 138.
[22] *Ibid.*, p. 142.
[23] *Gray's Croydon Directories*, 1851–1859.
[24] See ch. 5, pp. 117–19.

their agricultural estates at Croham Park and near Woodside had barely increased in value.[25]

The successes of both the Ecclesiastical Commissioners and the Whitgift Foundation in directing and controlling urban development to suit their own ends shows that corporate bodies may have had some advantage over private individuals in assessing and then manipulating market opportunities in building; however both bodies also started well ahead of other owners in the parish in terms of the opportunities available to them. The presence and activity of these two large corporate religious bodies certainly gave added weight and prestige to Anglicanism in the area, but were of little practical benefit to Anglicans: neither made grants of land for churchbuilding purposes; the Ecclesiastical Commission often donated money towards endowments, but were more concerned with the profit potential of their estates in Croydon and were clearly not inclined to divide or reduce them.

Demography

Although Croydon's population growth was under way by the end of the eighteenth century, it was in the second half of the nineteenth century that rapid expansion took off, reaching such a pace that it was to pose serious problems for the churches in raising resources and reforming their organisations in an effort to keep up with the growing population. In the early 1850s the town entered a protracted period of rapid, extensive expansion, reaching over 170,000 by the First World War. The period of the highest rate of growth was the four decades from 1851 to 1891, the population almost doubling between 1861 and 1871 alone from 30,240 to 55,652.[26] In 1851, therefore, it rivalled in size towns such as Colchester, Dover, King's Lynn and Reading. By 1881 it was equal to Derby. By 1911 it was the same size as Leeds in 1851 and more than twice the size of Reading in 1911. Croydon's rate of growth in the middle decades of the nineteenth century surpassed Manchester's peak rate (in the 1820s and 1830s). It was, on the other hand, easily matched by the growth rate of Middlesbrough, the iron town, in the 1850s and 1860s, although in absolute terms

[25] Statement of the Rents of the Charity called the Hospital of the Holy Trinity at Croydon, for the year ending 31st December 1867; Schedule of Whitgift Educational properties appended to a proposed scheme for the Whitgift Foundation for further alteration of the scheme of 1881, Board of Education 1906.
[26] Appendix 1 for this and subsequent census totals: table 1, p. 191.

Croydon was much the larger town in 1901, by some 43,000 people.[27]

A breakdown of these totals of growth confirms that between 1861 and 1891 the parish was expanding most rapidly in two principal areas, the town itself and its immediate environs (covered in 1861 by the districts of St James, St John's, Croydon and St Peter's) and the suburbs around Upper Norwood and South Norwood in the north-east of the parish (covered by the Anglican districts of All Saints and St Mark's).[28] St James's, for example, centred on a church built on the edge of Croydon Common about half a mile north-east of the town centre, vaulted from 7,590 to 27,404. All Saints, Upper Norwood, covered in 1861 a comfortable sized population of 4,060, yet by 1891 this district included 19,767 people. In dramatic contrast the semi-rural district of St John's, Shirley, two miles east of Croydon and populated mainly by agricultural labourers into the early twentieth century, remained virtually static, around the tiny figure of 642 in 1861. Christchurch, a poor district in 1861 covering most of the north-east of the parish, expanded at a relatively moderate rate from 4,203 to 9,283.

The changeover to the council ward as a unit of assessment for the census summaries instead of ecclesiastical districts makes direct comparison with the earlier period difficult and moreover reduces the choice of dates available to only two – 1901 and 1911. However, use of the burgess roll from its inception in 1883 at five-yearly intervals indicates very clearly how, in the closing decade of the nineteenth century and the early years of the twentieth, the main thrust of settlement switched from Croydon and Norwood to the intervening parts of the parish around Norbury, Thornton Heath and Selhurst;[29] here the area covered roughly by Christchurch district in 1861 increased by 234 per cent from 3,596 burgesses in 1883 to 11,995 in 1913. South Ward (covered by St Peter's in 1861) came nearest to matching it with an increase of 183 per cent. It is probable that this changing location of demographic growth reflected the falling social status of the borough as growth increasingly relied upon the artisanal and lower middle class groups who settled in the relatively low-lying areas to the north and north-east of the town centre and less upon the expansion of solid middle class 'villadom' at Norwood and the middle class estates around the town. From roughly the 1880s, therefore, although the pace of expansion overall in Croydon tended to slacken,

---

[27] Figures and comparisons taken from Yeo, *Religion and Voluntary Organisations*, p. 339; Briggs, *Victorian Cities*, p. 140; and B. I. Coleman, *The Church of England in the Mid-Nineteenth Century* (London 1980), p. 41.

[28] Appendix 1, table 2.

[29] *Ibid.*, table 3.

in certain areas it remained high and was of a kind – lower middle class and artisanal – which could imply diminishing resources for the churches. Yet it is also possible that the changing distribution of growth occurred because of saturation of previously developed parts of the parish. By the 1890s there were few open spaces close to the town and at Norwood where large-scale development was possible, and the successive acquisition of open land for recreation parks by the Local Board of Health and then the Council had closed some areas to the developer; building therefore had to move outwards from Croydon and Norwood.

Migration was the principal factor affecting Croydon's demographic explosion; its pattern was not without some significance for religion in the area, for though by late century a clear trend of movement outwards from London had become established, around mid-century there is evidence that levels of working class migration from the rural south-east were still very high, so that the religious character of the parish was affected as much by patterns of church-going in the countryside as by the metropolis.[30] By 1911 by far the largest proportion of migration to Croydon was accounted for by London: some twenty-six per cent of Croydon's inhabitants were born there, whilst the share represented by the rural south-east (all of Kent, rural Surrey and Sussex) was fourteen and a half per cent.[31] Dr Cox's intensive analysis of the 1851 and 1861 schedules provides some data for the earlier period of expansion.[32] Of 3,773 identifiable heads of household in 1851, twenty-three per cent were born in the Parish of Croydon; a further forty-seven per cent were born within thirty miles of Croydon.[33] A high proportion of the 1,749 under this forty-seven per cent would have been born in the towns and villages of rural Surrey, for Cox's figure for those born between five and ten miles from Croydon alone indicates some 285 out of a total of 763 as coming from rural areas.[34] The underlying tendency in mid-century was for working class immigrants to migrate towards the town from the villages of Surrey and for middle class immigrants to move outwards from London, since some fifty per cent at least of the working class heads of household counted came from rural areas, whereas some eighty-six per cent of middle class heads of household came instead from London and the suburbs of London. Cox's analysis also identifies two small Irish ghettoes: in Hill Street, Old Town, where just over half of the households were Irish, and Leather

[30] Chapter 3, pp. 41–3.
[31] Appendix 1, table 6.
[32] Cox, 'Urban Development and Redevelopment', ch. 3.
[33] Appendix 1, table 4.
[34] *Ibid.*, table 5.

Bottle Lane, near Broad Green at the northern end of the town, where four-fifths were Irish.[35] The Catholic chapel of St Mary's was built just north of the centre of Croydon, within easy walking distance of Old Town and Broad Green, after earlier temporary cottage chapels had been used close to Old Town and at Broad Green itself.[36] Irish settlers in Croydon were mostly labourers; many of them would have come to the town as navvies employed on railway construction.[37]

Economy and social class

Croydon's economic importance in the early nineteenth century was dual, as a coaching town on one of the main London to south coast roads, and as a market for agricultural goods. Though it continued to act as an agricultural market throughout the century, the scale and nature of its development reoriented its economy away from agriculture and its associated trades towards three principal areas. First industrial activity was not without some significance for its expansion. Large industries in the town in the 1840s and 1850s included gas works in the centre of the town, several large breweries, a bleaching works in the grounds of the old archiepiscopal palace, and several firms of coachbuilders.[38] Large concerns established within the parish by the 1860s and 1870s were in a wide variety of processes: a large boot factory near the High Street employing several hundred workers, a linoleum factory beside the Brighton Road in the south of the parish, clock-making and bell-making firms, a large brickworks at Woodside, and of course the building trade.[39] Several large processes, including an iron works, enlarged gas works and later still electricity works in the 1890s were established on the western border of the parish, to the north-west of the town centre.[40]

Yet though processing and manufacturing works could account for a modest proportion of townsmen's occupations in the second half of the nineteenth century, Croydon's growth as a retailing centre was of

[35] Cox, 'Urban Development and Redevelopment', pp. 322–3.
[36] W. H. M. McLaughlin, *The Foundation of St Mary's, Croydon* (Croydon 1938), p. 28.
[37] Cox, 'Urban Development and Redevelopment', p. 448.
[38] *Gray's Croydon Directory*, 1851–61; T. M. James 'The Inns of Croydon, 1640–1840', *Collections of the Surrey Archaeological Society*, lxviii (1974), 114; W. Page, 'My Recollections of Croydon Sixty Years Since' (mss. in C Ref Lib, 1880); L. Thornhill, 'From palace to washhouse: a study of the Old Palace, Croydon, from 1780 to 1887', *Proc CNHSS*, xvii (1987), 209–48.
[39] *Warren's Croydon Directory*, 1865–9; *Ward's Croydon Directory* 1874–1914; W. Benians, 'The trade and industrial development of Croydon', *Proc CNHSS*, xiii (1962).
[40] J. E. M. Martin, *Greater London: an industrial geography* (London 1966) p. 119.

greater significance for the town's economy. In the 1840s retail businesses were still concentrated in the High Street and the adjoining market area, with its narrow, cramped streets and open stalls on market day. Within the space of a mere twenty years, it seems, the retailing trade of the town switched away from the market area, towards High Street and its continuation at north and south (North End and South End), and in George Street, leading eastwards off the High Street. The change was almost certainly, as Pelton argued, due to the increasing volume of business, as expansion of premises was impossible in the cramped conditions of the market area, the narrow streets uncomfortable for large crowds, and the area situated on a downward slope behind the buildings on the western side of the High Street, off the main thoroughfare.[41] As retailing continued to expand throughout the Victorian period, the traders of the town centre became one of the most vociferous, powerful social groups in religious and municipal affairs.[42] The new-found status of retailing in the town in the 1860s and '70s was reflected in the foundation of a tradesmen's club, the holding of an annual tradesmen's ball, and the patronage by many employers of the early closing movement; finally the foundation of Croydon's Chamber of Commerce in 1891 set the seal on the systematic organisation of traders' interests in the town.[43] The High Street Improvement Scheme, carried out by the Council from 1890, by widening the High Street and demolishing part of the now run-down market area confirmed the changed pattern of trade in the town.[44]

The third 'growth' area in the parish's economic structure which needs to be taken into consideration is transport. It was of key importance for Croydon's growth because it enabled the settlement in and around the town of large numbers of the commuting middle class, as well as facilitating trading links both with the metropolis and with the rural south-east. Though coaching and the carriage trade continued well into the late nineteenth century, they were probably overtaken – at least for goods conveyance – by other forms of transport relatively early in the period. The Surrey Canal and the Surrey Iron Railway, neither of which were particularly successful ventures commercially, improved the transportation of goods to and

---

[41] J. O. Pelton, *Relics of Old Croydon* (Croydon 1891), p. 15.
[42] See, for example, complaints of traders about the local Board of Health's failure to widen the High Street: Minutes of the Croydon Local Board of Health for 28 Feb. 1860.
[43] *Ward's Croydon Directory*, 1901, p. lxxviii.
[44] R. C. W. Cox, 'The old centre of Croydon: Victorian decay and redevelopment', in A. M. Everitt (ed.), *Perspectives in English Urban History* (London 1973).

from Croydon before the 1840s.[45] The first steam railway line to Croydon was opened in 1839, running from London Bridge station through Croydon to Brighton; a further line was opened two years later, and both of the stations then built, West Croydon and East Croydon, were close to the town centre so that the lines rapidly became considerable carriers of passenger as well as freight traffic.[46] It can be said of Croydon perhaps more than of many other towns that the railways were a key factor determining urban expansion, for its accelerated rate of growth from the 1840s was very much affected by the attraction of the middle classes to Croydon, in other words those who moved out from Inner London districts precisely because, using railways, they could travel to work in London and yet live elsewhere. A further spate of railway construction in the 1860s, most of it consisting of 'filling-in' lines, meant that by the 1870s there were eleven stations in the parish, most of them constructed in areas where passenger traffic was likely to be heavy.[47] A further dimension to transport networks in the parish was added in the late 1870s, when four local tradesmen, headed by J. S. Balfour, building society boss and later to be the first mayor of Croydon, formed themselves into a company to construct a tramways system for Croydon.[48]

A relatively reliable statistical breakdown of Croydon's economic structure can be provided by an analysis of census data from 1861 to 1911, as reproduced in appendix 2. All of the tables inserted here have been drawn up closely following the lines set out by Stedman Jones, using the occupational classification established by the 1911 Census Summary Report to re-categorise the Croydon data for 1861 and 1891 as well as 1911. These figures need to be treated with some caution, as use of the summary reports makes it almost impossible to differentiate between some categories: retailing suffers particularly from under-representation, since more impressionistic material (town directories and newspapers) indicates that many small producers had retail outlets for their businesses, and yet the Reports class them strictly into manufacturing or craft production categories. Agriculture is over-represented in the 1861 figures, because these were based on the Croydon Union and consequently include several small rural parishes around the town. Nevertheless, as a broad indicator of

[45] Gent, *Croydon, the story*, p. 19; J. T. H. Turner, *The London, Brighton and South Coast Railway I: origins and formation* (London 1977), pp. 17–18; D. A. Bayliss, *Retracing the First Public Railway* (Croydon 1981), pp. 22–3.
[46] Gent, *Croydon, the story*, p. 20.
[47] *Ibid.*
[48] G. E. Baddeley, *The Tramways of Croydon* (Croydon rev. edn, 1983), p. 1. The four were F. M. Coldwells, J. Pelton, J. Allder and D. B. Miller; all four had High Street, North End or George Street businesses, and all served on the Council from its inception in 1883.

economic change in the period, the tables illustrate firstly the increasing proportion of middle and lower middle class occupations throughout the half century, particularly the rise of clerical occupations from 1.79 per cent of the adult male population in 1861 to 11.38 per cent in 1911, secondly the relative decline in significance of agriculture and agriculture-related crafts (such as the leather industry), and thirdly the existence (once the building and transport industries are considered apart) of a small but significant and diverse light industrial sector in the town (engineering works by 1911 accounted for some 5.03 per cent of the adult male population).[49] Employment of women was concentrated on domestic service (it was never less than half of the 'employed' adult female populaton), but the significant point here is that the relative importance of domestic service in the female labour market in Croydon over the fifty years was falling, and that the category of 'others' (mostly accounted for by wives and unoccupied daughters) rose by nearly ten per cent relative to employed categories.[50] The implications of this, coupled with the figures for male occupations, are that while Croydon throughout the period was very much a middle class area, growth increasingly relied upon those in lower middle class and artisan occupations: domestic service was falling in importance, clerical work and retailing were rising.[51]

Similar conclusions emerge when these figures are translated into an analysis of Croydon by social class, using the Registrar-General's five-class model established in 1951.[52] With class 1 representing over ten per cent of the town's male population in 1861, and larger than class 2, Croydon was clearly a fashionable area of settlement for professional men and the upper middle class. By late century its overall significance in the town's class structure had declined and had been easily surpassed by the growth of the lower middle class. By 1911, class 3, the skilled working or artisanal class, was also increasing in importance. Semi-skilled labour, class 4, declined rapidly between 1861 and 1891, but again this is an exaggerated figure because it includes a large number of agricultural labourers from other parishes in the Croydon Union in the 1861 figures. Class 5, the unskilled, remained remarkably stable during the period, falling only three per cent against the other classes, and all of this decline occurring before 1891.[53] Classes 1 and 2 are probably underestimated, again because of the impossibility of using the census

---

[49] Appendix 2, tables 1–6.
[50] *Ibid.*, table 6.
[51] *Ibid.*
[52] *Ibid.*, tables 7–12.
[53] *Ibid.*, tables 10–12 in particular.

reports to differentiate between large and small producers, and workers and employers. Croydon remained very much a middle class suburb, but its growth relied increasingly on the lower middle class and the 'respectable' working class; in comparative terms, by the 1900s its overall social status was falling. The social breakdown of employed women reflects this conclusion exactly, with classes 2 and 3 rising in importance, and class 4 (which includes most domestic servants) falling.[54]

Character, conditions and local government

Croydon's development in the nineteenth century can be characterised according to three stages of growth, which form the context in which the vicissitudes of organised religion in the area need to be set, with the crucial qualification that such a chronological framework can only be a rough description of leading features of change. A further qualification should be that the impact of change was not uniform, and did not affect all classes in the parish at the same rate; as will become clear, many of the changes described are particularly relevant to the controlling groups of the parish, and their effect on other groups is not nearly so apparent nor was it so immediate. What might be called the first stage of growth in Croydon would have begun sometime around the 1800s or 1810s; it was marked by modest population growth, and by the increasing importance of trading connections both with the wider net of rural east Surrey and with the metropolis. It was also a period, however, in which the administration of the town was concentrated in a small, compact elite of landowners, gentlemen farmers and traders in agricultural produce, or small-scale craft manufacturers. This elite was almost solidly Anglican and very largely Conservative in politics,[55] and it showed a constant failure to come to grips with problems of maladministration in parochial affairs and with the changing demands of town residents. By the early 1840s, towards the end of this first stage of growth, Croydon was facing a serious deterioration in sanitary conditions as population expansion put increased strain on the rough-and-ready drainage and watering system, based on the River Wandle and its tributaries, which had hitherto been used in the parish.[56] The existing public authorities were for the most part not inclined to take effective remedial action – due to the costs which would be involved – nor, had

---

[54] *Ibid.*
[55] See pp. 124–5.
[56] *Surrey Standard*, 24 Mar. 1849, Report on the Commission of Inquiry into the sanitary state of Croydon, held by W. Ranger.

they wanted to do so, did they have the power.[57] A pressure group of leading townsmen emerged ready to promote administrative reform locally with the intention of solving Croydon's sanitary problem.

The second stage in the town's growth began approximately in the late 1840s. The arrival of the railways and the rising attraction of Croydon as a residential commuter town began to displace the preponderance of the agricultural and landowning interest. Professional men, merchants and prosperous traders dominated the 'governing body' in the town, the Local Board of Health established in 1849, which in its political and religious complexion at first differed little from its predecessors, the Board of Surveyors of the Highways and the Town Improvement Commissioners.[58] Extensive schemes for water supply and sewage works carried out by the Board solved in the main the sanitary problems exacerbated by urbanisation, though its failure to tackle the problem of the narrowness of the High Street and the increasingly dilapidated market area signalled that its powers were limited.[59] The location of authority in Croydon in this period was ambiguous: parish authorities, the vicar, the churchwardens and then the ratepayers assembled in vestry, were still in a sense the ultimate court of appeal in the parish, and for this reason religious disputes centred around local political issues (church rates, parochial charities, parish appointments) were particularly intense, and confirmed by the disputes over religious teaching on the newly-formed School Board in the 1870s; yet the initiator of most public schemes in the parish was the Board of Health, insulated from a certain amount of public criticism by the property vote. With this divided authority, and under the pervasive influence of mid-Victorian notions of voluntarism and self-improvement, the sphere of public action by the authorities was anyway narrowly defined; this was a period when philanthropy was at its peak in the town, with wealthy residents active in philanthropic and missionary organisations as well as in churches, educational, literary and scientific societies and political associations. Stephen Yeo, whose 'phase iii' of Reading's development coincided largely with the second stage I have described for Croydon, highlighted similar features of participation and mass voluntarism as typical of this period.[60] Though town

---

[57] W. Ranger, *Report to the General Board of Health on a Preliminary Inquiry into . . . The Sanitary Condition . . . of the Inhabitants of Croydon* (Croydon 1849), p. 8.
[58] Ch. 5, pp. 124–5.
[59] This was confirmed in 1864 when the Board submitted a proposal for High Street widening to the Local Government Office, only to be discouraged from proceeding with the plan: C Chron, 5 Nov. 1864.
[60] C. S. Yeo, 'Religion in Society: a view from a provincial town in the late-nineteenth and early-twentieth centuries', unpubl. DPhil thesis, Sussex 1971, p. 85.

29

life was split by many tensions and divisions – over religion, politics, life-style, leisure activity – the elite groups of the town were still highly adaptable, many individuals taking upon themselves a very wide range of responsibilities; the progressive specialisation of the responsibilities and activities of leading townspeople which is in part the subject of this book had not yet proceeded very far.

It is difficult to pinpoint the beginning of what I have called the 'third stage' of Croydon's growth. It was associated with a declining faith in voluntarism as a medicine for society's ills, and with an increasing readiness to resort to collective action to supply what were perceived to be the needs of the town. In institutional terms, it was signalled by the incorporation of Croydon in 1883 after a campaign led by tradesmen and professional men, largely Liberal and Nonconformist, which had originated in criticisms of the ineffectiveness of the Board of Health. In the 1890s and 1900s the Council's field of responsibility in welfare matters, transport and town administration developed considerably. The ramifications (in terms of the structure and techniques of organisation) of a movement away from voluntarism and a faith in the virtue of moral influence, for churches, voluntary organisations, and political associations, as well as the Council, were such as to demand greater specialisation of resources and manpower to take on more responsibility in more closely defined areas and to demand more from members to meet these responsibilities. The compactness of the town's ruling elite before the 1880s began to disappear: council politics became at once the key source of power in the area and a time-consuming pursuit for those involved; church life similarly developed rather than retreated, but in ways which sought to extract more commitment and not less from membership. Underlining this change in Croydon was the coincidental change in urban growth: with the declining social status of the borough in the 1890s and 1900s as the upper and middle classes began to seek homes even further out than Croydon and as the development which occurred in the north and north-east of the borough for lower middle class and artisanal housing gathered pace, the numbers of the monied classes available to take an active, leading part in the social, religious and political life of the town could not meet demand and may actually have declined.

Local government in the first half of the nineteenth century was a curious, uneven mixture of tradition and innovation. The old manorial courts had withered into irrelevancy, retaining a largely formal existence into the 1900s.[61] The brunt of parish administration therefore fell into the hands of a complicated cluster of authorities

[61] *Victoria County History of Surrey*, iv (1902), p. 219.

which it is convenient to label the 'parochial system' of government, even though at first sight there was not much element of system. At the very centre was the vestry meeting, open to all resident male parishioners and summoned by the churchwardens; all the business of the parish, at least theoretically, had to be submitted to it for approval. There were no clearly defined limits to the authority of the vestry, and its jurisdiction in theory included supervising and approving expenditure on repairs to the Parish Church and district churches, sanctioning the levy of extra local rates for specific purposes, sanctioning the diversion of footpaths and supervising the management of parochial buildings such as the Town Hall.[62] It appeared to be a highly democratic institution, with all resident householders able to vote at a meeting, and votes so cast being equal in weight,[63] but in practice the picture was very different, for under Sturges Bourne's Act of 1818 any parishioner in vestry could, after a vote had been taken, demand a poll of the parish; this was then carried out under a property-weighted franchise, giving six votes in all to every householder with land assessed for poor rate at £150 or upwards, one vote to householders rated at £50 or less, and an intermediate number to those variously rated between £50 and £150.[64] Power under the vestry therefore ultimately resided in the hands of the propertied, unless a large number of small householders could be mobilised against them – a thing very difficult to achieve in prosperous, expanding Croydon in mid-century. Most of the business of the vestry was transacted at the Easter meeting when the parish accounts were read, the various subsidiary boards appointed, and select rates, including the church rate, generally approved.

The vestry was also responsible, however, for the appointment of the parish officers, the churchwardens, the overseer, the vestry clerk and the beadle and sexton. The churchwardens in particular were powerful figures. One in fact was chosen by the vicar and his choice ratified in the most formal manner only by the vestry; this practice seemed to rest on custom, but it was powerful custom, sufficiently strong to withstand an attack by Nonconformist critics in the 1870s.[65] The duties of the churchwardens extended beyond supervision of the Parish Church to include keeping parish accounts, managing

---

[62] Croydon Parish Church, Vestry Minutes, *passim*; see for example, meeting of 14 Apr. 1857 for Town Hall alterations; 31 Aug. 1858 for footpath diversion; 29 Dec. 1858 for creation of a Burial Board; and 8 Sep. 1863 for a resolution urging the Local Board of Health to provide public baths for Croydon.

[63] This was the aspect of the system which so attracted J. Toulmin-Smith, *The Parish* (London 1854), ch.1.

[64] B. and S. Webb, *English Local Government: the parish and the county* (London 1906), p. 155.

[65] *C Ad*, 11 Apr. 1874.

parochial buildings and property, and summoning vestry meetings. Their power of discretion was considerable: they could even refuse to summon a vestry as when requested to do so by the Local Board of Health in 1868.[66] The most important parochial officer after the churchwardens was the vestry clerk and, unlike theirs, his was a permanent appointment; he was responsible for the secretarial work in association with the vestry and with parochial business, as well as being expected to provide legal expertise of a kind in any disputes affecting the vestry. The three holders of the office during the period covered by this book were all solicitors: George Penfold, clerk from 1834 to 1852, John Drummond from 1852 to 1880 and Henry Seale from 1880.[67] Again the vestry clerk's power of discretion could be considerable: he could withhold or delay the publication of accounts, as John Drummond did during the disputes over parochial charities in the 1860s and 1870s,[68] and by confirming or denying points raised in discussion he could – temporarily at least – affect decisions taken; nevertheless he was in a sense more constrained by the vestry's opinion than the churchwardens were, because of the secretarial and not executive nature of his duties. The most influential figure of all in the vestry was an 'invisible' appointment, the chairman, by custom always the vicar of the parish or, if for any reason he was absent, one of the churchwardens. The chairman's ability to refuse a motion or a poll gave him a de facto power far greater than that of any of the parochial officers. The assumption that the vicar was ex officio chairman was also one challenged unsuccessfully by Nonconformists and Liberals in the 1870s.[69]

If ultimate power still resided in the vestry meetings, nevertheless by the 1840s the practical business of much parochial administration had been delegated to a series of subordinate boards. The first of these to be set up were the Trustees of the Waste Lands, established in 1801 under the Enclosure Act of 1797 to administer common land in the parish; they also became, in effect, part-guardians of the parochial buildings, the Town Hall and Butter Market.[70] The Trustees were the vicar, churchwardens and overseers (all ex officio), and six inhabitants of Croydon chosen annually by the vestry. In 1829, under a further parliamentary act for lighting, watching and improving the town, a Board of Improvement Commissioners was

[66] *C Chron*, 14 Nov. 1868.
[67] Croydon Parish Church Vestry Minutes, *passim*.
[68] See in particular *C Chron*, 11 Sep. 1869; 23 Apr. 1870.
[69] *C Ad*, 11 Apr. 1874.
[70] An Act for Dividing, Alloting and Improving the Open and Common Fields . . . within the Parish of Croydon, in the County of Surrey (27. Geo. III); D. W. Garrow, *The History and Antiquities of Croydon* (Croydon 1818), pp. 50–5.

formed, with the vicar again an ex officio member, and the other twenty members all householders elected by the vestry on an annual basis. The act defined the powers of the Improvement Commissioners widely, to cover provision for street-lighting, the employment of watchmen and police and the provision of lodgings for assize judges, to list labourers in the parish, to name and number the streets, and to raise rates to cover these expenses and other general parochial purposes as approved by the parish.[71] Though, as will be shown, the practical implementation of these powers was limited, their scope was sufficient to make it clear that the Board was the real precursor in the parish of the Local Board of Health. Finally another specialised body, the Board of Surveyors of the Highways, was formed in 1836 to supervise the public roads and footpaths in the parish; again its members were chosen by the vestry. It could appoint a salaried assistant surveyor, and its duties were strictly confined to highways business: whenever an issue arose over which its jurisdiction was uncertain, it invariably passed it either to the Improvement Commissioners or to the Trustees of the Waste Lands.[72]

The creation of a Local Board of Health in Croydon in 1849, under the previous year's Public Health Act, marked an important stage in the structural dismemberment of the parochial system, because the election of local representatives was taken out of the hands of the vestry and placed directly in those of the ratepayers at large, bringing about a certain separation between the principal governing body in the town, the Board, and the ultimate authority, the vestry. Elections were still carried out along property-weighted lines, much like polls of the parish, and there was a £1,000 property rating qualification for all would-be members.[73] The new Board possessed much more extensive rating and statutory power than its two predecessors, the Improvement Commissioners and the Board of Surveyors of the Highways.[74] It proved to be an active, progressive local authority; it implemented a systematic drainage and sewerage programme and an efficient

[71] An Act for Lighting, Watching and Improving the town of Croydon, in the County of Surrey . . . and for other Purposes relating thereto (10. Geo. IV, Session 1829).
[72] Minute Books of the Board for the Repair of the Highways in the Parish of Croydon, *passim*; e.g. meeting of 23 Sep. 1837, when the matter of water pumps was passed to the Improvement Commissioners, and 28 Jul. 1838 when the collection of gravel for roads was referred to the Trustees of the Waste Lands.
[73] The scale of votes property-owners could wield for the Board was broader than that for the vestry polls, with the lower limit for six votes starting at the higher assessment of £250; voting for the Board was regulated by the Poor Law Amendment Act of 1844, and not the Sturges Bourne Act of 1818: J. Redlich and F. W. Hirst, *The History of Local Government in England* (London 1903; reissued 1958), p. 147.
[74] B. Lancaster, 'The Croydon Local Board of Health and the "Croydon Case" 1849–1853', unpubl. MA thesis, Leicester 1981, pp. 5–14.

water supply for the town within a few years of its institution and continued to extend its provision of services and facilities into the 1870s, building parochial slaughter-houses and public baths, acquiring recreation grounds for the town, founding a voluntary fire brigade and developing an innovative farm irrigation scheme for the treatment of Croydon's sewage. Its operations were, however, increasingly marked by criticism from the 1850s, both for what it did not do (above all, widen the High Street), and for the way it did what it did (principally for the cost involved); by the late 1860s it was trapped in a circle of ambitious parochial projects, debts and rate increases.[75]

Two further developments in the history of local government in Victorian Croydon need to be described at this stage. The first was the formation of the Croydon School Board in 1871. Considering the history of sectarian disagreement on the Board, its origins were surprisingly harmonious, lying in a recognition by Anglicans as well as Nonconformists that some 2,800 of the parish's children were without adequate schooling in 1871.[76] It quickly became apparent however that the first elections to the eleven seats on the Board would be along sectarian lines, and a compact was reached between the Anglicans' and Nonconformists' Election Committees in an attempt to ensure a joint slate of eleven nominations, six of which in practice would go to Anglicans.[77] Other independent nominees were also put forward, however, including Croydon's Roman Catholic priest, and in the event five of the joint slate failed to be elected.[78] The practice of 'plumping', by which a voter could cast all or most of his eleven votes in favour of one candidate ensured a certain element of unpredictability in School Board elections in Croydon and, combined with sensitivities over religious education, created a situation in which strong pressures were exerted within denominations to sponsor candidates along sectarian lines. Nonconformists in fact were rarely in a majority on the Board. Some Anglican parishes even set up electoral machinery to exploit 'plumping': for example, the ritualist churches of St Michael's and All Angels and St Augustine's combined in 1897 and 1900 to nominate one candidate and urged their congregations to 'plump' for that candidate.[79] In the same year,

[75] Principal sources for these assertions are: B. Latham, *Report on the Permanent Sanitary Works and their Cost executed in the Parish of Croydon* (Croydon 1868); Minutes of the Croydon Local Board of Health, *passim*; C. M. Elborough, *Croydon, a Borough* (Croydon 1882); and Lancaster, 'The Croydon Local Board of Health'.
[76] *C Chron*, 14 Jan. 1871.
[77] *C Ad*, 18 Feb. 1871.
[78] Anon., *Old and New Croydon*, p. 88.
[79] St Michael and All Angels Parish Magazine, May 1900.

Croydon Parish Church was also urging 'plumpers' for its candidate, had formed its own electoral committee and was carrying out proper canvassing.[80]

The Board in fact proved to be an efficient organ of educational administration. Within four months of its first meeting it had already appointed a complement of honorary and full-time officers, had initiated an educational census of Croydon and had taken over two former voluntary schools.[81] By the end of the decade it had taken over or built seven schools in all, providing accommodation for 3,831 children. The Board's financial power, its ability to compel attendance, and its superior administrative organisation meant that by the 1880s it had already overtaken voluntary schools both in the scale and the quality of its provision.

The second major development in local government was perhaps the most significant of all, for the incorporation of Croydon in 1883 was to mark the beginning of a new stage in the centralisation and extension of local services. The new borough of Croydon followed closely the boundaries of the old parish, and was divided into six wards which in turn followed very largely ecclesiastical districts within the parish: the six were East, West, South and Central Croydon, Upper Norwood and South Norwood. A seventh, North Croydon, was added in 1905 by carving up West Ward.[82] Each ward elected six councillors; two aldermen for each ward were chosen by the councillors. Councillors served for three years, and then had to seek re-election; aldermen served for six, and could be re-elected by the councillors.[83] The Council came into being in June 1883, when the first elections were held; aldermen were then elected for each ward from the successful candidates and a round of by-elections held within three weeks to fill the now vacant places.[84]

The Council took over all the functions of the Local Board of Health, but it had wider compulsory powers and began with a clean financial slate, free from many of the debts which had bedevilled the Board. It was to prove a useful tool for Croydon's municipal leaders, as they sought to extend the functions and powers of local government. Nevertheless several schemes floundered in the mid-1880s because of insufficient support in the Borough at large; these included a proposal to establish a Free Library, a scheme for widening the High Street, a Jubilee fund established with the aim of purchasing the old archiepiscopal palace for the town, and a more

---

[80] St John the Baptist Magazine, June 1900.
[81] Croydon School Board Main Minutes, entries for 4 Jul., 1 Aug. 1871,
[82] Elborough, *Croydon*, pp. 22–3.
[83] *Ward's Croydon Directory*, 1906.
[84] Anon., *Old and New Croydon*, pp. 63–4.

ambitious proposal to purchase the Gas and Coke Company.[85] In the late 1880s, however, this phase passed: the Free Libraries Act was adopted, and in 1890 the Council was able to press for the Improvement Act which gave it rating and purchasing powers to enable it at last to widen the High Street, demolish and rebuild part of the old market area and build new municipal buildings on the site of the failed Croydon Central Station.[86] Further extension of municipal responsibility in the 1890s and 1900s included the purchase of the Tramways Company, the eventual purchase of the Gas Company and of the new Electric Company, the building of a mental hospital, the beginnings of large-scale council housing developments, and the acquisition of the powers of the School Board on its abolition in 1902.[87]

[85] Borough of Croydon, Council Minutes and Incidental Papers, *passim*; see also description of Council discussions and public polls in the following issues of the *Croydon Advertiser*: on Free Libraries, 6 Mar. 1886 and 26 Mar. 1887; on High Street widening, 9 Oct. 1886; on the failure of the Jubilee Fund, 25 June 1887; on the proposed purchase of the Gas Company, 15 Jan. 1887.
[86] Cox, 'Urban Development and Redevelopment', p. 255.
[87] Borough of Croydon, Council Minutes and Incidental Papers, *passim*.

3

The Churches in Victorian Croydon I

Churches at large: numbers and varieties

Members of the Church of England in Croydon in the nineteenth century were fond of claiming an exceptionally close relationship between the National Church and the town. They had some reason to do so, for there had been substantial connections between Croydon and the archbishops of Canterbury over the centuries: the archbishops were lords of the manor in Croydon, held valuable estates in the parish, wielded some local patronage, and continued to possess power over certain economic activities, such as the holding of fairs.[1] The strength of these historical connections and the continued scope for influence possessed by the archbishops enabled Anglicans to hold to what was a very one-sided view of the town's religious complexion: they were able to take up a particular version of history, one which rooted the historic rise of Croydon almost solely in its ecclesiastical institutions and which was therefore a valuable tool in attempting to buoy up Anglican influence in parochial affairs, and yet which inevitably provoked suspicion on the part of Nonconformists. J. B. Jayne was probably only voicing the views of many in 1877 when he alleged, during a public meeting organised by the Liberal, mainly Nonconformist movement for reforming the Whitgift Foundation, that: 'There were certain parties in Croydon who were anxious that Croydon should become a university town, that their noble church should become a cathedral, and that there should be a Bishop of Croydon.'[2]

The readiness of Anglicans to resort to this church-ridden perspective of history might have been a desperate reaction (at least on the part of some) to the knowledge that, in practice, Anglicanism did not have the predominance amongst churchgoers its followers would have liked it to possess, and even that its influence was deteriorating during the second half of the century. To members of the Church of England in Croydon in the late nineteenth century it

[1] Details from R. B. Bannerman, *Royal Croydon* (Croydon 1934), *passim*, and from the *Victoria County History of Surrey*, iv (1902).
[2] *C Chron*, 31 Mar. 1877.

37

must have seemed sometimes as if Nonconformity was a great hostile confederacy, ranged against the church in parochial affairs and formidably organised. The effective organisation of Nonconformists was cited, for example, by the Ruri-Decanal Conference in 1904 as a reason for the need for church councils for Anglican churches.[3] Yet though they were able to arouse concerted action in parochial affairs at certain points of conflict, in turn Nonconformists never formed such a cohesive entity as Anglicans sometimes liked to imagine. There were substantial differences of outlook, organisation and support between the various denominations – Congregationalists, Baptists, Methodists, Presbyterians and Quakers – which it is convenient to label 'Protestant Nonconformity'. Despite this variety, the defining characteristic of Nonconformity was, nevertheless, a political one, and, as will be seen, this raised tensions between the political demands the denominations put upon themselves which could imply that the attack on the Establishment was the single most important duty of Nonconformists, and their distinctive theological, structural and historical features, the development of which could require a more flexible approach to disestablishment.[4]

The complexities which lay behind these differing perceptions of the relative strengths of Anglicanism and Protestant Nonconformity in Croydon are highlighted in the only available systematic surveys of church attendance in Croydon in the period, the official religious census of 1851 and the *Daily News* census of 1902; unfortunately no local census was conducted in the intervening years, and the *British Weekly* survey of London churchgoing in 1886–7 did not extend to Croydon. The results of these censuses are set out in appendix 3, where I have only used the crudest of devices to eliminate 'twicers' from the figures; it cannot be claimed that these figures are an entirely accurate register of churchgoing, but rather that they are a useful way of assessing performance, firstly relative to an expanding population, and secondly by pointing up interdenominational contrasts. Anglicans in Croydon in 1851 could claim, on the basis of the total (adjusted for 'twicers') of 5,423 attendances (twenty-seven per cent of the population) to have a clear lead over all other denominations in the area, which together registered an adjusted total of 2,870 (fourteen per cent of the population).[5] The picture was a very different one by 1902. The adjusted total of Anglican attendances had risen to 19,963, yet as a proportion of the total population this had slipped to fifteen per cent; Nonconformists and

[3] Holy Trinity Parish Magazine, Mar. 1904.
[4] *C Chron*, 9 May 1863, for an example of a Congregational Church adapting parts of the *Book of Common Prayer* to cater for attending Anglican members..
[5] Appendix 3, table 1.

others, in contrast, had risen both in total attendances (adjusted figure) to 23,467 and in the proportion of attendances to population to seventeen per cent, overtaking Anglicanism in the process.[6] Overall percentages for church attendance had fallen from forty-one per cent in 1851 to thirty-two per cent. In the crudest sense, therefore, Croydon was becoming less churchgoing as a whole, but also less Anglican-dominated.

The varieties of Protestant Dissent – their differing impact and appeal – are mirrored very closely in the membership and attendance trends which can also be deduced from the censuses, and from supplementary material, including some membership series.[7] Four of these denominations could already be found in the parish by the 1830s, the Quakers, Congregationalists (Independents), Calvinistic Baptists and Wesleyan Methodists.[8] The 1851 census showed that these denominations, with the new Strict Baptist chapel in West Street founded in 1847, the Primitive Methodist chapel in Laud Street founded approximately in 1849, and Roman Catholics, presented no great challenge to Anglicanism as yet. The individual breakdown of the figures put the Independents or Congregationalists ahead of all the other Nonconformist denominations, with four per cent of the population attending, a total of 726 after adjusting for 'twicers'. Baptists were the second largest, with three per cent, or an adjusted total of 695 attendances. The Quakers were a sizeable congregation too with three per cent or some 633 attendances. Wesleyans achieved 316 attendances or one and a half per cent of the population, and the Primitive Methodists were a tiny group as yet with only 0.2 per cent.[9] The retreat of Anglicanism to an apparent minority position by 1902 tended to mask what appeared to have happened within Protestant Nonconformity itself. The lead of Congregationalists had been whittled away in the course of the half-century, placing them slightly behind the Baptists with three and a half per cent attendances to population compared with the Baptists' 3.7 per cent. In terms of absolute attendances, all denominations except the Quakers had increased considerably. The three largest Protestant Nonconformist denominations nationally, Congregationalists, Baptists and Wesleyan Methodists, now represented the three

[6] *Ibid.*, table 2.
[7] *Ibid.*, table 1.
[8] W. Beck and T.F. Ball, *The London Friends' Meeting* (London 1869), pp. 325–7; D. Finlow, 'A Study of the Religious Society of Friends at Croydon 1825–1875', unpubl. thesis, Coloma College of Education 1974, p. 12; E. E. Cleal and T. G. Crippen, *The Story of Congregationalism in Surrey* (London 1908); A. H. Stockwell, *The Baptist Churches of Surrey* (London n.d.), p. 81; transcript of Burial and Baptism Registers, Croydon Wesleyan Chapel, North End (deposited at C Ref Lib).
[9] Appendix 3, table 1.

largest locally as well, with percentage attendances within one and a half per cent of each other. Other denominations had appeared such as the Presbyterians and the United Methodist Free Church, though they were relatively small. The Primitive Methodists had increased percentage attendance to 0.5 per cent in 1902, or 676 attendances. Quakers alone had diminished in terms of numbers attending, from 633 in 1851 to 171 in 1902.[10]

Anglicanism and Protestant Nonconformity in 1851 dominated Croydon's religious life. Only a small Roman Catholic congregation, composed mostly of Irish labourers and their families, represented any alternative religious tradition in the parish. Yet Mudie Smith's census fifty years later showed that a considerable number of 'unorthodox' religious groups had appeared in the town. The timing of the establishment of these religious communities, so far as it can be deduced from street directories and newspapers, suggests that it was principally in the 1880s that they began to intrude upon Croydon's religious scene. Croydon seems to have been particularly susceptible to them. Including all the unorthodox religious bodies found in Greater London in 1902–3, the total percentage of all attendances they achieved was fourteen per cent; the figure for Croydon alone was almost eighteen and a half per cent. Again, the margin for some individual groups was even greater: the Brethren, for example, achieved 2.8 per cent attendances for Greater London, but four per cent for Croydon: the Unitarian church in Croydon and its associated mission hall accounted for almost half of the total of 694 Unitarian attendances in Greater London.[11] The Roman Catholics and the Salvation Army registered a pattern more in line with that of the larger Protestant denominations, with about one tenth of their Greater London attendances coming from Croydon.[12]

These two censuses of religious attendance pinpoint the local situation in 1851 and 1902 adequately, but the trends they identify need to be set in their national and regional contexts in order to grasp their significance for the development of organised religion in Croydon. No adequate national attendance series exists, unfortunately, to measure Anglican performance throughout this period. The Easter Day Communicant series presented by Currie, Gilbert and Horsley begins in 1885; a comparison between the figure for that year and that for 1902 shows a growth of forty-five per cent, a figure which contrasts with the growth rate of 268 per cent in Croydon attendances between 1851 and 1902, suggesting that Croydon was

[10] *Ibid.*, table 3.
[11] Mudie Smith, *Religious Life*, p. 446.
[12] *Ibid.*

faring much better than the church nationally.[13] For Dissent, denominational statistics make it possible to compare local with national rates of growth from 1851 to 1902 for the Methodist churches only, and predictably enough these put local growth well ahead of national growth: Wesleyan Methodists expanded by some 967 per cent locally, but only fifty per cent nationally; Primitive Methodists by 1,633 per cent locally, but by only eighty-one per cent nationally.[14] Locally, Baptists grew by 620 per cent, Congregationalists by 547 per cent.[15] Croydon's population boom accounted for the massive discrepancies between local and national rates of growth, but there was one sobering exception to the generally faster rate of growth in Croydon – the Quakers. The picture for the Society of Friends locally is clouded by the removal of the attached boarding school in 1879, but the adjusted attendance figure of 171 in 1902 would suggest decline at least from a peak membership of just over 230 in 1868. Actual decline was probably sharper than this seems to indicate, since the adjusted total of attendances in 1851, omitting the 118 school children, at 515 is much higher than the membership of about 160 for that year; if the same margin between attenders and members must be allowed for 1902, membership would have been around fifty to sixty.[16] This is a picture in reverse of the national trend: Croydon meeting increased fitfully at least until the late 1860s, and then (or soon after) seems to have begun to decline; nationally, the Quakers were declining to a low point in 1864, when they began a gradual increase which was sustained to 1914.[17]

If a contrast between national and local rates of growth, where possible, highlights the massive expansion of the churches' urban constituency in Croydon, it is the regional context which helps to pinpoint the way in which Croydon's growth as a commuter suburb was of particular relevance for the churches, for it suggests that the respective levels of attendance attained by the various churches in late century were due to Croydon's increasing reliance for population – especially for the middle and lower middle classes – on migration from London. Contrary to popular notions of overall Anglican strength in the south-east, the rural areas from which, as shown in chapter 2, much of Croydon's labouring population in mid-century was drawn were areas of unusually low churchgoing. The unadjusted total, tabulated by Coleman, put Surrey, with attendances at forty-

[13] Currie, Gilbert and Horsley, *Churches and Churchgoers*, p. 128.
[14] Local comparisons from 1851 and 1902 censuses; national from Currie, Gilbert and Horsley, *Churches and Churchgoers*.
[15] Local comparisons as previously.
[16] Finlow, 'Society of Friends', p. 9.
[17] Currie, Gilbert and Horsley, *Churches and Churchgoers*, pp. 156–7.

one per cent of the population, as the third lowest attending county in England in 1851, beaten only by Cumberland at 37.3 per cent and Middlesex at 37.2 per cent.[18] This should be a distorted figure, as it includes metropolitan Surrey; an unadjusted total for rural Surrey alone however makes very little difference, arriving at forty-two per cent, equal to Northumberland, and close to Durham with 42.6 per cent, but still far behind most other counties in England and Wales. Two of the Unions from which a high proportion of rural immigrants to Croydon would originally have come, Dorking and Reigate, registered extremely low attendances, both with a total percentage (adjusted for twicers) of thirty-four per cent attendances (of which around twenty-three per cent were Anglican).[19] In rural Surrey, in those areas where Dissent was relatively strong, it tended to be so in unions which contained a large town or several smaller towns: the Thames-side union of Chertsey was exceptionally strong Baptist territory, as was Godstone union, but elsewhere in the county the Baptists were weak. Wesleyan Methodists had established themselves all over the county, but overall were relatively weak. The Primitives' chapel in Croydon was the only one in 1851 recorded for the whole of the county, although the Quarterly Meeting Minutes indicate that often other areas were being missioned from Croydon.[20] The Friends were relatively numerous in East Surrey and on the metropolitan fringe, but with the exception of two meeting houses in Guildford Union were entirely absent from the west of the county.

If Alan Everitt's observation that Nonconformity in neighbouring Kent was principally an urban phenomenon is set beside Nonconformist views of rural Surrey as hostile territory, it becomes clear that it was an urban phenomenon in Surrey too, and that the roots of Nonconformist advance in Croydon in the second half of the century are to be sought in the town's urban development and the increasing tendency to draw immigrants from London, rather than in the remaining rural connections between Croydon and East Surrey.[21] As has been shown, the congruence between the relative position of the Protestant Nonconformist denominations in Croydon and in greater London as a whole by 1902 was considerable. In the 'inner' London district of Lewisham in 1902–3, already undergoing gradual social decline like Croydon, Anglicans registered a slight lead over Nonconformists, but the difference was not considerable;[22] in

---

[18] Coleman, *The Church of England*, p. 40.
[19] Appendix 3, table 2.
[20] Croydon Primitive Methodist Circuit, Quarterly Meeting Minutes 1851, *passim*.
[21] A. M. Everitt, *The Pattern of Rural Dissent: the nineteenth century* (Leicester 1972), p. 57.
[22] McLeod, *Class and Religion*, pp. 306–7.

Lambeth, also undergoing decline, and at a faster rate than Croydon, the same is true, although Croydon's overall level of attendance was higher.[23] There were parallels too between Croydon and London districts in terms of the overall decline of churchgoing, which suggests that Croydon's experience, though not as traumatic as some, was fairly typical. Attendance across all denominations in Croydon as a proportion of population fell by twenty-one per cent from 1851 to 1902; this was a figure matched by many London boroughs, including Hampstead, Wandsworth, Paddington, Kennington and South Newington in sixteen years alone from 1886 to 1902.[24] In late nineteenth century Croydon, then, the level of churchgoing was somewhat higher than it was in certain inner London districts south of the Thames, and this would have been related to Croydon's higher (though falling) social status, yet the pattern of Nonconformist encroachment was similar.

Underlying the trends identified by the two religious censuses were a variety of experiences of growth and decay felt by individual local churches. Particular local circumstances often played an important part in all this, as far as can be judged from occasional surviving membership and attendance records and from some impressionistic evidence, but whilst it is impossible adequately to summarise all these local developments, it is important to emphasise the extent to which, taken together, they illustrate the fact that by the beginning of the twentieth century there was a widespread perception that organised religion was undergoing a crisis. Six Anglican parishes registered this sense of crisis acutely: Christ Church, North Croydon, St Paul's, Thornton Heath, St Mark's, South Norwood, St Saviour's, East Croydon, St James, East Croydon, and Holy Trinity, Selhurst, were all to the north and north-east of the town centre and all facing rapid population growth in the late nineteenth century. At Holy Trinity, for example, the vicar was almost entirely dependent for his income upon pew rents, yet the falling social status of the district and its increasing population meant that his financial needs were increasing fast as the source of his income was diminishing; he also underlined that there was a serious shortage of church workers, particularly district visitors and Sunday School teachers.[25] In 1902 for the first time in ten years he recorded a slight increase in pew rents but this was not sustained.[26] The vicar of St James reported similar problems in 1889, and in particular a decrease in pew rents.[27] One of his

[23] Cox, *Churches in a Secular Society*, p. 25.
[24] McLeod, *Class and Religion*, p. 314.
[25] Holy Trinity Magazine, Annual Report 1900.
[26] *Ibid.*, Annual Reports, 1902, 1904.
[27] Visitation returns, 1889.

successors ten years later was still facing the same problem of prolonged decline and dependence on the diminishing returns from pew rents.[28] Problems of finance and manpower were also occurring at this time in other parishes in Croydon, though not on so acute a scale. Anglican strength in Croydon in the mid-nineteenth century was related to its middle class character; districts which contained a high proportion of solid middle class homes, such as Upper Norwood and Addiscombe, registered very high levels of church attendance. The vicar of St Matthew's, east of the town centre and on the edge of the affluent Addiscombe and Park Hill estates from which most of his congregation would have come, was nevertheless unusual in being able to claim in 1876 that none of his tiny parish of about 870 were labouring poor, and that his average congregation, at about eight hundred in number, was most of his parish. The only parochial institution he maintained at this period was a lending library for servants.[29] Yet even St Matthew's was reporting a third of its population as poor twenty years later and its income, again derived from pew rents, as gradually diminishing.[30] At Upper Norwood, by 1912, though congregations in the mainly middle class parish of St John's were large, the vicar was sufficiently concerned to invite suggestions from the church council as to how he could attract a larger congregation.[31]

Although Nonconformists stood to gain from the influx of the lower middle classes into the borough in the second half of the century, nevertheless by the 1900s many chapels were also registering financial difficulties and sometimes falling rolls. One interesting example is provided by the Primitive Methodists, who consistently recorded quarterly membership totals from 1867, with some scattered figures surviving from before that date; the circuit showed steady growth in the late nineteenth century, reaching 361 in 1902, expanded fitfully until 1908, and then began a sharp slump, falling to 324 by 1912.[32] Clearly the Mudie-Smith figures do not represent a fixed point in what was in fact a highly volatile picture of growth and decline amongst the Primitive Methodists in Croydon. At George Street Congregational Chapel membership increase was, unusually, sustained up until the First World War, but again it was fitful; a serious decline in attendances from 1897 onwards led to the wholesale resignation of all the church deacons in January 1900 to put pressure

[28] St James's Magazine, Mar. 1899.
[29] Visitation returns, 1876.
[30] *Ibid.*, 1898.
[31] Church Council Minutes, 30 Oct. 1912, St John the Evangelist, Upper Norwood.
[32] Croydon Primitive Methodist Circuit, Quarterly Meeting Minutes, *passim.*

on the minister to resign, and his two successors managed to rebuild the congregation.[33] But George Street was not typical, as it was in a sense the parish church of Congregationalism in Croydon: important denominational and interdenominational meetings were regularly held there, its pastors were generally men of some standing in the denomination, and it was attended by leading Congregationalists in the town, such as T. A. Johns, whose funeral service was conducted by Alexander Hannay, secretary of the Congregational Union, and Andrew Mearns, the Congregational social reformer.[34] So the social pull of George Street Chapel was likely to be much stronger in the 1900s than it would have been at other chapels. At South Norwood chapel, for example, a period of growth in the late nineteenth century was accompanied by a further rise in membership to 1907, when decline set in until the First World War; numbers of Sunday Scholars at the same church began to fall in 1902 from a peak of 320, declined sharply to the 200 mark in 1914, and then fell steeply again in the 1920s and 1930s.[35]

However, the Victorians did not measure a church's performance solely or even principally in the light of membership and attendance figures. Had they done so it is possible that more consistent, regular series would have been kept than those which have survived. Of greater weight to many contemporaries in estimating the influence of a church was the crude index of the numbers and scale of its places of worship, in other words the scale of accommodation for worship provided in the area. When the vicar of Croydon in the late 1850s participated in a brief local newspaper discussion about the published findings of the 1851 census, it was the question of accommodation on which he and the respondent to his letter concentrated, neither of them finding much on which to congratulate Anglican and Nonconformist churches. The vicar pointed out that in Croydon accommodation in the Established Church, at twenty-two per cent of the population, was well below the national average of twenty-nine per cent.[36] At the time he was writing there were already six Anglican churches in the parish, four of them perpetual curacies under a fifth, the Parish Church. All except the Parish Church had been built since the 1820s. The expansion of Anglican 'plant' in the form of church building continued at an even pace up to the First World

[33] R. A. Raymer, *The Congregational Church at George Street, Croydon: a history 1672–1964* (Croydon 1964), p. 25.
[34] *Ibid.*, p. 24.
[35] Anon., *South Norwood Congregational Church Centennial Brochure 1870–1970* (South Norwood 1970), p. 19 (membership chart).
[36] *C Chron*, 21, 28 Nov. 1857.

War.[37] From the 1850s onwards Anglican churches were put up at a constant rate, averaging three every decade, with the lowest number, two, in the 1890s matched by the highest, five in the following decade. The figures can be misleading – it could take up to ten years to begin 'working' an area, build a temporary church and finance and build a permanent structure – but they indicate that the momentum of Anglican expansion at least was maintained. However, by 1900 financial pressures and declining interest were taking their toll; twentieth century churches were all relatively small, cheap, brick buildings, nothing to compare with the magnificent structures designed by Pearson at St Michael and All Angels, North Croydon and St John the Evangelist, Upper Norwood, both of them designed and built in the 1870s. St Michael's in fact became a sad sign of declining religious interest, as sufficient money was never raised in the early twentieth century to complete the building altogether by adding the spire Pearson had originally designed for it.[38] By 1914 the original parish of Croydon had become subdivided into twenty-four parishes or ecclesiastical districts, with a further twelve mission halls built in lower middle class and working class districts of the town.[39]

In contrast for example to Hook's work at Leeds, Anglican church extension in Croydon ran more smoothly in that lay support and even lay initiative was readily forthcoming for the building of new churches;[40] yet a combination perhaps of the lack of a man of Hook's calibre and the weakness of the vicar of Croydon's financial position (reliant as he as upon a slender endowment, burial fees and collections and the readiness in the mid-century of middle class congregations to take up rented pews), meant that no concerted attack on pew rents was led by a vicar of Croydon. Even a systematic, modest programme of church extension in Croydon had to wait until the late 1890s, when a large bequest for church building became available to a new archbishop, Temple, with a more active interest in church provision in Croydon than his predecessor. Under the plan encouraged by Temple, two new parish churches were to be built, two new permanent missions to be established, several churches to be enlarged, and a rearrangement of boundaries carried out. Most of this programme applied to the areas of Thornton Heath, Selhurst, South Norwood and South Croydon, where growth at this period was

[37] I have based this assertion on the consecration dates of new church buildings, extracted from the prefaces to Croydon street directories and cross-checked where possible with local newspapers.
[38] N. Pevsner and B. Cherry, *Buildings of England: London 2: the south* (Harmondsworth, 3rd edn 1983), p. 210.
[39] *Ward's Croydon Directory*, 1914.
[40] W. R. W. Stephens, *Life and Letters of W.F. Hook* (London 1878), esp. ch. 6.

most rapid.[41] In Croydon, where a number of disputes amongst clergy and between clergy and laity occurred over issues of patronage which were bound up with church extension, Anglicanism in general was at least able to preserve some kind of united front on the question of church building. Even where clergy had a vested interest in opposing church extension because they were reliant upon pew rents for their income, as at All Saints, Upper Norwood, and St James, East Croydon, they were district clergymen, and so the effects of their obstructionism were extremely localised. Consequently, although serious shortages occurred in various areas from time to time, the lack of accommodation never reached crisis proportions. In 1851 three churches (excluding St John's, Shirley) had been available for a population of some 20,000, in other words one church per 6,670 approximately; by 1914 with a provision of thirty-six (including mission churches) for about 170,000, this figure had dropped to one per 4,720 approximately. The figure had actually been even lower in 1901, with about one per 4,000, the lowest proportion of churches to population throughout the period.[42]

The pattern of Nonconformist church building in Croydon reinforces the view of differential rates of growth which can be deduced for the denominations from the attendance and membership figures and which was affected by the developing social characteristics of the area. By 1902 Mudie Smith's reporters could record forty-six buildings for Protestant Nonconformity in the area: twelve Congregationalist chapels, fifteen Baptist chapels and mission halls, thirteen Methodist chapels (seven Wesleyan, two United Methodist Free Church, and four Primitive Methodist), five Presbyterian churches and one Quaker Meeting.[43] Weselyan Methodists and Primitive Methodists both began building in the 1850s, but their building rates remained relatively constant after a break in the 1860s. The Society of Friends extended the Meeting-house but saw no need to expand their organisation, understandably in the light of their modest size and probably decline late in the century. The most interesting contrast is that between the Congregationalists and the Baptists. Baptist church building peaked in the 1870s, with seven chapels appearing in these decades, tailing off to four from 1890 to about 1910; Congregationalists peaked earlier in the 1860s when six of their chapels were built, and had stopped expanding by the early

---

[41] Report of public meeting held under the presidency of the archbishop of Canterbury, *C Chron*, 18 June 1898.
[42] Comparison of numbers of places of worship (extracted from *Gray's*, *Warren's* and *Ward's Croydon Directories*, 1851–1914) with census report population totals for Croydon.
[43] Mudie Smith, *Religious Life*, pp. 383–5.

1880s. Both leading denominations were slowing by the 1880s, then, in terms of the extension of places of worship.[44]

Joshua Wilson's claim for the Congregationalists that 'our special vocation is to the middle classes of the people' was thus borne out by the performance of the Congregationalists in Croydon.[45] The pre-eminence they had attained within Nonconformity in the area by 1851 and their peak years of church building in the 1860s and 1870s coincided with the early years of Croydon's growth as a middle class commuter suburb; the fact that their appeal was to a distinct bracket within the middle class is shown by the subsequent success of the Baptists who caught up with the Congregationalists as from the 1880s the weight of urban growth tended to swing towards the lower middle class, and Croydon began a gradual social decline. Congregational-ists in the area did not build mission halls for the poor and mostly supported chapels in middle class residential districts such as Addiscombe and South Norwood; Baptists on the other hand by 1902 had mission halls and chapels situated in the poorer areas of the town as well as in the residential districts. Quakerism also mirrored the curve of Croydon's social development closely: the membership of Croydon Preparative Meeting expanded from the 1820s with the arrival of wealthy, middle class Friends such as Peter Bedford, the silk merchant, and John Morland, umbrella manufacturer; by 1865 where the occupations of Croydon members were known, nearly half were gentlemen, professional men, merchants or large manufactur-ers, and this proportion would be a much higher one if teachers employed in the Friends' School were omitted from the analysis:[46] but the numbers of the Friends began to decline in late century as the appeal of Croydon to the wealthy middle class declined. Methodist growth also illustrates social change: first Wesleyan and Primitive Methodists who nationally are supposed to have had a differential class appeal, that of the Primitives being slightly lower than the lower middle class base of Wesleyanism, established themselves in the town and then expanded as the town grew. The United Methodists, who nationally did not have a class appeal markedly different from Wesleyanism, built two chapels in lower middle class districts, though one of them was disused by 1906.[47]

[44] Details of church building rates collected from *Gray's*, *Warren's* and *Ward's Croydon Directories*, 1851 to 1914; details of dates of building and costs were inserted for each new chapel in the compendium of local information printed at the front of the directories.

[45] *Congregational Year Book*, 1861, p. 63.

[46] Finlow, 'Society of Friends', p. 16.

[47] *Ward's Croydon Directory*, 1906.

The building of chapels and the expansion of the various denominations in the area, linked to the social evolution of Croydon, produced what was a rich and complex religious pattern by the 1900s. Urbanisation, if it produced or strengthened many obstacles to church activity, also increased religious opportunities for the potential churchgoer. The very varied social roots of Nonconformity were not necessarily a strength, for the resilience of the denominations depended upon maintaining their appeal within fairly specialised social categories. The absence of strong sectarian competition between the Protestant Nonconformist denominations needs to be understood as a consequence of differential social support: they were not necessarily in direct competition amongst the same social groups. And yet for the same reason, if support amongst a denomination's traditional social constituency began to decline, the sense of crisis would have been multiplied; all the more serious, for example, must have appeared the Primitive Methodists' falling membership in the late 1900s, for this was a period of lower middle class and working class growth in the area which should have been favourable to them.

The transformation of the Anglican Church

Two countervailing views of the vicissitudes of the Anglican Church at parish level have become commonplace in the historiography of Victorian religion. One is that parish life successfully combined the preservation of the historic traditions and continuities of Anglicanism with an infusion of new inspiration from a rediscovered Catholicity so that, whatever difficulties the church might have faced nationally, pastorally at least it was regenerated. The judgement, for example, of Roger Lloyd was that 'the Church entered the [twentieth] century with palsied limbs and hardening arteries. Its heart was still beating strongly, for at the centre of the whole frame lay then what has always lain, the ideal of faithfulness in the parochial ministry'.[48] Against this is the view that the parochial machinery of Anglicanism was an obstacle to the development of the church in urban areas, and yet one to which churchmen clung obstinately. As Kent has expressed it: 'Anglican history has been written on the principle – it is far more than an assumption – that the parochial system is the ideal type of the ecclesia; this belief is deeply rooted in the institutions as they are, and

---

[48] R. Lloyd, *The Church of England in the Twentieth Century* (London 1946), p. 25.

has been transmitted to generation after generation of priests.'[49] Both views are in fact wide of the mark. At the local level the Church of England could be much more flexible and innovative than these arguments suggest; parish life was marked by more intense doctrinal conflict than Anglican historians have tended to note, but at the same time the parochial system proved to be much less of an impediment to the activities of churchmen – and to the growth of different religious traditions within Anglicanism – than their critics have sometimes supposed.

Under the impact of doctrinal and liturgical change, in its attempts to meet the demands of rapidly urbanising areas the parochial ministry of the Church of England was transformed in the Victorian period. Church life became much more vigorous and parish organisation more complex; where the sense of failure crept in was in the perception that, ultimately, the church was becoming marginalised in relation to society at large. Its attempts to rid itself of political controversy led to its withdrawal from entrenched positions of authority, and yet its engagement with local issues of welfare and control was proportionately reduced. The efforts of High Church proponents to reform liturgical practice alienated some, and served in the long run to emphasise the authority of the church in a specialist field of spiritual endeavour rather than in the wider society. Thus the attitude which Wickham saw as symptomatic of the church's failure to engage adequately with industrial and urban society – 'theological error that narrowed the claims of God and the concern of the church from the dimension of the Kingdom to the dimension of "religion" ' – was paradoxically a result of the church's attempt to do precisely that.[50]

The changes which underlay this overall reorientation of the Church of England were of particular significance in Croydon in five principal areas: the conflicts over the rise of the High Church in Croydon, the general field of theology and liturgical practice, the efforts made to recruit new members, the organisation and management of the parish, and the role and status of the clergy.

The course of the controversy over Tractarianism and Ritualism was very much affected by the structure of patronage in Croydon, and Low Churchmen relied on the manipulation of patronage as a

---

[49] J. Kent, *The Unacceptable Face: the modern church in the eyes of the historian* (London 1987), p. 95; this view is considered at some length in Inglis, *Churches and the Working Classes*, pp. 24–30.
[50] E. R. Wickham, *Church and People in an Industrial City* (London 1957), pp. 192–3; for an attempt to appraise Wickham's book in the light of recent historical research, see J. N. Morris, 'Church and people thirty-three years on: a historical critique', *Theology*, xciv (1991).

means of maintaining their influence. Had church extension proceeded solely as a result of initiatives on the part of the vicar and his district clergy it is very difficult to see how the High Church could have gained a footing at all in the parish before the appointment of the moderate High Churchman J. M. Braithwaite as vicar of Croydon in 1882. Yet the participation in church building by wealthy, influential members of the town elite in the 1850s, 1860s and 1870s and the scope which existed to some extent for externally-initiated church extension enabled Ritualism to appear in Croydon as early as the late 1850s. The rise of High Churchmanship thus has much to say about the practical limitations to the authority of the vicar, and by implication for the degree of central control wielded by the Anglican hierarchy over what was happening in rapidly urbanising parishes like Croydon. It also suggests that in the middle decades of the nineteenth century the religious sensibilities of leading laity, reliant as the church was on such people for the financial support and to some extent the social prestige which would enable it to adapt to the changing conditions of urban areas, were every bit as important in determining the ultimate course of church policy and the complexion of the Anglican Church as were those of the hierarchy itself.

This is best exemplified in a network of three High Anglican churches which were partly founded by the same group of laity, though it could also be illustrated from other High Churches in the parish. The three concerned were St Andrew's, near the Old Town, St Saviour's, near Croydon Common, and St Michael and All Angels just north of the town centre. The foundation of St Andrew's in 1857 took place with the active support of the vicar of Croydon, John Hodgson, but the initiative was an external one, coming from the rector of the neighbouring rural parish of Sanderstead, who retained the patronage.[51] Under the first priest-in-charge St Andrew's adopted High Church forms of worship; subsequently a curate from St Andrew's moved to a mission church, St Saviour's, in the parish of St James, where he was followed by at least four influential members of St Andrew's congregation. This curate's death in 1869 raised anxieties that the vicar of St James, Henry Watson, would not appoint the congregation's choice of a successor, the Rev R. W. Hoare, and so guarantee the continuation of High Church forms of worship at St Saviour's.[52] In the face of the vicar's obstinacy, a group of laity – including those who had originally moved from St Andrew's

[51] C. G. Paget, *Seventy-Five Years of Progress: St. Andrew's Church, Croydon 1857–1932* (Croydon 1932), p. 10.
[52] Anon., *Memorials and Correspondence respecting the Recent Appointment of an Incumbent for St. Saviour's Church, Croydon* (Croydon 1869).

– mounted a campaign to procure a church in Croydon for Hoare. This they eventually managed to do under Peel's 1843 Act, and despite opposition from the vicar of Croydon.[53] Hoare was licensed as a minister-in-charge by Archbishop Tait in August 1870, yet even though the new parish did not have a suitable site for the new church.[54] There could be no better illustration of the impatience of laity concerned to protect and extend provision for worship according to their doctrinal beliefs with the niceties of the Anglican Church's system of authority. A similar pattern of attempted resistance to High Churchmanship occurred at Norwood, where it led to the formation of a new Ritualist church, St John the Evangelist's, in the early 1870s, again at the instigation of a group of High Church laity, reinforcing the impression that opposition to active lay interest in the propagation of a specific doctrinal view in mid-century was ineffectual.[55] Unwittingly the growth of the High Church party in Croydon had been fuelled by those who had sought to contain it.

Despite the criticism which greeted the advance of High Churchmanship in Croydon at every step, what had happened by the 1880s was that a church party highly unpopular in the 1850s had not only gained a footing in the area but had become one of the more dynamic features of church life. In the 1880s it must have seemed at times as if the Anglican Church in Croydon was divided into two hostile camps. Two rival networks certainly existed. Ritualists took pains to maintain close connections between their churches in Croydon. Already St Andrew's had been recognised in 1870 as the 'parent of St Saviour's, and . . . is destined to acknowledge other descendants in Croydon', a reference to St Michael's.[56] They exchanged preachers on some occasions, and participated in the formation of a branch of the English Church Union in 1876.[57] In 1879 an East Surrey district of the ECU was formed to include Croydon, holding its annual meeting at the Public Hall in Croydon; business principally covered discussion of issues affecting the church nationally.[58] A similar network of evangelical churches existed, Christ Church, St Matthew's, St Luke's, Woodside and St Mary Magdalene at Addiscombe being the most consistently 'Low' though others (including St James) were sometimes described as such.

[53] F. N. Heazell, *The History of St. Michael's, Croydon: a chapter in the Oxford Movement* (Croydon 1934), p. 50.
[54] *Ibid.*, p. 51.
[55] H. W. Bateman, *A Short History of the Church of St. John the Evangelist, Upper Norwood 1871–1937* (Croydon 1937).
[56] *C Chron*, 9 Jul. 1870.
[57] *C Ad*, 1 Dec. 1877.
[58] *Ibid.*, 10 Jul. 1880.

Croydon-wide branches of the Church Association, the Protestant Reformation Society and the Protestant Evangelical Mission attracted evangelical support, as well as less militant, evangelising bodies such as the Society for Promoting Christianity amongst the Jews.[59]

Given this apparent organisation of extremes within Anglicanism, one might have expected tension to have reached the point where it could have erupted over specific issues such as education and seriously split the church in Croydon. This did not happen. Instead what occurred was that on both wings of the church from the 1880s some sort of accommodation was made with the alternative doctrinal traditions; Low Church criticism of Ritualism declined, High Churchmen lost their early near-conversionist zeal and began to be seen regularly on platforms with Evangelical clergy. There were no bitter conflicts from the 1890s onwards between laity and clergy of the kind that had surfaced in the founding of Ritualist churches in the 1860s and 1870s. There were still occasions when laity criticised clergymen for ritualistic innovations, but when they did so they were in a small minority and failed to raise much support from the rest of the congregation. A leading member of St Andrew's congregation accused the Rev Randolph of introducing a number of 'extreme' ritualist practices at the church in 1891, but Randolph was able to show that he had exaggerated the significance of these or mistaken their meaning, and that he was not supported in his protests by any other members of the congregation.[60] At St Augustine's in South Croydon the very ritualistic John White in 1908 and 1909 was severely criticised by several of his congregation for, amongst other things, introducing a cope into church, wearing a biretta, having a sanctus bell and holding views favourable to intercessory prayers, but even these extreme practices did not stir up prolonged opposition, and when the most outspoken critic put himself forward for re-election as a churchwarden in 1909, his rival for the position crushed him easily by twenty-six votes to four at the vestry meeting.[61]

No doubt the declining intensity of doctrinal conflict within the Anglican Church from the 1880s owed something to what might be called the 'liberalising' of theological and liturgical traditions in the late nineteenth century, the second major area of change. The 'Liberal Catholicism' of which *Lux Mundi* was by far the most influential statement was already being anticipated in the 1880s in Croydon (though only at a practical level) by J. M. Braithwaite,

[59] *C Chron, passim*, for example 23 Jan. 1875 and 8 Apr. 1876.
[60] Benson papers (Lambeth Palace Library), ic 307–12.
[61] Vestry Minutes, St Augustine's Church, 24 Apr. 1908 and 16 Apr. 1909.

liberal vicar of Croydon, known for his High Churchmanship, and yet one for whom 'outward divergencies' between Anglicans and Nonconformists were not as important as their shared 'love of Christ and zeal for His glory'.[62] It is possible to trace a similar easing of tension within Evangelicalism. Statements of evangelical principles from the 1880s tend to be more pliant, more moderate and accommodating in tone than in mid-century. A curate at Christ Church in 1891 praised the recently dead wife of the evangelical vicar, O. B. Byers, as an examplar of 'the Christianity of the English gentleman and the English lady, the Christianity which is quiet, unobtrusive, kind, considerate and charitable'.[63] There was no weakening of evangelical doctrine, but rather a less strident tone in its proclamation. As it was said of Arthur Easter's evangelical ministry at St Matthew's: 'Such a ministry as this was bound to succeed. It was a ministry of prayer and humility. Of myself, he told me, when leaving home for a time, I am of little account; all that I am and have has been through helping and sympathising with others. This, after all, should be the ideal of every faithful minister.'[64]

If the influence of theological change had something to do with this sense of accommodation, it also must have owed much to recognisable changes in liturgical practice in the church. Here the dynamic impetus was derived ultimately from the High Church revival. Firstly the scale of provision for worship – the number of services – increased greatly at Anglican churches in the area. That this was as much a priest-inspired change as a response to actual demand in the form of over-crowded services can be seen by the elaborate provision made for week-day services, most of which were badly attended. Every Anglican church in Croydon registered this change to a greater or lesser degree. The most extreme example was the ultra-High St Michael's, by 1900 holding four celebrations of the Eucharist on Sundays (at 7 am, 8 am, 9 am, and 11.45 am) as well as Matins, Litany, a children's service and evensong, and Matins daily at 8 am, preceded by Holy Communion, and Evensong, also daily.[65] At the moderate or middle-of-the-road St Paul's, Thornton Heath, the two Sunday services held in 1869 had risen to four by 1900 (including two celebrations of Holy Communion), with daily Matins as well and

[62] Rev Canon Benham, *Sermon preached in the Croydon Parish Church on Sunday July 7th, 1889, on the occasion of the death of the Rev J.M. Braithwaite* (Croydon 1889).

[63] Rev J. K. Hawker, *A Sermon in Memory of Catherine Byers Preached on Sunday 2nd August 1891* (Croydon 1891).

[64] Rev A. J. Easter, *Memoir of Arthur Joseph Easter* (Croydon 1919) p. 25.

[65] Details of services for St Michael's and other churches extracted from *Gray's, Warren's*, and *Ward's Croydon Directories*, 1853–1914, confirmed as far as possible from parish magazines.

extra Communion Services on the second and fifth Sundays in the month. Even at the evangelical Christ Church the two Sunday services held in the 1850s had increased to four by 1900 (one celebration of the Holy Communion), with three week-day services; the week-day attendances were very low, about twenty on average.[66]

Secondly, in practically every sphere of liturgical practice what were regarded as ritualistic innovations in the 1850s and 1860s were gradually accepted as necessary features of church life, for many carrying no explicit doctrinal connotations and yet by their very adoption signifying that some sort of accommodation to the existence of the High Church party was taking place. John Hodgson defended his introduction of a full surpliced choir at the Parish Church in 1869 on the grounds that they had appeared all over London, that they did not imply specific doctrinal formulae, and that 'owing to the advance of taste, and the increased attention now paid to the details of Divine worship, the propriety of some suitable garb for persons directly engaged in conducting the services has been generally felt'.[67] The *Croydon Advertiser* interpreted his action less charitably as a turn around from his earlier opposition to 'full-blown' Ritualism.[68] The offertory, favoured by the Tractarians as a solution to the problem of raising money in the absence of church rates, was gradually introduced throughout Croydon and by the 1890s made a substantial contribution to the incomes of many churches.[69] Other changes included the use of stone altars, the introduction of Hymns Ancient and Modern, the use of lighted candles on the altar and decorative tapestry work which featured crucifixes or images of Christ and the saints.[70] The evangelical St Mary Magdalene (amongst other Croydon churches) was already advertising for ladies for its surpliced choir in 1871, and when about thirty years later A. J. Easter introduced a surpliced choir at the equally Low St Matthew's he was able to do so without raising any serious objections.[71]

A third sign of the increasing influence of High Church practices and ideas was the emphasis which came to be placed upon the importance of Communion as a vital act of worship. Chadwick put the turning point in Anglican attitudes to the Communion in the 1840s and 1850s, but in Croydon most churches in the late 1850s and

[66] Visitation returns, 1898.
[67] Letter to the *C Chron*, 19 May 1898.
[68] Anon., *Croydon Crayons* (reprinted from the Croydon Advertiser, 1873), p. 10.
[69] See replies to questions about source of income in Visitation returns. Even at evangelical Christ Church by 1889 one-fifth of the vicar's income was derived from the Easter offertory.
[70] See for example *C Chron*, 30 Mar. 1878 for criticism of candles and tapestries at St Peter's in South Croydon.
[71] *C Chron*, 21 Jan. 1871; St Matthew's Parish Magazine, May 1899.

early 1860s still only celebrated Matins and Evensong on Sunday.[72] Ritualist churches founded in the 1860s adopted Communion almost immediately, it seems, but the Parish Church did not advertise separate Communion services until the mid-1870s.[73] St James started around the end of the 1870s, and was holding five celebrations by 1882; probably the rapid change was due to the death of the evangelical incumbent, Henry Watson, in 1879. Other evangelical churches followed suit in the 1870s and 1880s. Only in ritualist churches is it likely that the 'High' notion of Communion was explicitly enunciated: 'instead of one in five being Communicants, *all ought to be so* [original italics]; and none who are not so, can be considered in a healthy or happy condition, as regards their state in GOD's sight, and as regards the hope of their everlasting salvation in the world to come'.[74] But it seems equally likely that the implications of placing greater emphasis on communion were not altogether lost on the Low Church as well. Low Church clergy, like their High Church brethren, came to regard the numbers of those communicating as the acid test of a church's growth by at least the 1890s; so it was quite natural when, in 1902, a chapel-of-ease, St Philip's, was established at Norbury in the parish of Christ Church, that its growth over the ensuing nine years should be measured in terms of Easter and Christmas communicants.[75]

The third significant area of change was in the various enterprises associated with the recruitment of new members: the methods employed remained essentially the same throughout the period, but there was change in degree and in relative success. Methods of recruitment fell broadly into two categories: endogenous recruitment, in other words the 'religious socialisation' of children who would, it was hoped, move naturally into regular participation in the church when they became adults, and exogenous recruitment, namely missionary activity and the work of conversion.

The subject of religious education was of such importance to churchmen that it would be impossible to give it adequate treatment here; the wider implications of educational policy and sectarian conflict over education will be examined in their turn elsewhere. Though other agencies were employed, the greatest attention of Anglicans was directed to maintaining Sunday schools and day schools. Sunday schools were an integral part of the parochial system; no church was without them and the establishment of a Sunday

[72] Chadwick, *Victorian Church*, i, 514.
[73] Details about communion services extracted from directories, and cross-referenced where possible with parish magazines.
[74] Anon., *St Andrew's, Croydon: a church for the poor* (Croydon 1858), p. 24.
[75] Christ Church Magazine, Nov. 1911.

school invariably followed closely on the heels of the founding of a new church. At St Michael's, for example, one was opened within six months of the erection of the temporary church in 1872; with no parochial room in which to hold classes, the church itself had to be used.[76] The provision of Sunday school teachers was a serious burden on churches; their shortage was one of the first signs that a church was facing difficulties in keeping its agencies going, as occurred at Holy Trinity, for example, in the late 1890s.[77] The formal importance of Sunday school teachers was confirmed in the early 1880s when an association of Sunday school teachers was organised for Anglican churches, centred on the Parish Church.[78] Church day schools naturally drew heavily upon the financial support of the churches rather than upon manpower; again the impression is that they were regarded as integral to church activity in the period and not supplementary to it. It was admittedly more difficult – because more costly – to establish a day school than it was a Sunday school, but very few churches chose to ignore perceived responsibilities in this direction. By 1881 thirteen of the sixteen Anglican churches then existing in the town supported them.[79]

Yet there is much incidental evidence to suggest that whilst the value of church schools for 'recruiting' attenders must have been considerable, it was not as great as many clergymen hoped. In terms of numbers alone undoubtedly Sunday schools were successful: at a meeting of the Sunday School Teachers' Association in 1888 returns for each school indicated a total of 4,587 children being educated by some 339 teachers, and this was a figure which omitted the two Upper Norwood churches of All Saints and St John the Evangelist's, so the total would in fact have been nearer 5,000.[80] This was one half of the 10,215 children under fifteen years of age recorded in the Borough by the 1891 census,[81] though probably the returns reflected numbers on the rolls and not regular pupils. Church day schools on the whole fared worse. Returns submitted to the Borough Inquiry in 1881 showed that within ten years of the inception of the School Board they had already yielded precedence to the new Board schools: whereas the Board could claim 3,957 children on its books and average attendances as 3,383, the Anglican schools could claim only 3,604 on their books and an average attendance of 2,434.[82] The narrow margin

---

[76] Heazell, *History of St Michael's*, p. 10.
[77] Holy Trinity Magazine, Annual Report, 1900.
[78] *C Ad*, 18 Oct. 1884.
[79] Details from street directories and visitation returns.
[80] *C Chron*, 16 June 1888.
[81] *1891 Census Report for England and Wales* (1893), iii, 35.
[82] Elborough, *Croydon*, pp. 22-5.

between the Board's enrolled numbers and its attendance, in comparison with the Anglican gap of twice the size, showed how its rating powers and its powers of compulsory attendance were taking effect. Furthermore Anglican accommodation, at 3,661 places, was being seriously under-used, whereas Board accommodation was already over-crowded at all but one of their schools, the exception being the large Mitcham Road schools opened only a year previously and therefore not yet taking on their full capacity.[83] The financial strain of maintaining day schools was telling on churches by the 1880s and 1890s. Croydon Parish Church National Schools were already running at a deficit in the early 1880s, and special steps had to be taken (a committee formed and a special appeal launched) to ensure their survival.[84] Holy Trinity's National Schools faced the same problem by the mid-1890s, Christ Church and St James by the early 1900s.[85] Visitation returns show that in almost every parish where a Board School was opened the incumbent feared his church school would suffer. In 1898 the Rev Randolph of St Andrew's, for example, claimed that the new Board school recently opened close to his church was 'Designed to please agitators. It has had no effect so far on our National Schools. Ragged School has suffered. In long term it cannot fail to lower the number of children desiring to be admitted to National School.'[86] The returns also indicate what might have been an equally damaging trend, namely the lukewarm response most clergymen gave to the question 'Are you able to retain your young people in the Sunday School after they have left the Day School?' Typical answers were 'sometimes', 'in some instances', 'yes but very few', 'yes to some extent in Bible Classes' – these all from the 1876 Returns alone:[87] the picture was no different twenty years later.[88] The unavoidable conclusion, on this evidence, is that religious education was in itself no reliable method of ensuring regular commitment to church membership. K. D. Wald has recently argued that the declining share of elementary school students who were educated in church schools was directly linked to the falling away of Anglican and Nonconformist affiliations in electoral behaviour, but that the change did not take effect until 1918;[89] the evidence cited

[83] *Ibid.*, p. 25.
[84] Croydon Parish Church Magazine, Nov. 1882.
[85] Holy Trinity Parish Magazine, Parochial Report 1894; St James' Parish Magazine June-Sep. 1904; Christ Church Parish Magazine, 54th Annual Report, 1906.
[86] Visitation returns, 1898.
[87] Visitation return entries for All Saints, St James, St Luke's, Woodside and St Mary Magdalene.
[88] Visitation returns, 1898.
[89] K. D. Wald, *Crosses on the Ballot: patterns of British voter alignment since 1885* (Princeton 1983), pp. 250–1.

above suggests that, by the 1890s, even in church schools 'religious socialisation' was not so persuasive that it could be relied upon to perpetuate and extend Anglican membership. The church's influence was being edged out of the field of education by an alternative agency, and the consequence was that in this, as in other fields Anglicanism was gradually being driven in upon itself, so that even its principal source of recruitment was operating within gradually narrowing boundaries.[90]

A similar conclusion emerges from a consideration of the always more random Anglican attempts at exogenous recruitment, in other words conversion of non-Anglican adults. This chiefly meant missionary activity of various kinds, of which two strands in particular are of relevance. First, there was the mission church movement; the pattern of mission church-building was a patchy one, not always responsive to the greatest perceived need with the greatest available effort because the initiative lay entirely with the local incumbent. A clergyman like Henry Watson at St James, whose role as the unintentional proponent of High Churchmanship in Croydon has already been discussed, could resist with ease any attempts to set up a mission church in his densely-populated parish; this in fact was also what happened at Christ Church for many years. Most of the fourteen mission churches and halls recorded in the Mudie Smith Census of 1902–3 in Croydon had been built since 1880. St Saviour's, for example, established the two mission churches of St Luke's and St Stephen's in 1889; only St Stephen's 'grew up' to become a parish church, due, above all to its being sited in the rapidly growing area of Thornton Heath.[91] The practical effect of this provision was to add another dimension to the increasingly complicated structure of urban parishes, requiring again more time and effort on the part of church members, without being a response to an actual demand for the services provided. In Stephen Yeo's terminology, these were very much 'for' institutions rather than 'of'.[92] Nor do the attendance figures supplied by the Mudie Smith Census inspire much confidence that their services were widely

---

[90] See, for example, Marsh, *Victorian Church in Decline*, p. 81: 'Rate-financed board schools had robbed the Church of some of the substance and much of the lustre of being England's schoolmaster: they had left voluntary schools dominant only in the countryside.'

[91] Anon., *Historical Notes on St Stephen's Church, Norbury and Thornton Heath* (Croydon 1949).

[92] Yeo, *Religion and Voluntary Organisations*. Yeo describes a 'for institution' as arising from provision, an 'of institution' as arising from participation. Hence his comment on religious organisations in Reading around 1890: 'By a variety of provisions for people, they were trying to render themselves of unlimited numbers of people to the deepest extent possible': p. 2.

appreciated; St Alban's at Thornton Heath, for example, a mission church of St John's, Upper Norwood, recorded 156 attendances, but only six of these were men and women; the rest were children from a Sunday school.[93] A similar situation obtained at most of the others: at Pitlake Mission, for example, one of the oldest (opened in 1887), the total congregation of 188 for the day contained 118 children, again most of them from the Sunday school.[94]

A novelty to late nineteenth century parish life were parochial missions, which were in effect institutionalised revivalistic campaigns, generally a week or two long and marked by special mission services for which preachers were invited from outside Croydon; the 'missionary' would hold services, address meetings and carry out a certain amount of visiting during his stay. One was held at the Croydon Parish Church as early as 1874,[95] but it was from the 1880s onwards that they became a regular feature of parochial life. The intention of a mission was to reach out to all who lived in a parish – 'every house in the parish must in one way or another be touched'[96] – but the wider numbers of non-believers or non-attenders were impossible to catch by this means and the principal effect of the missions seems to have been to strengthen the commitment of those who were already attenders: 'I know that the spiritual life in many has been deepened. But alas! I also know that we have done little more, as to the great mass of the indifferent, than to touch its outer edge.'[97] The value of these missions in converting people to Anglicanism was probably minimal, then, and their continuation is much more likely to have been related to the positive signs of interest they would have aroused among existing attenders or infrequent attenders: an Anglican clergyman might interpret a rise in attendance consequent upon a mission as successful evangelising activity, whereas in fact it was probably a temporary expedient only for making irregular churchgoers into regular ones.

The Victorian period also saw a change in the role and status of the clergy. Several decades of national awareness of the need for church reform, a belief that the church had so far failed in its mission to draw in the poor, dissenting pressure for disestablishment, and the intensity of doctrinal clashes within the church had combined by the 1850s to make the parish priest a figure whose actions were subject to close public scrutiny. The position he occupied was therefore a vulnerable one: though his status within society as a whole was high,

[93] Mudie Smith, *Religious Life*, p. 382.
[94] *Ibid.*
[95] Croydon Parish Church Magazine, May 1874.
[96] St James' Parish Magazine, Sep. 1889.
[97] Croydon Parish Church Magazine, Mar. 1874.

public interest in his performance of his duties meant that failure and controversy in his pursuit of them could lead to acute criticism. The difficulties clergymen faced, quite apart from public sensitivity to doctrinal and political issues, have to be understood as questions affected by clerical income and the degree of control a clergyman exercised over his district. The two problems were inter-related, since financial weakness could to some extent be offset by a degree of clerical power, principally through the use of patronage and legal right to limit and control church extension in a district and to attempt to resist any other developments which could wean away part of a congregation from a church. A liberal endownment, such as that provided at St Michael's for R. W. Hoare,[98] gave a clergyman not only security of income but more scope to develop parochial agencies as he pleased, and although church extension as such was not needed at St Michael's, it could be carried out with relative ease in other parishes similarly well provided for, such as St Peter's.[99] A good illustration of concern over the level of the clerical stipend was the Parish Church itself, where by 1889 the churchwardens reported that the vicar's net income had fallen over the years to £250 p.a., due to a reduction in virtually every source of the stipend (the principal contributions came from tithes, rent on glebe, the Easter offertory, and surplice fees); their solution was to form a special committee to raise money by voluntary subcription and to use this fund to acquire a grant from Queen Anne's Bounty, the joint sum forming an endownment in addition to the existing sources of income.[100] The status of the vicar of Croydon depended on something other than wealth if in 1889 the position of influence he occupied had comparatively so small an income; in his case his prestige rested on his powers of patronage and the central position he occupied in church life in Croydon. The same was not generally true of his brother clergy, whose chances had to some extent been cramped until John Hodgson's resignation in 1879 by an arrangement whereby the larger share of the district church burial fees went to the vicar of Croydon himself.[101] Clerical status for most of Croydon's clergymen in mid-century was dependent above all on what they could command in the way of patronage and income.

These problems were particularly highlighted in a long and bitter controversy over church extension in Addiscombe, east of Croydon town centre. The early stages of the dispute bore some resemblance to

[98] Heazell, *History of St Michael's*, ch. 2.
[99] J. H. White, *A Short History of St. Augustine's* (Croydon 1919), pp. 11–20.
[100] *C Ad*, 13 Jul. 1889.
[101] Anon., *Croydon Crayons*, p. 8.

what happened at St Saviour's.[102] An evangelical curate at St Matthew's church, Maxwell Machluff Ben-Oliel, proved to be so effective a preacher that he attracted to the church worshippers from the wealthy middle class residential district of Addiscombe in the neighbouring parish of St James. His supporters procured a site and built a church for him in Addiscombe, but met fierce resistance from Henry Watson, vicar of St James; Archbishop Longley, petitioned by the Addiscombe residents, attempted at first to take a conciliatory stance, but really could do little more than uphold the undoubted legal right of Watson to absolute control of all appointments in his district. The protracted correspondence, marked by bitter criticism on both sides, was regularly printed in the *Croydon Chronicle*; when St Paul's Church, Addiscombe was finally completed in mid-1869, still without a licensed priest, the new archbishop, Tait, like his predecessor could only accept Watson's side of the case. St Paul's was opened as an unofficial Anglican church in September 1869, with Ben-Oliel as its priest. Watson founded a rival church in Addiscombe, but St Mary's attracted a tiny congregation and could make little headway against the popularity of Ben-Oliel at St Paul's. The uneasy rivalry continued until June 1872 when, in an extraordinary volte-face, Ben-Oliel suddenly embraced High Church opinions and, introducing a ritualistic form of service, prompting a walkout by most of his congregation, who at once transferred to St Mary Magdalene. Practically and doctrinally, Ben-Oliel's position was now an impossible one: though he now owned the church, he was reliant on offertories for his income and so, in alienating his congregation, had deprived himself of his financial support. Tait readily accepted his offer of submission, and he was forced to abandon all hope of remaining at St Paul's; the building was eventually acquired and consecrated as the permanent church of St Mary Magdalene.[103]

What the dispute implied for the role and status of the clergyman in the mid-Victorian period first of all was that he was much less of a participant in a systematic policy of urban religious supervision, much more dependent upon specific local conditions and local demands than has sometimes been supposed was the case: church extension in Addiscombe occurred almost in spite of the clergyman responsible for the district, Henry Watson. The dispute pinpointed

[102] See pp. 51–2.
[103] Details in this paragraph from the Rev J. Wright, *Addiscombe Parish Church: its History and Jubilee* (Croydon 1927), but above all from the lengthy exchanges between Ben-Oliel, Watson, the archbishops, and the Addiscombe residents, published in *The Croydon Chronicle* between 1866 and 1874, for which see the following issues in particular: 3 Jan. 1866; 12, 19, 26 Jan., 2 Feb., 9, 30 May, 4 Jul. 1868; 25 Sep. 1869; 11 Feb. 1871; 19 Apr., 3 May, 28 June, 13, 20 Sep., 29 Nov. 1873.

all the weaknesses of the Anglican system of authority: the inability of the bishop of a diocese to direct the affairs of a sitting incumbent and its corollary, the near total autonomy of an incumbent; the absence of central church-building initiatives which would have provided a means by which the district of Addiscombe could have been catered for; and the strong practical reliance, in the absence of central funding, on the pockets of wealthy laymen. The dispute also confirmed that key conditions affecting the status of the clergyman were his income and his power. Watson may initially have opposed church extension because he was reliant on pew rents for his income, and may have feared an extra financial burden; Ben-Oliel in turn was hampered by his source of income, to the extent that it eventually made it impossible for him to preach altered views.

What happened at Addiscombe also highlights the way in which laity in the mid-century were taking an active role in church affairs, prepared to go even to the lengths of separating themselves officially from the church in this case to obtain the preacher they wanted. Again, this explosive combination of lay enthusiasm and an intransigent clergyman supported by the structural inadequacies of the Anglican Church had led some Anglicans almost to the point of a wholesale condemnation of key features of their own church's polity. One correspondent, for example, concluded from the Addiscombe dispute that the current system of patronage was a serious fault in the church: 'There is a worldly, money-making air about it that jars upon our feelings. Things temporal and things spiritual are too much mixed up together.'[104] Others preferred to concentrate on the failings of the vicar of St James, some even going so far as to accuse him of 'uncharitable' and unchristian behaviour;[105] a more damaging letter was one which drew a comparison between the Addiscombe dispute and the Colenso affair, accusing the archbishop himnself of inconsistency.[106] Where does this leave the position of the clergyman? Though the Anglican system gave little scope for lay participation and assistance in the spiritual work of the parish priest and his curates, the practical exigencies of the church in an area such as Croydon meant that it was more than ever reliant upon the laity for financial support and for the social influence lay urban leaders could command for programmes of church extension. In practice, if not in an official sense, the ties between clergy and wealthy members of a

---

[104] *C Chron*, 1 Dec. 1866.
[105] See, for example, the sentiments expressed by several speakers at a public meeting in Addiscombe early in the dispute: *Ibid.*, 12 Jan. 1867.
[106] *Ibid.*, 2 Feb. 1867.

congregation were very close, and the clergyman was far from standing isolated from what his congregation thought.

The physical constraints of the clerical office – the source of income and the extent of a clergyman's power – changed little in the course of the nineteenth century. It was only in the twentieth century that reorganisation of diocesan finance took place in such a way as to reduce the weaknesses of many clerical livings, with the introduction of standard salary scales and a quota system of finance which amounted to cross-subsidy of parishes.[107] Yet some of the more intangible constraints weakened or disappeared. The easing of doctrinal conflicts from the 1880s onwards meant that clergy became less subject to vociferous criticism from their congregations on doctrinal grounds alone. The steady spread of High Church practices, even in their more diluted form, ensured that sensitivity over the way in which a clergyman performed his liturgical functions declined. This was evidently accompanied by a decline in lay interest in church affairs; at least, evidence of the volatility of lay reactions seen in the Addiscombe dispute and in the course of the growth of Ritualism in Croydon traced earlier ceases from roughly the same period. This was not without significance for the role of the priest. It seems that what was happening operated at two levels: the active involvement of clergy in the wider affairs of society – political life, philanthropy, social life – was receding, and their relative prestige in this area seems also to have been declining; yet within the church the status and authority of the clergyman was increasing. Long-term effects of the reform of clerical training – professionalisation of the clerical office – may have contributed something to this.[108] Sheer pressure of work must also have done something towards it. In urban areas in particular an increased sense of clerical responsibility was evident in the frequent complaints that clergy were overworked. John Hodgson in the early 1870s referred to the 'cares and anxieties' of the parish of Croydon,[109] and Henry Watson's death in 1879 was put down to overwork.[110] The vicar of Croydon confided to Archbishop

---

[107] Lloyd, *Church of England*, pp. 343–5.

[108] Opinions are divided over the issue of professionalisation: B. Heeney, for example, considered it an unquestioned fact, in *The Woman's Movement in the Church of England 1850–1930* (Oxford 1988), pp. 77–8; Alan Haig saw the priesthood more as a form of service than a profession, in *The Victorian Clergy* (London 1984), pp. 16–18; R. O'Day, from a longer-term perspective, has recently questioned the applicability of the notion of 'professionalisation' at all, but she does not doubt, however, that significant advances took place in the organisation of clerical training: 'The Clerical Renaissance in Victorian England and Wales', in G. Parsons and J. R. Moore (eds), *Religion in Victorian Britain: I Traditions* (Manchester 1988), pp. 184–212.

[109] *C Ad*, 19 Apr. 1873.

[110] *C Chron*, 11 Jan. 1879.

Benson in 1883 that he thought the vicar of St Andrew's was suffering from exhaustion and ought to be given a quiet country living instead.[111] The change was also apparent, however, in the way in which the initiative in church extension and indeed in most church affairs was gradually falling into clerical hands altogether, with the laity retreating into a more passive role. This can be seen particularly in the case of church building. Clerical initiatives there were in mid-century, and they were highly important ones, but they were sufficiently patchy, and lay interest was sufficiently high, for scope for lay concern to be great as well. Lay activity was prominent, for example, in the founding of St Michael's, St John's, Upper Norwood, St Paul's, Thornton Heath and St Mary Magdalene's (initially as St Paul's). Later in the period only one church can be so attributed, Emmanuel, an evangelical church founded by the Misses Watney, daughters of the brewer.[112] In any case, the major programme of church extension proposed by Archbishop Temple and executed under the supervision of the vicar of Croydon in 1897 confirmed clerical domination of future church building movements.[113]

The changing role and prestige of the clergy within the church need to be seen in the context of the parochial system, for only then will it become apparent just how elaborate the duties of the parish priest had become, and how this had drawn the clergyman further into concern with church work rather than pushing him out into participation in extra-church affairs. The typical Anglican urban parish of the 1900s was a highly sophisticated unit, composed of many interlocking agencies designed to cater for the various perceived needs of the population of the parish and to relate these to the church. In seeking to adapt the church to urban society, clergymen had added agency after agency to the parish, benefit societies, mutual improvement societies, schools, and temperance societies amongst others. The total effect of this proliferation of parochial organisations was paradoxically not to broaden the appeal of the church on any significant scale but to strengthen existing ties of loyalty and commitment within it, to demand more attention and more energy from lay support, because it was taking place against – and was in part a deliberate response to – a background of political, intellectual and social change which was tending to reduce the wider appeal of organised religion. The picture is not necessarily one of an unthinking inflexibility which led to

---

[111] Benson papers, vol. 2, 340.
[112] Heazell, *History of St Michael's*; Wright, *Addiscombe Parish Church*; Anon., *St Paul's Church*; Anon., *Emmanuel Church, South Croydon 1899–1949* (Croydon 1949).
[113] Temple papers (Lambeth Palace Library) vol. 10, 382.

absolute decline. It could be argued that the methods employed registered some successes at least in buoying up interest in the church amongst Anglicans, and so helped to preserve influence for the church into the twentieth century. It could also be argued that, though many agencies 'failed', many others attracted sufficient members (even though many of them might have been church members already) for them to create and sustain a belief that they were a success. Something has already been said about some of the penumbra of parochial organisations, mainly about schools and missions. There is insufficient space to discuss all other organisations: some, such as the temperance societies, will be touched upon in later chapters; others, such as the mutual improvement societies and bible classes, have left behind too little evidence to merit much more than a passing reference where necessary. In three areas in particular, however the tendency towards increased provision and improved organisation was especially evident and significant.

One of these was the gradual spread of societies which were designed to band together existing believers, the communicants' guilds and associations. These were in origin a High Church innovation, and possibly owed something to the extensive religious societies and guilds in existence in France and other Catholic countries.[114] By the late 1870s some of the ritualist churches in Croydon already had them – St John the Evangelist at Upper Norwood at least by 1877, for example.[115] From the 1880s they gradually spread to other Anglican churches, becoming a regular feature of most by 1900. St Andrew's for example started a communicants' association in 1880, St Augustine's and the Parish Church in 1885, Holy Trinity in 1889, and St James in 1899.[116] Even at ritualist churches 'innovation' in a sense continued, for smaller sub-guilds and societies sprang up around the main one: St John the Evangelist, for example, by 1900 supported no less than six in all: the Guild of St John the Evangelist, the Confraternity of the Blessed Sacrament, the Ward of the Sanctuary (for men), the Ward of St Agnes (for women), the Ward of St Mary (for women in service) and a Band of Church Watchers.[117] Guilds were short-lived at some churches: St Matthew's 'revived' a guild in 1900, St Andrew's the

---

[114] See, for example, M. Agulhon, *Pénitents et Francs-Maçons de l'ancienne Provence* (Paris 1984).
[115] St John the Evangelist's Parish Magazine, Aug. 1877.
[116] St Andrew's Magazine, May 1880: Guild of St Augustine's Minute Book, p. 1; Croydon Parish Church Magazine, Nov. 1885; Holy Trinity Parish Magazine, Nov. 1889; St James' Parish Magazine, Mar. 1899.
[117] St John the Evangelist's Parish Magazine, Jul. 1900.

year before.[118] The aim and function of a guild was to maintain the religious interest of existing church communicants, and to strengthen the church by drawing communicants and church workers closer into a sense of solidarity; this was to be achieved by regular meetings at which religious affairs would be discussed, so that in method and purpose the guilds were a logical extension of the Sunday school and the bible class. The range of subjects discussed at St Augustine's Guild varied considerably, though most papers related to religious affairs and many were concerned with the minutiae of worship – an A. L. Ryder, for example, read a paper on 'Evening Celebrations of the Holy Eucharist'.[119] More intriguing is the way in which it is clear that the guild also functioned as a consultative body, almost a church council, discussing and reaching decisions upon various matters of church business submitted to it by the vicar; at St Augustine's these included the provision of altar frontals, arrangement of times of services, the formation of a Band of Hope, resolutions and petitions on the education issue, and the formation of a Men's Institute.[120]

The second area of innovation concerns the reorganisation of the administration of the parish, and here the guilds may well have acted as useful precursors of a change which began to take place in the 1900s: the formation of church councils. Those known to have been in existence by 1914 were mostly in parishes which would have felt the problems of dwindling resources and increasing population acutely; at St Paul's, Thornton Heath, for example, the church council was reorganised in 1913, with members to be elected from amongst the communicants and the council to control, through a Finance Committee, all of the funds not reserved by the vicar and churchworkers to meet immediate expenses; the vicar hoped the change 'will bring home the sense of responsibility to a larger circle of our actual worshippers. If this is not its result, it will be all in vain'.[121] The council formed at St John the Evangelist's, Upper Norwood in 1905 devoted itself in the main to relatively mundane matters such as the lighting of the church and the building of a new vicarage.[122] The reasons for the initial impetus to the movement are unclear: if, as at St Paul's, membership was invariably recruited from the communicants and not from the parishioners at large, then the near universal adoption of communicants' guilds by the late 1890s could have

---

[118] St Matthew's Parish Magazine, Jul. 1900; St Andrew's Parish Magazine, Sep. 1899.
[119] Guild of St Augustine, Minute Book, 12 Nov. 1886.
[120] *Ibid.*
[121] St Paul's Parish Magazine, Jan. 1913.
[122] St John the Evangelist, Church Council Minutes, 1905ff.

influenced it; as early as 1901 a council was suggested for St John the Evangelist, though not immediately formed, and the same for St Augustine's in 1902.[123] In 1904 the Ruri-Decanal Conference passed a resolution recommending all churches in the deanery of Croydon to form parish church councils, but the resolution was linked to a criticism of the apathy churchmen displayed in municipal issues and an encouragement to them to sponsor church candidates in elections, so that church interests, particularly in the field of education, could be defended. Although it recognised the advantages to be gained from church councils, then, the resolution was not directly linked with whatever was the origin of the movement. In fact it seems that only Holy Trinity immediately implemented it.[124] Like the communicants' guilds, the church councils further strengthened the participation and commitment of existing membership by giving them a more regular say in the administration of the parish than the annual vestry could provide.

Just as the communicants' guilds and church councils were effectively placing parochial administration on a new basis, one which brought the members of the church as defined by the act of communion into closer contact with the source of authority in the parish, so in a third area of innovation the complexity of the parochial unit was becoming enhanced by its inclusion within a hierarchy of representative church bodies in the late nineteenth century. At diocesan level the Diocesan Conference discussed church affairs and sent representatives to the House of Laymen, which sat at the same time as Convocation; of greater importance from the angle of local church affairs was the tier below it, the Ruri-Decanal Conference, to which all churches in the Rural Deanery of Croydon sent elected representatives. It is difficult to trace the origins of the Conference, but it was certainly in existence by 1885.[125] In the absence of surviving minutes, it appears from reports of the proceedings published at various times in parish magazines that the functions of the Conference, predictably enough perhaps, were two-fold. In the first place, it was a deliberative body, discussing national church affairs and framing resolutions accordingly, covering a range of subjects such as the Salvation Army, social purity, the small attendance of men at Holy Communion and the interpretation of the Old Testament.[126] Secondly, it took some initiative in formulating

[123] St John the Evangelist, Vestry Minutes, 9 Apr. 1901; St Augustine's, Vestry Minutes, 1 Apr. 1902.
[124] Holy Trinity Parish Magazine, Mar. 1904.
[125] Benson papers, xxix, 29, 350.
[126] Guild of St Augustine, Minute Book, 18 Feb. 1891; Benson papers, lxxvi, 376.

what might be called local church policy, resolving for example to form a branch of the Church Reading Society in Croydon in 1887[127] and supporting the 1898 scheme of church extension in the area.[128] In theory it was a large, inclusive body: all Croydon clergy could attend, and large numbers of them seem to have done so (thirty-eight in 1887, for example);[129] and if the number of five lay members selected at St John the Evangelist in 1910 is anything to go by, it would have contained by the 1900s upwards of 100 lay members.[130] Just how influential a body in fact it was is difficult to ascertain, and there are some signs that it was not as well attended as it should have been: there were complaints of apathy in the election of lay representatives for the Parish Church in 1902, for example.[131] That delegates were elected by special meetings of communicants and not by the parishioners in vestry once again illustrates how in this field, as in others, participation in Anglican affairs was becoming restricted to a more precise definition of membership than that formerly used in the vestry meeting; the whole structure of Anglican administration within which the parochial system nestled was being tightened up, placed on a more secure but narrower basis.[132]

The elaboration of the various organs of the parochial system along the lines described here was a necessary response of clergymen to the problems of administration with which urbanisation presented them. The presence of the urban poor provided the chief stimulus, because those parishes with a high concentration of poor faced the conflicting requirements of more services with less resources. However, albeit on a less urgent plane, the same innovations and pattern of development were also to be found in predominately middle class parishes, so it is not a question of 'response' alone, but also of a changing attitude towards what constituted the legitimate sphere of activity of the church, what the purpose of associated agencies were, and what was the position of the 'church in society'. D. E. H. Mole has argued that the model for Anglican programmes of church building in urban areas in mid-century was a rural one, which elevated the priest into the 'father' of a small community and attempted to bring in available upper class followers to supervise and strengthen work amongst

127 Benson papers, xliii, 244.
128 St Michael's Parish Magazine, Dec. 1898.
129 Benson papers, xliii, 244.
130 St John the Evangelist, Church Council Minutes, 24 Feb. 1910.
131 Croydon Parish Church Magazine, Nov. 1902.
132 The use to which confirmation was put in parishes as a sign of full church 'membership' is perhaps one important but neglected aspect of the debate over church 'franchise' for the parochial church councils established under the Enabling Act of 1919: see F. A. Iremonger, *William Temple* (London 1948), pp. 258–60.

the poor.[133] If this was the case, not only was the ideal inappropriate and not being fulfilled, but it was being positively abandoned in late-century in favour of a more complex vision, in which the church, whilst still providing the same welfare services as its rural counterparts, sought to involve committed laity in the administration of the parish and renounced some of its extra-congregational aspirations. The enhanced status of the clergyman within the Anglican Church, a product of the gradual adoption of High Church ritual with its renewed emphasis on the sacramental function of the clerical office, was thus accompanied by a reassertion of a spiritual definition of church membership, the act of communion, which was in turn made the condition of participation in the newer forms of administration within the parish. It seems that the behaviour of congregations was changing anyway, as they abandoned the principle of territoriality in attending church and made churchgoing much more a matter of personal taste, choosing a particular church according to its doctrinal bent or the character of its clergymen. The vicar of Holy Trinity, Selhurst, put it like this: 'Parochial boundaries are little recognised, or even known by many, all over Croydon except as regards the very poor and that mainly for relief purposes, the congregational system has superseded the Parochial.'[134] Amongst the very class to whom the geographical appeal of the Anglican parish would have had most relevance – the working class with its 'neighbourhood consciousness' as described by McLeod[135] – churchgoing habits were in any case poor. The middle class were certainly selective in their churchgoing. At St Saviour's, during the dispute with the vicar of St James, it had already been recognised by the churchwardens in 1869 that 'there are many regular attendants who do not reside in the district'.[136] It made sense therefore in urban parishes, where attenders at a parish church often were not residents of the parish, to base church activity on 'membership' rather than the traditional, localised affiliations of Anglicanism. This was especially attractive when a parish was located in a district which contained a high proportion of working class people or was undergoing a deterioration in its social status. It was through his church council that the Rev A. W. Bedford, vicar of St John the Evangelist, Upper Norwood, sought advice on how to put his living on a firmer basis.[137]

---

[133] D. E. H. Mole, 'The Victorian town parish: rural vision and urban mission', *Studies in Church History*, xvi (1977).
[134] Visitation returns, 1898.
[135] McLeod, *Class and Religion*, ch. 3.
[136] Anon., *Memorials and Correspondence*, p. 17.
[137] St John the Evangelist, Church Council Minutes, 17 Sep. 1906.

What was happening to the parochial system helps to put into perspective what was happening in the Anglican Church at large. Gradually severing the politial responsibilities it had carried earlier in the century, the church was seeking to adapt itself to urban conditions by the 1880s by concentrating its energies on the cultivation of forms of worship and church government which were designed at the same time to widen the church's popular appeal and to strengthen existing bonds of loyalty on the part of churchgoers. The changes described in this section carried the significance they did because they occurred within a particular social context, that of nineteenth-century society; not only Anglicanism, but all forms of religion, though as yet losing little in terms of numbers of followers, were finding themselves, by the end of the century, confined to a narrowing definition of their role, as alternative agencies in politics, welfare and leisure usurped functions formerly performed by the churches.

4

The Churches in Victorian Croydon II

Protestant Nonconformity: from Peculiar Minorities to the Free Churches

Though they started from very different positions, and thus development within them followed different courses, sufficient was common to both Anglicanism and Protestant Nonconformity to indicate that they were subject to the same kind of sociological pressure and that, as religious organisations, to survive their responses in many ways had to be similar. Anglicanism began with what many regarded as a dead weight of hierarchy and organisation; Nonconformity, the Society of Friends and Wesleyan Methodism perhaps considered apart, could not boast the same degree of elaborate denominational organisation at mid-century, and its growth in the early decades of Croydon's urbanisation was character-ised above all by informality. Even in this however there were comparisons with what was happening in the Anglican Church, and similar patterns of change may be detected in the ways in which new congregations were founded, in the role of ministers, in missionary and educational activity, and in theology.

The relative absence of strong centralised hierarchies in Noncon-formity meant that growth in mid-century depended very much on local initiative. One probable exception to this was provided by Wesleyan Methodism, where the arrangements required to maintain the itinerant ministry demanded efficient central organisation, and here expansion was more likely, in consequence , to be 'connexion-led' rather than to arise from below.[1] Even in Wesleyanism, however, the heavy dependence on voluntary, lay finance meant that local support ultimately counted for everything where expanding and maintaining the connexion's activities were concerned. There were two principal methods in mid-century by which Nonconformist growth occurred, both of which gave great scope for lay initiative. The first and often the most difficult to trace was informal, unplanned

[1] For example, the initiation of Wesleyan missionary work at Addiscombe was consequent upon the establishment of a mission station and a resident minister: *The Wesleyan Methodist magazine*, xvi (5th Series, 1870), 1138.

growth, whereby a small cause might be started by a preacher or layman, often with a tiny following or even no following at all, and – if 'successful', that is – would only gradually develop into a larger circle of worshippers, who eventually might find themselves large enough and wealthy enough to begin to raise finance for a permanent building. Meetings might be held in the open air, or in a house or cottage, and would then progress to a small hall or an iron, temporary church. So the 'cottage' religion typical of early nineteenth century Nonconformity, which it has sometimes been argued disappeared in Victorian urban areas, could still in fact be traced as the origin of many mid-century chapels. At South Norwood in the late 1850s 'a few devoted souls' formed a Congregational church in a small mission hall in Portland Road, and later moved to South Norwood High Street; the cause did not flourish and seems to have disappeared by the mid-1860s; then in 1870 it was re-started in an upper room in a house in the High Street, later moving back to the hall in Portland Road and then to the South Norwood Public Hall. When it was formally constituted in December of that year it had twenty-three members.[2] Primitive Methodism in the area also progressed very much by these methods. Early in 1869 a new lay preacher at the Croydon station, Joseph Odell, began preaching at a cottage in Cross Road, near Croydon Common; within a few weeks he had formed a class there, though only of six people at first, and read them the rules of the Primitive Methodist Connexion. At the same time he also started another class on Croydon Common, and could soon boast a mission band at Cross Road, nicknamed 'Odell's heavy artillery'; though he soon left Croydon, he had formed the nucleus of what was to become Cherry Orchard Road chapel.[3] The small cause which could suddenly spring up in a house or even in the room over a shop in a street, perhaps just around the corner from a parish church, must have been what was at the heart of the Anglican 'contagion theory' of the spread of dissent.[4] It was a means of growth which thrived on lay interest in church work and on a relatively relaxed, informal attitude to church organisation on the part of existing churches who would often be called upon to support these causes.

In mid-century Nonconformity also grew by another means, which by contrast thrived on powerful tensions within existing congregations, namely growth by schism; here direct parallels can be traced with what was happening at the same time in the Anglican Church.

[2] Anon., *South Norwood Congregational Church*, p. 11.
[3] Notes from Joseph Odell's Journal (mss. at C Ref Lib).
[4] The vicar of St James complained in 1889 of 'The large amount of dissent which has been allowed to plant itself in the Parish years back': Visitation returns, 1889.

In general the doctrinal conflict of High versus Low which was a divisive but dynamic feature of Anglican life was lacking in Nonconformity, solidly Protestant and at this period evangelical. Yet there was plenty of scope for conflict in the nature of the relationship between a minister and his congregation, given that (as in the Anglican Church) lay interest in Nonconformist church affairs in mid-century was very extensive. The particular problem for Nonconformists sprang from reliance upon voluntary finance to maintain their churches and pay their ministers' stipends. Since they were unable to adopt decorative ritual as a means for holding or attracting congregations, they were forced back upon the powerful popular preacher as a means of doing so. The simple consequence of falling membership, falling subscriptions, was sufficient to jeopardise the position of many Nonconformist ministers, particularly in those denominations – the Baptists, Congregationalists and Presbyterians – in which the appointment and dismissal of the minister was largely or totally in the hands of the church members. The financial problem was at the root of George Street Congregational Chapel's regular disputes with successive ministers.[5] The same chapel serves to illustrate that schism could also occur for doctrinal reasons. In 1877 a minister who had been there for four years and had encouraged a costly chapel rebuilding scheme ran into trouble with his congregation and diaconate over his gradual abandonment of distinctive Congregational forms of church government (he proposed, for example, the admission of people who were not full church members to the diaconate); he was censured at a church meeting and forced to resign, taking part of the congregation with him to form a new church on the Addiscombe estate.[6] As the *Croydon Advertiser* was to see it when the debt on the rebuilt George Street Chapel was finally cleared ten years later in 1887: 'The Church was of the old "Independent" character, and could not brook the vagaries of an autocratic priesthood.'[7] Thus at George Street adherence to the congregational form of church government, readiness on the part of leading members of the congregation to defend it, and suspicion of the ambitions of a minister together had indirectly led to the founding of another church. Congregationalism was particularly susceptible to schism in this period and to the resulting foundation of churches by the schismatic ministers or their followers. Trinity Chapel, for example, was also founded in 1858 by seceders from George Street,

---

[5] The Rev William Park's resignation in 1897 was forced upon him by the diaconate because of a serious falling off in subscriptions and attendances: Raymer, *The Congregational Church*, p. 26.

[6] *Ibid.*, pp. 10–12.

[7] *C Ad*, 7 May 1887.

as was the London Road Chapel in the mid-1850s, which eventually became West Croydon Congregational Church. The reasons for these two secessions are not known, but the impression that Congregational affairs in these years were volatile is reinforced by Waddington's comment that 'The peculiar trials experienced by the churches in Croydon within the past seven years only served to prove the elasticity of Congregationalism.'[8] Nor were Baptists free from this kind of dispute: Derby Road Chapel was founded in 1876 as a result of a dispute over the form of service at Tamworth Road Strict Baptist Chapel.[9] In other organisations as well – the temperance movement and the London City Mission, for example – the same pattern of extension by schism could be traced in mid-century.[10]

Nonconformity was particularly well adapted to giving practical expression to lay interest, through cadres of deacons and elders in the case of Old Dissent and through the lay preachers of Methodism. But these were forms of office which carried considerable responsibility and made serious demands on the time of their holders, and which, by virtue of the power they commanded, carried an especial attraction for the wealthy and socially prestigious within the denominations. The deference which, according to Bagehot, saturated the social structure and sustained the mid-Victorian constitution, sustained Nonconformist as well as Anglican forms of church government, even though Protestant Nonconformity was fond of parading its identification with ecclesiastical democracy.[11] When Arnold Pye-Smith, wealthy grandson of a famous Congregational minister, arrived at Croydon in the mid 1870s he attained the diaconate at George Street almost immediately, over the heads of other attenders of the chapel.[12] The interest of men like him in church affairs was not fuelled or spurred on by renewed doctrinal conflict, however, and here there is a distinct difference from Anglicanism. Instead it was the product of the specific historical position of Dissent in mid-century. The removal of dissenters' disabilities, the Reform Act and the Municipal Corporation Act, had in national terms removed the obstacles to Nonconformist participation in public affairs; even in a parish like Croydon, dominated in the 1820s and 1830s by Anglican, Conservative landowners, professional men, and merchants, the mid-century marked a distinct rise in Nonconformist

[8] J. Waddington, *Surrey Congregational History* (London 1866), p. 193.
[9] *C Chron*, 13 May 1876.
[10] For schism within the LCM see *C Chron*, 12 Jan. 1861; within the temperance movement, for example, *C Chron*, 13 Mar., 22 June 1861.
[11] W. Bagehot, *The English Constitution* (1867; World's Classics edn. London 1955), pp. 235–40.
[12] Raymer, *The Congregational Church*, p. 11.

participation in parochial government. The tendency of wealthy Quakers to take up public office from the 1830s, noted by Isichei, for example, was true of Croydon too.[13] By mid-century Dissent had not lost its sense of pride in its reliance on lay activism, and yet those same activists were now also taking on responsibility in other fields; furthermore, issues such as church rate and education still gave participation in chapel affairs some political and social relevance.

In the course of the late nineteenth century this transitional stage was gradually abandoned, as Nonconformist laity found themselves, like Anglicans, increasingly forced to make a choice between political activism and religious activism, most of the socially prestigious opting for municipal affairs. Consequently church extension, again as in Anglicanism, gradually fell into the hands of ministers as they assumed an ever more elevated position within their denominations. Growth became 'minister led'. A good example was St Paul's Presbyterian Church, South Croydon, founded on the initiative of the Church Extension Committee of the Presbytery of London South in the late 1890s, and supervised by Rev A. N. Mackray of St George's Presbyterian Church in Croydon. None of the committee appointed to assist him were prominent in the town's political and social life.[14] West Croydon Baptist tabernacle was the typical example of a church built in the first place in the 1860s because a group of lay Baptist townsmen felt there was a need in Croydon for a Baptist church on open lines; yet the very success of the chapel and its preacher, a brother of C. H. Spurgeon, ensured that the initiative in schemes of further expansion based on the church passed to its minister.[15]

Although in doctrinal terms there was no significant influence encouraging an elevated conception of the ministerial office amongst Nonconformist denominations by the 1900s, there were practical reasons for attaching an increased importance to it. Declining readiness on the part of laity to volunteer funds for church building sometimes made denominational organisation to extract resources of money and manpower more important. At Woodside Baptist Church recurrent financial shortages and a consequent failure to pay off debts led to the takeover and administration of the chapel in 1901 by the

[13] E. Isichei, *Victorian Quakers* (Oxford 1970), ch. 7; three wealthy Quaker members of the Local Board of Health, for example, were Richard Sterry, an oil merchant, John Morland, the umbrella manufacturer, and Alfred Crowley, a local brewer: anon., *Old and New Croydon* cross-referenced with town directories and local press.
[14] R. S. McMinn, *These Twenty-Five Years: St. Paul's Presbyterian Church, South Croydon* (Croydon 1926).
[15] Stockwell, *The Baptist Churches*, p. 83.

Baptist Pioneer Mission, and the resignation of the pastor.[16] In other cases, the personality, motivation and attitude of the minister became of crucial importance for a struggling congregation, because his salary was their most significant annual outlay. Throughout the 1890s South Norwood Congregational Church faced severe difficulties in balancing income and expenditure: the pastor's stipend was cut in stages from £300 to £175 in 1891, and then brought back up to £200; treasurers resigned on two occasions because of a perceived lack of commitment on the part of deacons and pastor to resolve the financial problems of the church; and even elections to the diaconate were suspended when laity refused to put themselves forward during a particularly difficult period from May to November 1897.[17] The appointment of a new pastor in 1901 marked the beginning of a general improvement in the church's fortunes, but in the following year the church was still considering applying to denominational sources for a £100 loan to cover a predicted deficit.[18] The potential pre-eminence of the minister was already implicit in reliance upon his abilities and his preaching to attract congregations sufficient to sustain the financial burdens of a church. In the mid- and later 1870s Croydon Primitive Methodist Circuit passed through an acute crisis, with a falling membership, a rapid turnover of superintendants, and a crisis of confidence amongst its lay preachers, whom its Quarterly Meeting in the period constantly had to censure for failing to meet their preaching appointments. In 1880 the Meeting chose the Rev W. E. Crombie as superintendent; it was a fortunate choice. Almost immediately membership began to increase and the income deficiencies which the Meeting had reported to disappear; at the same time Crombie appears to have imposed some sort of discipline on the lay preachers, for cases of their neglect of appointments fell dramatically.[19] His success was such that he was invited to remain year after year, passing a remarkable ten years in all as superintendent of Croydon. If the potential influence of the ministers was as great as this, then it would become all the more openly recognised as leading lay support for, and interest in, church affairs receded. An awareness of the burden of responsibility the Congregational minister carried by the early 1900s, and an implied reproach to congregations who failed to realise this, was voiced by the Rev R. B. Brindley at George Street Chapel in 1903:

16 Woodside Baptist Church, Church Meeting Minutes, 20 Feb. 1901.
17 South Norwood Congregational Church, Enmore Road, Church Meeting Minutes, ii, 1884–1901, *passim*.
18 Enmore Road, Church Meeting Minutes, iii, 1902–4, entry for 3 Dec. 1902.
19 Croydon Primitive Methodist Circuit, Quarterly Meeting Minutes, 1880–90, *passim*.

The relationships existing between the Independent ministry and churches it serves are exceedingly delicate. When a church calls a man to be its pastor, and hands over its pulpit to him, it does him the greatest possible honour, because it lays on him a great trust. His usefulness and happiness depend on many things. Think how the people must trust him for the right and diligent use of his time, and for the methods of work he shall follow, for aspects of truth that he shall emphasize in his ministry, for his wisdom and tact in managing affairs and managing people, for exemplary behaviour in all the varied social relations of life. I believe the position of a Congregational minister is in these days one of the most difficult of all clerical positions.[20]

Urban growth presented opportunities for Protestant Nonconformity but the denominations could attempt to seize these only by developing their organisations and methods of operation in certain ways. Specifically, like Anglicanism, they sought to lock into the processes of change by enlarging and developing the various services – welfare, social, leisure – which a chapel could offer, although to do this required greater levels of commitment within the denominations. The result, in a setting of increasing occupational and social specialisation in late nineteenth century urban society, was that Protestant Nonconformist religion was transformed from a phenomenon which saturated all human activity in the mid-century and in which laity participated because in a sense it was inconceivable to them not to participate, into a highly specialised activity in its own right. Nonconformity changed itself in the process of adapting to change, and in doing so marginalised itself.

The methods by which the denominations sought to attract new members illustrates this process of change very well. There had always been a tendency for Nonconformity to lean more heavily – at least overtly – on familial ties than did the Anglican Church; this after all was a logical corollary of the 'peculiar people' outlook of early Dissent, the feeling that the denomination was an outcast minority which could not undertake extensive conversionist endeavour without raising acute tensions between the sect's followers and the wider society (particularly as embodied in political and ecclesiastical authority). Methodism supplanted but did not altogether destroy this sense when it reintroduced evangelistic enthusiasm into Dissent. Combining strong, historic denominational identities with Evangelicalism in the early and mid-nineteenth century, Dissent threw

---

[20] R. B. Brindley, *The Darkness Where God Is, and other sermons*, 'The Congregational Pulpit', v (Croydon 1903–4), p. 146.

itself wholeheartedly into domestic missionary activity. Missionary societies like the London City Mission, for example, attracted Nonconformist support in large numbers: most of the committee members of the Croydon branch of the LCM were Dissenters.[21] By mid-century even the Society of Friends was active in the LCM and other missionary groups, co-operating openly with Baptists, Methodists and Congregationalists, and thereby illustrating the influence of the rise of Evangelicalism within the Society, as traced by Isichei.[22] The co-operation Protestant Nonconformity achieved in precisely the areas of recruitment where one might otherwise have expected competition to be most acute suggests that Nonconformists themselves, though holding to a denomination-centred view of religion, did not perceive their differences to be significant except on certain specific points of organisation and doctrine.

The same conclusion can be deduced from a consideration of Dissenters' educational work. As early as 1812 a non-denominational school in Croydon was founded under the auspices of the British and Foreign Schools' Society, supported at first principally by Independents and Baptists, but later by other Nonconformists.[23] By 1881 it had 656 children on its books for the Mixed Infants, Girls' and Boys' schools, and 475 on average in attendance.[24] The composition of its committee shows that it received active backing from many influential Nonconformist laymen in Croydon, such as the brewer Alfred Crowley, a Quaker and Liberal.[25] Reports of Her Majesty's inspectors on the quality of teaching in the school were eulogistic in late century.[26] Similarly, Nonconformists co-operated in the founding and operation of the School Board in Croydon from 1871, forming a joint committee before the first election to engineer the election of favourable candidates and thereafter a permanent Nonconformist Committee to supervise their interests in education.[27] But, with the great exception of Sunday schools, there were significant limits to Nonconformist participation in educational activity. Shortage of financial resources meant that they were not able to support day schools on the same scale as did Anglican parishes; in fact the British Schools in Tamworth Road were the only 'Nonconformist' schools in Croydon, although the Ragged Schools in Old Town, run by the London City Mission until their acquisition by the Anglican parish of

[21] For example, *C Chron*, 10 Mar. 1860; *Ward's Croydon Directories*, 1874–1914.
[22] Isichei, *Victorian Quakers*, ch. 1.
[23] Garrow, *History and Antiquities*, pp. 136–7.
[24] Elborough, *Croydon*, p. 25.
[25] *Ward's Croydon Directories*, 1874–1914, *passim*.
[26] For example, *C Ad*, 2 Jan. 1892.
[27] See pp. 90–1.

St Andrew's in 1892,[28] had mostly Nonconformists on its committee and probably admitted a large number of Nonconformist children. Furthermore, although winning a number of controversies in the early years of the School Board, including the suspension of the payment of fees for compulsory attendance at voluntary schools,[29] Dissenters never achieved ascendancy within the Board, possibly because, without summoning Catholic help (unthinkable in relation to the religious arguments over education), Nonconformists within the borough could not actually out-vote Anglicans; the Anglican party were thus usually able to command a majority on the Board in the 1880s and 1890s.[30]

Most chapels maintained Sunday schools and bible classes, as well as Mutual Improvement Societies, the Christian Endeavour movement, Literary and Debating Societies from around the 1880s, and from the late 1890s the Pleasant Sunday Afternoon movement, all designed to reinforce the ties between church membership and the wider circle of potential church members. These organisations could not have been very effective, however, in recruiting from outside this periphery. They were church-centred, did not carry religion out to people but relied on some initial interest in the life of the church at least, and many of them relied upon some level of educational and intellectual attainment as well. Furthermore there are some indications that even the exogenous recruiting activity of the Nonconformists, the plethora of evangelising initiatives and agencies they supported, was slowing down by the 1880s. The heyday of the LCM in Croydon was in the 1860s and 1870s, when it was able to support six missionaries; later it began to run into financial difficulties.[31] There was a noticeable decline in informal missionary, revivalistic activity, the use of theatres and halls for missions, for example, and although the ostensible interest of the denominations in converting the working class did not decline, the methods used began to approximate more to the church-centred methods of Anglicans. Baptists, for example, built and supported a number of mission halls in the area, and most Nonconformist churches participated in regular church missions.[32] The Primitive Methodists, who in mid-century were the most aggressive proponents of evangelising activity amongst the working class, had by the 1880s a small but well-established

---

[28] St Andrew's Parish Magazine, Oct. 1892.
[29] C Ad, 3 Feb. 1877.
[30] See tabulated election results in appendix 1 of R. J. M. Lister, 'The Electoral History of the Croydon School Board 1870–1903', unpubl. BA thesis, Leicester 1972.
[31] See C Ad, 26 Apr. 1884; 30 Apr. 1887; 28 Apr. 1888.
[32] See, for example, West Croydon Baptist Church Magazine for 1903 on a United Free Church Mission in Croydon.

following in Croydon, and had begun to abandon the love-feasts and regular open-air preaching typical of their earlier phase of growth.[33] They were already beginning to move back towards the position of Wesleyan Methodism, a move which of course ultimately made reunion possible in the twentieth century, and which entailed an increasing formality and institution-centred atmosphere in the connexion. Something of the flavour of this change can be caught from the answers John Whittock gave to the series of questions he faced when he submitted himself as a candidate for the Preacher's Plan in 1912:

I have never been converted as some take conversion to mean an extremely radical change. I have always been a Christian, have been brought up in a Christian home by Christian Parents . . . I have been a member of the Primitive Methodist Connexion since infancy, although of course not a full, member. I mean I was baptised in a Primitive Methodist Church, my parents attending the Primitive Methodist Church.[34]

What was actually being preached in Nonconformist chapels also changed, although again the change was not so much one of substance as of manner. The Evangelicalism of mid-century Protestant Nonconformity was a strident, demanding religion, which tended to set believers apart from the world at large and which read the hand of divine guidance or retribution into almost every field of human activity. As the evangelical Quaker, John Sharp, superintendant of the Friends' Croydon school, said of his missionary work at Croydon fair in 1840, 'I returned home with the feelings of one somewhat relieved from a burden, and with a grateful sense of the mercy of my Heavenly father in making hard things easy.'[35] The Strict Baptist Francis Covell, who founded a chapel in West Street in 1847 and was pastor there until his death in 1879, believed God had worked in his soul to wean him away from Anglicanism, had cured him of a stammer soon after he first took up preaching, and thereafter watched over his life at every step, 'It having pleased the Lord to bring me to see and feel my lost estate as a sinner, and to reveal His

---

[33] Croydon Primitive Methodist Circuit, Minutes of Quarterly Meetings, *passim*; for a wider discussion of changes within Methodism, see R. Currie, *Methodism Divided: a study in the sociology of ecumenicalism* (London 1968), pp. 125–31.

[34] John Whittock's 'Statement of Doctrine', papers of Croydon Primitive Methodist Circuit.

[35] Anon., *Memoir of John Sharp, Late Superintendent of Croydon School* (Croydon n.d.), p. 40.

dear Son to me, before I had heard the truth preached.'[36]
Evangelicalism promoted a sense of God as ever-present, demanding
of a minister a constant dialogue between the thoughts of his earthly
life and his communication with God; as it was said of John Nelson,
Congregational minister of Pump Pail Chapel from 1868 to his death
in 1873: 'He lived as one on the border-land of heaven. To converse
of this was his delight, and he never wearied of it. Ready to go –
awaiting the summons home – he yet was willing to labour on and to
do his best until the hour of release struck.'[37] Whether within the
predestinarian exclusiveness of the Strict Baptists or the Arminianism
and moderate Calvinism of mainstream Protestant Nonconformity,
human life could be depicted as a constant and unremitting war with
evil; preachers were 'exercised' by their struggles with temptation,
victory was due to the Lord alone, failure to man alone. The intensity
of this struggle, the absolute conviction that salvation was to be found
within a specific ground of biblical evangelical Protestantism, as well
as a backwash of accumulated tradition about the historical
development of the churches, were what fuelled the acerbity of
Nonconformist reactions to Catholicism and the advance of ritualism
within the Church of England.

Though unchallenged in the hold it had over the practical forms of
worship, yet Evangelicalism within Nonconformity was also subject
to stresses of an intellectual and doctrinal nature in the late nineteenth
century, and these stresses were of a liberal nature rather than High
Church, since Nonconformist fundamentalists had to face scientific
theory and scriptural exegesis just as much as Anglicans. What took
place in Nonconformity was no outright abandonment of Evangelicalism in favour of some alternative religious viewpoint, but again a
loosening of its tension, a spirit of accommodation. Already by the
1880s dissentient voices within Nonconformity were expressing a
sense of dissatisfaction with the rigidities of orthodox Evangelicalism.
Lindon Parkyn, the Congregational pastor forced out of George
Street Chapel because of his unorthodox views on congregational
church government, must have felt that some doubts should be raised
about a narrow, exclusive approach to religious truth: 'He thought
that they might consider themselves an eclectic church . . . Life was
far larger than dogma or creed, and they all felt that they enjoyed the
most perfect freedom from any thraldom at all.'[38] The very plasticity
of late nineteenth century Evangelicalism, its lack of sharp points of

---

[36] W. G. Covell, *A Brief Account of the Lord's Dealings with the Late Mr. F. Covell, Minister
of Providence Chapel, Croydon* (London 1880), p. 17.
[37] Obituary of John Nelson, *Congregational Year Book*, 1874, p. 348.
[38] Speech on opening of Christ Church Congregational Church, Addiscombe: *C
Chron*, 12 Jan. 1882.

friction with other religious traditions, and the all-pervasive influence it gradually came to acquire, make it very difficult to outline the course of its diffusion. Henry Solly, a Unitarian prominent in various voluntaristic movements to improve the condition of the working class, moved to Croydon in 1877, tried out various churches in the area and eventually settled at George Street Congregational Church for the 1880s and early 1890s, finding the moderate doctrine there to his liking and hoping 'that both the Congregational and Baptist denominations may continue to free themselves – as the English Presbyterians of the last century did – from the unscriptural heresies which have too long usurped the name of orthodoxy'.[39] Even when George Street reverted to 'orthodox' evangelicalism with the appointment of R. B. Brindley in 1900, the changes of the last twenty years or so could not simply be erased; his successor, the equally orthodox W. Major Scott, believed that even strict Evangelicalism had to come to terms with the complexities of modern life and that religion could no longer be one of 'spirit' alone, but must involve intellect as well:

> I for one do not believe that the mental and moral and social anarchy of our age is an accidental thing. It is no chance product. I believe it is in many instances a peverse expression of spiritual desires and needs; but a manifestation none the less – which may be translated into the movement of the Eternal Spirit of God . . . I insist that there is an urgent need on behalf of the Church of Jesus Christ to give more concentrated thought to these deeper perplexities and problems which drive men to-day oft-times, as it seems, beyond our reach, though not beyond the arm of the Eternal Love.[40]

The consequences of practical and theological change within Protestant Nonconformity were epitomised in their understanding of the nature of a church. Alan Gilbert described early Evangelical Nonconformity as characterised by the priority accorded to evangel-ising activity aimed at making converts, by itinerancy and village preaching, and by reliance on the considerable support given by laymen.[41] At mid-century all three could still be found to a greater or lesser extent in the Nonconformist denominations, but by the 1880s the situation was changing. The denominations were not becoming more insular as such. They already possessed stricter definitions of 'membership' than the Anglican Church, and their course of

---

[39] Henry Solly, *These Eighty Years* (London 1893), ii, p. 531.
[40] W. Major Scott, *The George Street Congregational Pulpit* (Croydon Aug. 1912), p. 63.
[41] Gilbert, *Religion and Society*, p. 53.

development, while subject to some pressures and responses similar to those faced by that church, started in a sense from an opposite position, that of sect-like cohesiveness, and began to converge on a point which, could the logic of its development have been followed through, the Anglican Church would also have reached: a voluntarist church with a clear definition of membership, and relatively self-contained, 'inward-looking' organisations. What typified Nonconformist reactions to social change was a gradual elevation of the corporate identity of their denominations. The status of the minister was raised as with improved ministerial training, the opening-up of university education to Dissenters, and the regularisation of income in some cases, he began to be considered not just a religious rival to the Anglican clergyman but his social equal as well, taking the same role in public movements or public platforms. As John Whittock's Statement of Doctrine suggests, the pride of Nonconformists in the government and principles of their particular denominations was not lost, yet in doctrine and method the denominations were in fact much the same by the 1900s.[42] Nonconformist chapels sported welfare agencies – coal clubs, blanket and clothing clubs, relief agencies, savings banks – and leisure societies as much as did Anglican churches.[43] For example, within a year of opening its new, temporary iron building Brighton Road Baptist Church counted amongst its connected agencies adult classes, a Sunday school, Provident Clubs, Mothers' and Dorcas Meetings, and a Tract Distribution Society.[44] As will become apparent in the next section, where religion impinged upon political life Nonconformity acquired the organisation which set the seal on its evolution towards a sense of being churches rather than sects. Naturally, the range of responses varied considerably. Though the development of the Society of Friends illustrates some of the tendencies I have described – the abandonment of distinctive dress and customs in mid-century, the end to the prohibition on marriage outside the sect, the gradual (if limited) elevation of the status of the 'minister', the liberalising of evangelical Quakerism – it remained very much a detached component of Nonconformity. Congregationalism, on the other hand, changed rapidly and early: Trinity Congregational Church in Dingwall Road, opened in 1863, was designed along well-established 'chapel' lines, shaped like a Greek temple, but the London Road Church, West Croydon, opened three years earlier, had followed a

---

[42] See p. 81.
[43] See lists of chapel agencies printed for some chapels in *Ward's Croydon Directories*, 1874–1914.
[44] *Ibid.*, 1892.

new style in Congregational building, modelling itself on neo-gothic Anglican designs. C. E. Mudie stressed the significance of this change at the ceremony of the laying of the foundation stone: rejecting the use of the terms 'chapel' and 'meeting house' he went on to say:

> Ours, and every place of worship, is a Church – a house of God . . . although to some it may savour of affectedness, or of pretension to adopt this title in preference to the one generally given to Nonconformist places of worship, we prefer this word, and purposely designate our building by this name, to which we shall adhere, not only because it is an ecclesiastical structure, but as more truly significant of the purpose of its erection.[45]

Nonconformists were beginning to take on board a conception of their particular religious communities as 'churches', analogous to Anglicanism, at the same time as they were gradually abandoning their earlier aggressive missionary zeal and sect-like exclusiveness; theological change played its part in this process, as well as a practical recognition that this had to happen if Nonconformity was to remain an influential force rather than the refuge of dwindling minorities. An explicit endorsement of the spirit of accommodation was uttered by R. B. Brindley at George Street Congregational Chapel in 1903: 'No Englishman can excuse religious neglect from being unable to find a type of worship or pulpit teaching to his taste. There are some who would reduce all Christian worship and teaching to one pattern. A short-sighted policy indeed!'[46]

The political dimension of religion

Nonconformists were fond of pointing out that Anglicans who accused Dissenters of being mere 'political dissenters' in fact betrayed themselves into admitting that the Established Church was not just an association of like-minded believers, but was a projection of certain political and social ideals.[47] The behaviour of Anglican clergymen and leading laity in the quarrels and conflicts which bedevilled both church life and the political life of the community at large in Victorian Croydon cannot be understood fully without reference to the series of assumptions implicit in the idea of Establishment as it was held by

[45] *C Chron*, 19 Nov. 1865.
[46] Brindley, *The Darkness Where God Is*, p. 99.
[47] See Edward Miall's jibe at the 1861 vestry meeting that he was a political dissenter because 'you are political churchmen': *C Chron*, 21 Dec. 1861.

churchmen and criticised or only accepted in part by Nonconformists. The connection Anglicans made between nationality and Establishment was a valuable weapon in their attempts to refute criticisms made by Dissenters. They were not able to claim that Dissenters were unpatriotic, but they could allege that the uproar over, for example, church rates or disestablishment was socially disruptive and factious, liable to impair good relations in the nation at large and to prevent the churches working together to regenerate urban life. Dissenters were depicted as party men, Anglicans as seeking harmony and mutual respect between different religious groups in national life.[48] However the Establishment was also deemed to have a local existence as well as a national one, and it was this which enabled Anglicans to feel that they were representatives of something postive in Croydon, something worth defending, and Dissenters to feel that the 'National Church' was a very real threat to their existence. Political authority in the town, through the intermingling of civil and ecclesiastical administration, was principally in the hands of Anglicans in mid-century. This was reflected in the composition of the ruling elite in the town, for Croydon's market-based economy and rural hinterland still gave landowners, tradesmen and professional men, who were mostly Conservative and Anglican, prominence in the town's affairs. What the Establishment was able to effect in the way of practical political power in the area was consequently legitimised by the acquiescence of the town's social leadership. There were other circumstances peculiar to the locality which confirmed this trend. The long-standing connection of the see of Canterbury with Croydon certainly lent the weight of historial tradition to the over-riding influence of Anglicanism, and this was reinforced by the existence of church estates in the parish.

The political meaning of the 'Establishment' in Croydon was thus a powerful one, reinforced by history and by landowning interests. Had this been all that the Establishment meant in a local sense one could expect the stance of Nonconformists to have been a very rigid, hostile one, excluded as they were by religion from almost any say in the running of the town's affairs. Certainly this was in part the case, but the picture of sectarian conflict this implied was to some extent clouded by a more diffuse understanding of Establishment, which gave some scope for Dissenters to work alongside Anglicans in religious, political and philanthropic movements. It entailed a recognition that not only was Anglicanism synonymous with political power in Croydon, but it was also in a vaguer, but equally potent

---

[48] A frequent charge of supporters of church rates, for example, was that Dissenters were introducing 'party' spirit into local affairs: *ibid.*, 11 Sep. 1858.

sense, the 'official' face of religion. This was particularly apparent in the appointment of clergymen as chaplains to the various public institutions of the town – the workhouse, the Whitgift Hospital, the new Whitgift grammar school, and the Croydon general hospital founded in 1866. Dissenting hostility to the Church of England, when it emerged into open conflict, concentrated upon those issues which involved the use of financial resources, above all the issues of church rate and the payment of fees to the denominational schools after the establishment of the School Board in 1871. No-one seemed to mind that the salaried chaplain to the workhouse, for example, was always an Anglican.[49] Yet in return for official status, Anglicans promised equal accessibility to Nonconformist ministers. When in 1866 Thomas Edridge, magistrate, proposed that the vicar of Croydon, John Hodgson, should be chaplain to Croydon general hospital, a voluntary body, at a meeting of donors and subscribers in the Public Hall, the Rev Frederick Stephens, a leading Congregational minister, supported Edridge on the grounds that Hodgson had already made it clear that ministers of all denominations would be permitted to enter the hospital.[50] An equally striking illustration of the almost 'representative' status accorded to the Established Church was the readiness of Dissenters to forward voluntary contributions for the upkeep of Anglican churches in place of compulsory church rate before its abolition; when the old Parish Church was completely gutted by fire in 1867, Dissenters formed a committee to resist a church rate should the vicar choose to levy one, yet proved themselves willing to contribute voluntarily towards the rebuilding when Hodgson decided to rely on voluntary funds.[51]

A little more needs to be said about the role of the vicar of Croydon before some assessment of the changing nature of the meaning of the Establishment can be made. John Hodgson's long experience and work in the demanding parish of Croydon had probably influenced his view of the nature of the clerical calling; at all events at a testimonial meeting on his retirement in 1879 this was how he described it:

> The clergyman was the most public man of all, and especially in so large a parish as Croydon. There were other public men but any one of these could at any time retire into private life. It was not so with the clergyman. He had to take up his line. He had adopted his

---

[49] The vicar was chaplain until the resignation of Hodgson in 1879; thereafter the Guardians appointed their own chaplain, still an Anglican: minutes of Croydon Union, 1879, *passim*.
[50] *C Chron*, 3 Nov. 1866.
[51] *Ibid.*, 19 Jan. 1867.

profession, and so long as he lived a fierce light must beat on him every year of his life.[52]

Hodgson in fact was the last vicar to play a major role in parish administration. As chairman of the vestry he had had to preside at the stormy meetings which accompanied the Nonconformist campaign to abolish church rates in the parish in the 1850s and 1860s, and many of the meetings at which the Liberal and Nonconformist groups ascendant in the town's politics by the mid-1870s had sought to reform parish government and the parochial charities. His immediate successors caught the tail end of the latter campaign, but vestry meetings by the mid-1880s were generally tame affairs, and to all intents and purposes the main burden of town affairs had switched first of all to the Board of Health and then to the Corporation. The vicar's influence had also been derived very much from his social prestige: there was scarcely a significant philanthropic, educational or social movement in which Anglicans could participate in the 1850s and 1860s and in which Hodgson was not prominent. In most of them he occupied a position of importance, such as president, vice-president, or director.[53] In general his successors attempted to maintain this tradition – one particularly prominent in town affairs was J. M. Braithwaite, an enthusiastic supporter of most of the council's schemes for municipal reform and improvement in the 1880s, and a member, like Hodgson before him, of the School Board[54] – and yet their involvement overall was not as extensive as Hodgson's. There were three particular reasons why the vicar's social role shifted. First, church extension in Croydon both increased his burden of pastoral responsibility and (through the exercise of patronage) tended to enhance his prestige within the diocese. Thus the vicar appointed to four churches directly, and to a further five indirectly through the patronage of churches which in turn, by subdivision, had acquired patronage themselves.[55] In 1859 his authority was given official confirmation by his appointment as rural dean, a position which was subsequently held by all his successors.[56] By 1914 he supervised some sixty-five clergy in all, about two-thirds of them junior clegy.[57] Furthermore, the frequency with which his opinions were sought both by Croydon clergy and by the archbishop

[52] *Ibid.*, 9 Aug. 1879.
[53] *Ibid.*, and *C Ad*, *passim*; also the lists of committee members for local societies published in *Gray's*, *Warren's* and *Ward's Croydon Directories*, 1851–1914.
[54] *Ibid.*, *passim*.
[55] Patronage details from Visitation returns, and from Vestry Minutes, 1823–68.
[56] C Chron, 3 Sep. 1859.
[57] Numbers of clergy extracted from *Ward's Croydon Directory*, 1914.

in affairs affecting the Anglican church in Croydon testified to the elevated position of trust he was seen to occupy; until the formation of the suffragan bishopric, and in some ways even after then, he was in effect the archbishop's right-hand man in Croydon.[58] Second, the development of parochial organisations in the late Victorian period, discussed in the previous chapter, increasingly drew the vicar into a more exclusive concern with church affairs. Finally, a very real alternative figure of prestige in the town's political and social life had emerged in the form of the mayor of the new Corporation. By the late 1880s the mayor was undertaking many of the municipal responsibilities which Croydonians had previously looked to the vicar to perform, in the absence of any other municipal figure head. The prestige a mayor would bring to the town had indeed been one of the very arguments employed by the pro-incorporation movement.[59]

The social prestige accorded to the vicar in the 1840s and 1850s, along with the scale of church involvement in philanthropic and educational movements, and the relative weakness as yet of Dissent, meant that the Establishment in Croydon was probably as close to Coleridge's ideal of religion – 'the centre of gravity in a realm, to which all other things must and will accommodate themselves'[60] – as it could be in any rapidly expanding, medium-sized town in England. To many it must have seemed that the Church of England was in practice as well as in theory the moral and functional centre of their community. This understanding of Establishment became increasingly untenable in the course of the second half of the nineteenth century; it was attacked both nationally and locally by militant Dissent. By the mid-1870s the influence of the Nonconformist Liberal camp in Croydon was seriously challenging Anglican hegemony and, by associating the Parish Church with the form of parish government which Liberals and Dissenters claimed was inadequate for Croydon's needs as a rapidly urbanising area, was by the 1880s able to create some distance between the new, Liberal-dominated Council and the older parochial elite.

Two developments facilitated this process. First, the Nonconformists evolved organisations through which they could co-ordinate local Dissenting political activity. Some form of organisation appeared during the church rate disputes of the late 1850s and early 1860s, namely an ad hoc committee to manage the anti-rate campaign

---

[58] See frequent references in Benson and Temple papers at Lambeth Palace Library: for example, in 1885 J. M. Braithwaite was reporting to Benson on the conduct of elections for the Diocesan Conference (Benson Papers, xxix, 350).

[59] Elborough, *Croydon*, pp. 57–9.

[60] S. T. Coleridge, *On the Constitution of Church and State* (1830; Dent edn, London 1972), p. 53.

annually, which printed circulars and attempted to manage dissenting opinion during the inevitable poll of the parish.[61] The movement died out in 1863 after a succession of humiliating defeats at the poll,[62] and the anti-church rate committees seem to have had no connection with the Nonconformist Committee permanently established in Croydon ten years later to monitor the activities of the School Board and to press for the implementation of Nonconformist demands on it.[63] The institution of a permanent committee was a natural response to the regular meeting of the Board, but the organisational implications of this simple point of difference – the need for permanent officials and for regular contact between the different churches – marked a significant step towards regular Nonconformist co-operation. Already in 1871, during the first Board elections, temporary committees had been formed to produce a list of Nonconformist candidates.[64] The first chairman of the permanent body, J. S. Balfour, Liberal MP and later to be the first mayor of Croydon, explicitly linked the committee's work to opposition to Anglicanism:

> Croydon was a very ecclesiastical parish, and among those selected to manage its affairs there were but very few drawn from the ranks of the Nonconformists. It was therefore thought desirable that a committee should be formed to watch over the interests of the parish as they affected the Nonconformists, and take an active part in regard to the School Board and other matters.[65]

The committee was formed at an appropriate time for Nonconformists in Croydon, marking an early point in the rising tide of Liberalism in the area; most of its leading figures, including Nonconformist clergy, were politically Liberal, and many were active in the newly-formed Liberal clubs and associations and in other reformist movements in the locality. Yet it did not become a regular political organ of Liberalism in Croydon, since the remedy of the greatest Nonconformist grievance in education was achieved in 1874 with the local abolition of the payment of fees to denominational schools (where attendance was compelled) in return for a voluntary fund, and thereafter religious controversy on the Board receded; the committee seems to have ceased meeting sometime in the late 1870s.[66]

[61] For example, *C Chron*, 19 Sep. 1857.
[62] *Ibid.*, 3 Sep. 1859; 1 Dec. 1860; 21 Jan. 1861; 18 Oct. 1862.
[63] *Ibid.*, 19 Apr. 1873.
[64] *C Ad*, 18 Feb. 1871.
[65] *Ibid.*, 6 June 1874.
[66] The last *C Chron* reference I have found is 3 Feb. 1877.

Either in the 1880s and early 1890s it proved too difficult to raise interest in a permanent Nonconformist body for electioneering purposes, or (as seems more likely) Liberal Nonconformists were sufficiently satisfied both with the arrangements reached at the School Board and with the Liberal majority on the Council not to feel much concern over the Anglican majority on the Board for much of that period, for no permanent body seems to have been in existence until 1897, when the Croydon Free Church Council was formed.[67] That body, like other Free Church Councils throughout the country, was aimed as much at strictly religious co-operation as at electioneering activity.[68] It organised united weeks of prayer, and evangelistic missions, as well as debating issues which affected Nonconformity generally; for Nonconformists, then, it was the equivalent of the Anglican Ruri-Decanal Conference.[69] It also seems, significantly, to have been a minister-dominated organisation.

Second, the tendency (noted by other writers) of the denominations to develop strong central organisations in the Victorian period created firm structures which could support and co-ordinate local effort.[70] Denominational organisations developed for many reasons other than strictly political ones, but they were useful for 'political' mobilisation, and yet would not significantly have affected the way an individual church or chapel ran itself. All the major denominations had regional or sub-regional organisations linked with individual churches or meetings, which acted as a means for co-ordinating political just as much as strictly religious activity, and through which individual ministers and their congregations could be informed of events, opinions, and decisions. Regional associations like the Surrey Congregational Union, formed in 1865, provided a forum for debate on social and political issues believed to be of relevance to Nonconformity; they were a minister's main link with the trend of opinion amongst his fellow ministers.[71] The quarterly meeting of Croydon Primitive Methodist Circuit, in addition to making decisions affecting the relatively mundane business of circuit management, passed resolutions on a range of political issues, condemning, for example, the Conservative government's licensing proposals in 1904, supporting the Liberal Government's educational and licensing bills in 1908, and in the same year electing delegates to

---

[67] *Ward's Croydon Directory*, 1898.
[68] For a brief reference to Free Church Councils, see Gilbert, *Religion and Society*, p. 196.
[69] For example, *C Chron*, 19 Apr. 1899.
[70] See, for example, Chadwick's discussion of the impact of the formation and work of the Congregational Union; Chadwick, *Victorian Church*, i, 401–7.
[71] Waddington, *Surrey Congregational History*, pp. 135–40.

act as representatives at a peace conference to be held at West-minster.[72]

The situation of political Nonconformity in Croydon by the 1900s suggests a paradox of increasing political provision and organisation at the same time that, within the denominations which were eventually subsumed under the general description of the 'Free Churches', changes were taking place which were locating church effort in activities associated exclusively with the church and not with the wider society. In fact what was happening was that political agitation which, in the mid-century and before, had seemed to represent the very essence of Dissent was becoming a particular activity of Nonconformists. Solution of some Nonconformist griev-ances tended to undermine the immediate relevance of political points of tension anyway, and this was especially so in a local context with the abolition of church rates since the annual voting of a rate had made the vestry the focus of sectarian conflict in Croydon. The issue of education kept tension high, but within a relatively circumscribed area of activity. There were two substantial matters on which sectarian disagreement on the School Board was intense: the first was the question of religious teaching in Board schools, and the second was the payment of fees to denominational schools. On both Anglicans, despite their narrow dominance of the Board for most of its history, were to make some concessions to Nonconformists. An attempt to restrict religious education to a vague, scripturally selective teaching was defeated by a combination of Anglicans and evangelical Nonconformists in 1871, but with the result that the interpretation of nondenominational education was somewhat looser than some Anglicans would have wished.[73] Subsequently, Anglicans had to fight off attempts by some Dissenters to ban collects, certain prayers and hymns, and the display of the Ten Commandments from schools on the grounds that these were 'denominational' articles or that, in the case of display of the Ten Commandments, they amounted to religious 'indoctrination'.[74] The fee issue, settled by a compromise in 1871 which recognised that in cases of hardship fees could be paid to denominational schools, was resurrected by Nonconformists in 1874 who managed to overturn the original decision on the grounds that only £3 10s. had been paid in fees to denominational schools in the past year and that a private fund could easily bear this expense.[75]

[72] Croydon Primitive Methodist Circuit, Quarterly Meeting Minutes, entries for 6 June 1904; 2 Mar., 1 June 1908.
[73] Croydon School Board, Main Minutes, 13 June 1871.
[74] *C Ad*, entries for 13 Jul. 1872; 26 Apr. 1873; 17 May 1873.
[75] *Ibid.*, entries for 25 Nov. 1871; 4 Apr. 1874.

Along with the fact that Anglican influence in schooling was falling in relation to the rising activity of the School Board, their comparative success on the Board endeared it to Nonconformists. For this very reason Nonconformist reaction to Balfour's Education Bill abolishing School Boards was intense, but two considerations are significant here: the first is that the resolution which Liberals on the Croydon Council in 1902 narrowly pushed through condemning the proposed abolition of the School Board did not receive unanimous support from Nonconformist council members, several of whom opposed it on the grounds that it introduced party politics into the council chamber;[76] secondly, that the effect of the bill was to take even education out of the immediate arena of religious conflict, extending at the same time the power and responsibility of the Corporation. It abolished at one sweep the local roots of political Nonconformity; Nonconformists' objections looked a little lame in face of the undoubted fact that the unsectarian state-aided religious education they had come to advocate had surpassed the importance of the Church of England in education long before, and the rapid passing of protest owed something to a realisation that the situation they had feared in 1870 had not materialised.[77]

It is possible to exaggerate the political significance of Noncon- formity: many Dissenters themselves tried to separate their political activism from their religious behaviour. C. H. Spurgeon warned Baptists at West Croydon Tabernacle in 1872 against allowing political agitation to overshadow the rest of the church's work, asserting that the strength of Nonconformity lay in spirituality and that Dissenters should seek above all to win souls.[78] A similar warning issued from George Street Congregational Chapel thirty years later, where the pastor claimed that the words 'My Kingdom is not of this world' applied to even 'the most democratic Nonconformist, so open to temptation to adopt worldly schemes for the support of unendowed means of grace'.[79] Yet inasmuch as Dissent existed at all, it did so by virtue of conscious opposition to the State Church and was, at root, therefore a political question. The deepening sense of denominational commitment Nonconformists required of their church members in

---

[76] *Ibid.*, 11, 18 Oct., 1 Nov. 1902.
[77] There was only one notable case in Croydon concerning 'passive resisters', when 83 burgesses appeared before the County Court for non-payment of rates; it was settled by mutual agreement to pay only towards the £2,000 which the town clerk reckoned to be the excess expenditure by the new Education Committee over what the School Board would have spent: *C Chron*, 26 Mar. 1904.
[78] G. H. Pike, *James Archer Spurgeon* (London 1894), p. 133.
[79] Brindley, *The Darkness Where God Is*, p. 23.

the late nineteenth century, though it took place against a background of easing tensions of a doctrinal or theological nature within Nonconformity itself, may have contributed to a renewal of the sense of separateness of Nonconformity, because at the same time that political conflict over the issues of education and disestablishment continued, the institution against which Nonconformists defined themselves, the Church of England, was gradually adopting the tenets and practices of a High Church tradition most Dissenters found repellent. An approximation of methods and forms of organisation did not therefore imply a lessening of Nonconformist sensitivity to the issue of the Establishment. The problem is rather that the politico-religious disputes between Anglicans and Nonconformists in the 1880s and 1900s tended to obscure the shifting basis of Nonconformist support and structure. The issues concerned remained similar to those in previous decades, centring on the struggle for resources which Nonconformists believed Anglicans had an advantage in pursuing because they could use the lever of State support and power. Education by this period was therefore the real area of discord, because it was the one remaining activity for which Anglicanism could in fact attempt to claim State support (through payment of fees to denominational schools). However the complex intertwining of ecclesiastical tradition, myths about the origins and value of religious endowments, and genuine perception of the social prestige and power of Anglicanism, also served to keep alive Dissenting interest in the possibility of more wide-sweeping reform, as is evident in the abortive move to disestablish the Welsh Church in 1894 and the successful attempt of 1912–14. Ostensibly the arguments behind Dissenting agitation in these campaigns were the same as those used in mid-century over the abolition of church rates, the abolition of University Tests and the disestablishment of the Irish Church. In fact, the context of these disputes was changing and, at least locally, their effectiveness was being reduced; by the 1890s they were becoming increasingly isolated from municipal politics, as other issues were taken up by a Council which was extending gradually its field of responsibility in welfare, housing and transport in the area. The success of the School Board in Croydon and the rapidity with which it took over voluntary school provision confirmed this trend, reducing the overall importance of the Established Church in educational affairs in the Borough. The waning of the sectarian basis of British politics in the early twentieth century was therefore not solely a question of religious socialisation, as claimed by Wald,[80] nor

---

[80] Wald, *Crosses on the Ballot*, p. 203.

was it a simple product of congregational decline within Nonconformity, for though decline did occur before the First World War it was not on so significant a scale as to merit such a conclusion; it was a structural question as much as anything, with the respective spheres of political and religious life pulling apart and forming their own largely independent realms, and with political Nonconformity dropping through the gap in the middle.

A similar process was at work within Anglicanism, reorienting church life away from an arena in which religion was understood to carry inevitable sectarian associations, towards one in which it could eventually, later in the twentieth century, become essentially depoliticised. It was a question, first, of structures: the disentanglement of ecclesiastical administration from civil administration, the gradual abandonment of church involvement in political issues which could only serve, in a context of conflict, to discredit it, and the evolution of alternative forms of civil administration, all of this for a host of social, political and economic reasons. It was also a question of pressures, namely those exerted on churches with their existing structures and traditions by the demands of social change, taking the form of demographic change, declining resources of manpower and money, changing patterns of work, and the rise of leisure activity and political activism. From this angle it is all too easy to depict Anglicanism as a passive victim of forces beyond its control. A sobering reminder that this was not strictly the case is provided by the third reflection, that the changes so far described were also attributable to doctrinal or ideological struggles within the church, an arena within which conscious decisions about the role and future of the church were made. The pattern of adaptation within the church, given these three, was a complicated one in Croydon, affected by the abilities and disposition of individual clergymen and the latitude they possessed (or did not possess) for carrying out their intentions. Overall, leading features emerge from an analysis which tend to concentrate the drift of change in the 1880s and onwards: the gradual disappearance of the bitter disputes between clergy and laity which tended to dog church extension in mid-century, the gradual adoption of High Church ritual and practices throughout the church, the declining intensity of doctrinal conflict, the softening of evangelicalism, the elevation of the spiritual authority of the clergyman within the Church, the declining active interest of the lay urban leadership in church affairs, the rise of a new means of defining membership, and the appearance and elaboration of new systems of parochial management. The process could be – and has been by some authors[81] – described as one of denominationalisation, but this could only be at best a partial description: in retaining its traditional role with regard to the rites of passage as well as formal, less contentious Establishment claims, the Church of England continued to give some practical evidence in support of those who still believed it to be the National Church.

Unorthodox Croydon and Roman Catholicism

Anglicanism and Protestant Nonconformity remained far and away the dominant religious traditions in Victorian and Edwardian Croydon, but by the late nineteenth century they did not monopolise worship, for a number of separate, independent religious organisations had established themselves in the Borough. With the exception of Roman Catholics and Unitarians, these religious bodies were only marginally involved in the complex of religious activity and municipal and political life which forms the principal subject of this study. However, they merit some independent discussion, for their growth illustrated both the inability of the larger Protestant churches by late century to comprehend between them all religious sensibilities in an urbanising area and the process of diversification in religious practice which is an underlying theme of this study and which, it is argued, was a product – or rather a necessary corollary – of the collection of changes which went together to form 'urbanisation'. In terms of numbers alone 'unorthodoxy' in Croydon could claim to be a significant voice in the town's religious life by 1902: total attendance at all places of worship apart from the Anglican and Protestant Nonconformist churches amounted to 9,767, or nearly one-fifth of total attendances, throughout the Borough.[82] The census figures may if anything understate the importance of these groups because they omit many small unorthodox congregations which may have appeared before or after the census, which may have been short-lived, and whose existence can only be established sometimes from passing references in newspapers and directories.

Why was Croydon such favourable ground for these groups? Their proliferation in the 1880s and 1890s suggests a direct link between the kind of urban growth which relied increasingly on an influx of lower middle class and artisanal residents into the borough, and the appearance of religious organisations which clearly thrived on

---

[81] For example, Gilbert, *Religion and Society*, esp. ch. 7, 'Church and chapel in denominational relationship'.
[82] Mudie Smith, *Religious Life*, pp. 382–5; appendix 3, table 3.

dissatisfaction with the forms of service provided by the larger Protestant denominations. The pace of development was outrunning the ability of Anglican and Nonconformist churches to maintain religious and other provision to the same extent as they had done in mid-century, and the locations of most of the small, unorthodox places of worship lay in the lower middle and working class areas of the town – the Old Town, North Croydon, Thornton Heath, East Croydon and Selhurst – where the larger denominations were particularly suffering. Middle class Norwood and Addiscombe were generally free of them. Along the Brighton Road, where development occurred after the 1880s and was mostly poor or lower middle class, for example, several small meeting houses were established either on the main road or in the side-streets leading off it, and the Salvation Army built a small hall there in 1912.[83] Yet it would be misleading to interpret the growth of unorthodox Croydon as a result solely of the 'failure' of the larger denominations, since these small religious groups often seem to have been characterised by highly distinctive theological systems which would have separated them from Protestant Nonconformity even in its most strident form. Millennial views were sometimes voiced – 'addresses were delivered by a reverend gentleman who predicted the end of the whole cosmic scheme in 1896', it was said of a Gospel Messenger's meeting[84] – and some groups preserved an extremely rigid idea of membership which would have excluded many even had they sought to join: the Plymouth Brethren, for example, expelled one member in 1882 because of alleged untruthfulness, and then two more for failing to support his expulsion.[85] So amongst some of these groups at least, apparently drawing support from lower middle class and artisanal believers, there was to be found the sort of frustrated social expectations and lack of status which gave rise to closely-knit, distinctive religious communities, typical of what Weber regarded as the religion of disprivileged classes, and Troeltsch as composing a sect-type of religious organisation; the intensity of the religious bond and the powerful sense of an exclusive special gift of salvation would have compensated for the relative lack of success in worldly affairs.[86]

This seems to hold good for small groups such as the Brethren, the Gospel Messengers, and perhaps even the Salvation Army, but it is not the whole picture: some groups thrived on educated middle class unorthodoxy instead. The Unitarian community, Croydon Free

[83] *Ward's Croydon Directories*, 1874–1914.
[84] *C Chron*, 21 Nov. 1891.
[85] *Ibid.*, 28 Jan. 1882.
[86] M. Weber, *The Sociology of Religion*, ed. T. Parsons (London 1965), esp. ch. 7;
E. Troeltsch, *The Social Teaching of the Christian Churches* (London 1931).

Christian Church, was very much of this order. Its founding committee members in the early 1870s were all wealthy, middle class, professional men, gentlemen or merchants and manufacturers, many of them prominent in other political and social movements in Croydon – hardly the kind of people one could regard in any sense as 'disprivileged'.[87] The congregation at the Free Christian Church was relatively small, and solidly middle class, not an overwhelmingly wealthy one, to judge by the problems experienced in raising financial support for a mission hall in the late 1880s, but one sufficiently well-educated to attract and support a succession of capable, eminent Unitarian ministers, including E. M. Geldart, C. J. Street, W. J. Jupp and John Page Hopps.[88] Davies thought there was a 'distinct theistic tone tracable throughout' the service there.[89] One of the regular attenders, J. H. Mitchiner, councillor and author, was also in the 1870s and 1880s a spiritualist, as well as president of a debating society formed at the church, the Croydon Socratic Society.[90] Two of the church's pastors, W. J. Jupp and John Page Hopps, were prominent in the the Brotherhood Church movement in Croydon.[91] The conscious intellectualism of the pastor and some of the congregation of the Free Christian Church is a little out of step with the pleasure-loving, sociable picture F. W. Moore drew of the life of the church, but both were vastly different from the religious world of the Brethren and the Salvation Army; 'unorthodoxy' in Croydon derived support from as wide a social spectrum as did Anglicanism and Protestant Nonconformity.

The strength of these religious movements in Croydon may also have been related to regional, demographic factors. Several of them would have received impetus from immigration from London, where an extremely wide range of small denominations and religious groups could be found. Close as it was to the metropolis, Croydon had already in the 1870s received the attention of William Booth and the Christian Missionaries.[92] Rural immigration may also account for something of the complexity of Croydon's religious sub-culture even in late century. The relative weakness of churchgoing in rural Surrey

---

[87] F. W. Moore, 'Croydon Free Christian Church: its early days', typescript (1923) at C Ref Lib; C. M. Davies, *Unorthodox London* (London 1875), p. 102.

[88] Moore, 'Croydon Free Christian Church'; Croydon Domestic Mission, Minute Book 1888-9.

[89] Davies, *Unorthodox London*, p. 292.

[90] Book of cuttings compiled by J. H. Mitchiner, deposited at C Ref Lib.

[91] M. Tichelar, 'Labour Politics in Croydon 1880-1914', unpubl. BA thesis, Thames Polytechnic 1975.

[92] *C Chron*, 16 Mar., 5, 12 Oct. 1872; *C Ad*, 5 Apr. 1879.

need not have ruled out the existence of small eccentric religious communities; Everitt concluded that neighbouring Kent showed a remarkable proclivity for small independent sects, such as the Mormons, the Catholic and Apostolic Church (who established a congregation at Croydon in 1912),[93] the Plymouth Brethren, the Bible Christians (who had eight congregations in West Surrey in 1851, though none in East Surrey)[94] and the Huntingtonians.[95] It may consequently be argued that geographically Croydon was favourably situated for the proliferation of marginal religious communities, drawing most of its immigrants – in a period of very rapid demographic growth – from areas typified both by relatively low rates of orthodox church attendance and by relatively high interest in the smaller, sect-like religious groups.

The growth of unorthodox Croydon can reveal more about the pressures to which churches were subject than can a simple description of the increasingly complicated pattern of Croydon's religious life, for where sufficient evidence is available the same process of development and elaboration of church life found in Anglicanism and Protestant Nonconformity in the late nineteenth century can be traced even within some of these smaller groups. The smallest or most sect-like, such as the Brethren, embraced exclusive theological systems which would not have encouraged the cultivation of agencies designed to extend a church's influence; in a sense they were an entirely different kind of religious organisation from the larger churches. But those in which membership was relatively open clearly fall in line with what was happening in Protestant denominations. At the Free Christian Church a debating society, a free library and discussion and social groups for young people were founded in the late 1870s, then in the 1880s children's services were begun, a new permanent church built to replace the temporary iron building used formerly, congregational soirées organised, and a mission hall built for the poor in Dennett Road.[96] The dependency of the church upon a minister, and the importance this implied for the status of a minister, was illustrated by an attempt in 1910 and 1911 to run the church without a permanent ministry, accepting temporary preachers only; the result, according to Francis Moore, was disastrous, with many old members ceasing to attend; the situation was saved only

[93] *Ward's Croydon Directory*, 1912.
[94] 1851 Census of Religious Worship in England and Wales (Report) Division 11, pp. 10–11.
[95] Everitt, *Pattern of Rural Dissent*, p. 61.
[96] Moore, 'Croydon Free Christian Church', *passim*.

with the appointment of a permanent minister in August 1911.[97] The
growth of the Ethical Movement and the Brotherhood Church in
Croydon illustrates similar themes. The Fellowship of the New Life,
'the religious counterpart of the Fabian Society', formed in 1882 or
1883, was effectively centred on Croydon, where the editor of its
journal *Seedtime* and its secretary lived.[98] By 1898 it had merged
locally with the Ethical movement, a similar synthesis of vague theism
with ethical radical politics, and had supported a labour church at
Broad Green in North Croydon from 1894.[99] It was an intellectualist
movement, drawing support principally from middle class radicals,
some of whom later left Croydon to found a utopian Tolstoyan
community in the Cotswolds, and though it supported the Labour
Movement in Croydon was not directly associated with it.[100] A
Fellowship Guild was formed in 1893 to organise meetings and
classes; Harold Oakeshott, son of the secretary of the Fellowship, took
a leading part in the running of the Guild, and wrote an article in
Seedtime describing, first of all, how the ambitious schemes of the guild
had gradually been scaled down from building a community of
artisans' cottages with a central Fellowship Hall to the hiring out of a
small mission hall in Mansfield Road; he then described how sub-
agencies had been formed within it, first a kindergarten, then a
weekly social to 'capture' the adults (a largely unsuccessful venture,
he admitted), then boxing and gymnastic classes for young men, and
then in 1895 evening classes, readings and a swimming club.[101] The
Fellowship had been formed to give practical effect to an opinion J. F.
Oakeshott voiced that 'Theological dogma and doctrine have now
. . . been dethroned in favour of a social practical Christianity which
recognises that the importance of this world is greater than that of the
world to come',[102] but the development of its work closely mirrored
that of the orthodox churches; furthermore, his son described the
opposition of some members of the Guild to a narrow, closed
conception of its work in language little removed from that of
conventional religious ideology: 'Others, however, desired for the
Fellowship the broadening and strengthening influence of more
extended social work, and the feeling was expressed that the mission

[97] *Ibid.*, pp. 61–2.
[98] P. Thompson, *Socialists, Liberals and Labour: the struggle for London 1885–1914*
(London 1967), p. 33.
[99] *C Chron*, 13 Nov. 1897; 'H.T.B. Muggeridge' in *Dictionary of Labour Biography*, v
(1979), .
[100] N. Shaw, *Whiteway, a colony in the Cotswolds* (London c. 1934); Tichelar, 'Labour
Politics in Croydon', ch. 3.
[101] *Seedtime, The Organ of the New Fellowship*, 3 (Jan. 1897), p. 9.
[102] *Ibid.*, 19 (Jul. 1896), p. 7.

of keeping the springs pure was ineffectual unless those springs could be brought to contribute to the needs of the thirsting multitude.'[103]

The diversity of religious groups to be found in unorthodox Croydon testifies to the range of differing religious ambitions which could exist within an urbanising area in the late nineteenth and early twentieth centuries. Their impact was strictly limited: they were small groups in the main, and only those which drew upon educated middle class support can be said to have played much part in municipal political and social life; significantly, these were the groups whose membership was least restricted. The sect-like organisation of the Brethren, for example, almost by definition could not become a 'mass' movement, and for the same reason – its exclusiveness – it could not wield much influence within middle class circles. The extensive social contacts required of those who sought to participate in municipal life would have excluded members of sects which sought to shun contact with the outside world and preserved what, from the point of view of prevailing ideas amongst the middle class, would have been eccentric theological views. The tensions between sect-like exclusiveness and the demands of the wider social world of the middle class which Gosse described in *Father and Son* had local significance as well, therefore. Unorthodox Croydon represented no great threat to the Protestant denominations; orthodox church life was not disintegrating. What the growth of these small groups does indicate, however, is that urbanisation opened up religious opportunities and made it increasingly difficult for the orthodox denominations to control the religious colouring of the borough. Those sects which, like the Brethren, represented the extreme form of a tight religious community, could draw on some support in a suburban commuter town like Croydon, but lived as it were in the interstices of urban society: the sect-like mentality could make little headway against a middle class culture which itself was defining more closely and more narrowly the functions of a church, and giving greater prominence to political and social institutions.

Roman Catholicism, as always, is the exception in almost any attempt to classify nineteenth century religious denominations: it drew some support from the middle class as well as from the lower classes, and its congregations contained some municipal leaders even though, theologically and to some extent socially, it stood apart from the rest of church going Croydon. Even so, most of its support was drawn from a single lower class immigrant group, the Irish, and its influence was consequently strictly limited. In the second half of the

[103] *Ibid.*, 31 (Jan. 1897), p. 9.

nineteenth century, Roman Catholicism did not significantly enlarge its share of worship in Croydon: in 1851, at 461 (adjusted) attendances, it accounted for 2.27 per cent of the population; by 1902, this proportion had shrunk marginally to two per cent, although attendances had risen to 2,685 (adjusted).[104] It is possible, however, that the census figures are a little misleading, because the 1900s marked a stage of substantial institutionalised expansion for the Roman Church, as the original two chapels in the borough, St Mary's, Wellesley Road and the chapel attached to the Convent of Virgo Fidelis at Central Hill, Upper Norwood, were joined by a further three (at South Norwood, Thornton Heath and South Croydon) between 1904 and 1908.[105] These later chapels were built in predominantly lower middle class and working class areas which apparently did not have a high proportion of Irish residents, whereas St Mary's had been founded near to Irish settlements in Old Town and at Broad Green, and had subsequently moved to a more prestigious site a little nearer to the town centre.[106]

Throughout the Victorian period Roman Catholics in Croydon had to contend with the same hostility and lack of understanding they encountered elsewhere in Britain. However there is a lack of evidence of positive discrimination and hostility from the 1890s on, which may suggest a decline in the intensity of anti-Catholic feeling along the lines described by E. R. Norman.[107] Branches of the Protestant Reformation Society and the Society for Irish Church Missions to the Roman Catholics were in existence in Croydon at least by the late 1850s: although these were chiefly fund-raising bodies, nevertheless through regular meetings and lectures they helped to perpetuate local anti-Catholic feeling.[108] The local press from the 1850s through to the 1880s frequently carried letters denouncing 'popery', although local anxieties were chiefly centred around perceived Romanistic tendencies in the Anglican church. Anti-Catholicism was even supported by principal local leaders. The vicar of Croydon, for example, in 1864 claimed that his observations of Roman Catholicism convinced him how 'completely the second commandment was cut out, and pictures really worshipped'.[109] In 1881 a local *cause célèbre* was the attempt by the vicar of St James to seek an injunction preventing the Catholic

---

[104] Appendix 3, tables 1, 3.
[105] *Ward's Croydon Directories*, 1905–8.
[106] McLaughlin, *The Foundation of St. Mary's*, pp. 25–8.
[107] E. R. Norman, *Anti-Catholicism in Victorian England* (London 1968), ch. 1.
[108] Earliest references are: *C Chron*, 10 Oct. 1857 (Protestant Reformation Society), and *ibid.*, 20 Nov. 1858 (Society for Irish Church Missions to the Roman Catholics).
[109] *Ibid.*, 19 Nov. 1864.

rector of Croydon, the Rev Alphonsus David, from speaking to his son.[110] Earlier, a proposal to admit Roman Catholic priests to the workhouse was vigorously opposed by several members of the Board of Guardians, one even claiming that Catholicism was 'a great ecclesiastical confederacy for resisting the extension of light and liberty in the world'.[111]

Despite the all-pervasive nature of this hostility, Catholics were not altogether excluded from local municipal life. Two individuals in particular secured for them a say in the town's administration. One was John Hubert Schmitz, a Catholic who was active in Croydon Liberalism from the late 1870s, secured election to the Council in 1883, became mayor in 1889 and subsequently served as alderman until his retirement in 1902.[112] As councillor, Schmitz represented Central Ward, which included Old Town and therefore one concentration of Irish Catholics; he was top of the poll in 1883 and unopposed in 1885, but it is difficult to establish whether his success was due largely to sectarian or to party political voting.[113] The picture is clearer in the case of the Rev Alphonsus David, priest and rector of St Mary's from 1850 to 1893, who served on the School Board in the early 1870s and owed his electoral success very much to the solidity of Catholic voting.[114] On particular issues such as the appointment of officers and the use of the bible in religious teaching, he sided with Anglican-Conservative members against Nonconformist-Liberals.[115] This was also true in the case of the payment of fees to denominational schools; the Board's compromise of 1871 whereby fees in necessitous cases only could be paid at all public elementary schools, including denominational schools, would appear to have achieved David's principal objective, for he did not trouble to stand for election again.[116]

Roman Catholics were able to acquire some influence in municipal affairs, but the comparative poverty and small size of their following in Croydon meant that this influence was strictly limited. They were of little significance in the religious and political struggles between Anglicans and Nonconformists, and in any case their public presence was an ambivalent one: regarded as

---

[110] *Ibid.*, 10 Dec. 1881.
[111] *Ibid.*, 28 Jan. 1865.
[112] Details from *C Ad* and *Ward's Croydon Directories*, 1874–1914, *passim*.
[113] Anon., *Old and New Croydon*, p. 64.
[114] Lister, 'Electoral History of the Croydon School Board', appendix.
[115] Croydon School Board, Main Minutes, entries for 16 Mar., 13 June 1871.
[116] *C Chron*, 25 Nov. 1871.

'dissenters' by some Anglicans, they were the victims of hostility and prejudice across all denominations, and sided with Anglicans over religious education, and yet their only influential municipal figure was a Liberal most of whose political colleagues were Protestant Nonconformists. Their following was simply too small to sport the wide range of leisure, charitable and other organisations typical of the Catholic 'ghetto' in some other Victorian cities, and in religious terms they were completely isolated from mainstream church life in Croydon.[117]

[117] D. H. McLeod, 'Building the "Catholic Ghetto": Catholic organisations 1870–1914', *Studies in Church History*, xxiii (1986).

5

The Parochial System of Government

As the Victorian churches sought to adapt their organisations and techniques to catch and retain believers in urbanising areas, a separation began to take place between the practical influence of the churches and the organisation, methods and ethos of local government. There were several strands to this: developments within the churches themselves; an accumulating criticism of the partisan basis of what Keith-Lucas has called the 'unreformed local government system', which in turn fuelled demands for radical reform and democratisation of local government;[1] the apparent failure of voluntarist remedies for urban problems, remedies which the churches were particularly active in promoting; the contrasting success, growth and increasing sophistication of reformed municipal authorities in the late nineteenth century; and the behaviour of municipal leaders themselves, as they gradually switched their attention away from denominational activism towards municipal life.

This process was particularly acute in towns, such as Croydon, which were not incorporated until late in the century and were instead governed by an unwieldly combination of parish authorities and specialised boards which became the focus of bitter political and sectarian rivalry. It is true, as Keith-Lucas asserts, that the growth of specialised, ad hoc boards such as the Croydon Improvement Commissioners is a sign that 'the traditional system of the open vestry and the unpaid annual officers was proving inadequate for the needs of the time',[2] but it does not follow that the authority of the vestry necessarily was diminished as a result; the vestry remained the final arbiter in parish affairs, annually selecting the membership of the boards in the first place, and also having the final say in most of the important decisions they had to take, in other words those which involved raising public finance. However the parochial system was one in which civil government was inextricably intertwined with ecclesiastial administration. It assumed religious uniformity: the exclusion of Disssenters from public office by the Test and

---

[1] B. Keith-Lucas, *The Unreformed Local Government System* (London 1980).
[2] *Ibid.*, p. 101.

Corporation Acts had been one implication of a system of government in which those who supervised the running of the parish church were also those at the top of the 'civil' administrative hierarchy in the parish, and which indeed used the same organ, the vestry, to raise what was in effect a civil rate – church rate – for religious purposes. The parochial system of government was therefore very much the practical aspect of the Church of England as by law locally established. The vicar was the key figure in Croydon's civil administration, as well as religious government. Consequently religion was inseparable from politics, and the removal of Dissenting disabilities in 1828 did not give Nonconformists a clear path to local power. The gradual rise of Nonconformity in Croydon from the 1850s, as the town entered its fastest phase of urban expansion, meant that Dissenters increasingly came into conflict with the vestiges of the parochial system which still existed in the parish even after the formation of the Local Board of Health in 1849.

Religion was not the only motivating force behind political activism in the early Victorian period, but it was an important source of alignment in political affairs. Sectarian alignments were clearly registered time and again at vestry meetings, because that was the forum through which appointments to public office were made and to which proposals to levy church rate were put. Twenty-six individuals were elected at the Easter vestries as people's warden between 1830 and 1870, and for seventeen of these it has been possible to establish religious affiliations: all of them were Anglicans, and yet in seven cases out of the seventeen where it has also been possible to identify political allegiance, six were Conservative and one Liberal.[3] The composition of the Improvement Commissioners in the 1830s and 1840s also suggests that religion was a more important factor in determining membership than were political affiliations.[4]

It is important to note a number of qualifications. First, on many issues sectarian alignments were non-existent because they were not issues which directly affected particular denominations rather than others. This is particularly true of the work of the various ad hoc boards which undertook specialised responsibilities in the parish in the 1830s and 1840s: there was, for example, no specific denominational perspective to the issue of sanitary reform in Croydon. Although the structure of authority under which these boards were

---

[3] Churchwardens' names found in Croydon Parish Vestry Minutes, *passim*, cross-referenced for political and religious affiliations with the *C Chron* (church and political committees) and J. Ward, *Croydon in the Past* (Croydon 1883) (burials in the Anglican portion of Croydon Cemetery).
[4] See p. 124.

appointed – the parochial system – was itself a focus for Nonconformist criticism, the issues dealt with by these boards were substantially
ones on which disagreement occurred along other lines. Second,
potential sectarian divisions were to some extent marginalised by the
sheer weight of Anglican dominance in Croydon. The rising affluence
and assertiveness of Nonconformists focused in particular on church
rate in the 1850s and 1860s, and in the 1870s began imperceptibly to
shade into a Liberal critique of local government, but time and again
they were defeated in vestry meetings and in polls of the parish; in
mid-century they were a vociferous but impotent minority. Third, it
is impossible to identify with precision exactly what were 'political'
and what were 'religious' elements in the motivation of local
notabilities. Church rate and Establishment were political issues, and
yet their contentiousness depended upon differing religious perspectives; the same was true of controversies over education. Contemporaries did not make a formal separation between the civil and religious
functions of the parish until later in the century, when church rate
had been abolished, alternative agencies of local government had
been established and religion had begun to be stripped of many of its
more ambitious, 'secular' connotations.

Nevertheless, the vestry represented the nexus of religion and
political activism under the parochial system of government. Local
notabilities were bound together by economic interest, and to some
extent by shared political values, but they were also linked by
religion. If religion was not necessarily the only determinant of their
behaviour, yet it provided an important part of the framework within
which their ambitions were articulated, because religious responsibilities were attached to the key parish offices. A clear recognition of this
can be found much later in the century. The *Croydon Chronicle*
highlighted the Parish Councils Bill in 1894, since it finally separated
civil administration from church government by taking remaining
civil functions out of the control of the vestry; it referred to the Easter
vestry of 1894 and went on to say:

> The annual gathering, therefore, was significant from one point of
> view only, *viz*, that it was the last of the old-fashioned vestry
> meetings, wherein Church matters were mixed up with charities
> that were claimed to be as much parish affairs, outside legitimate
> ecclesiastical control, as the election of Overseers and the collection
> of poor rates. No longer is the Church to be found the leading
> figure among the various subjects.[5]

---

[5] *C Chron*, 31 Mar. 1894.

In 1901 the vicar of Croydon felt able to look back on the former intermingling of religion and civil government as an age well past, when he spoke of the annual ceremony of beating the bounds of the parish, and called it one of a number of customs which 'remind us of the close tie that there was, in older times, between the church and all matters of public interest and importance'.[6]

The operation and breakdown of the parochial system of government

It is a common assumption that the parochial system of administration 'broke down' in the nineteenth century in expanding towns like Croydon because it was in origin a rural method of government and therefore by definition unsuited to coping with the complicated business of an urban area.[7] The problem with an assumption of this nature is that it is likely to obscure a close study of the reasons why the system came to be replaced. It is true that it was more likely to succeed – to carry influence and to operate efficiently – in areas where the ruling elite was relatively compact and allied to the religious establishment, a situation which did not generally prevail in urbanising areas in the nineteenth century. Yet it was not in itself an inflexible system: the principle of specialised boards to carry out administrative functions supervised by a central representative body, the vestry, could in theory at least combine provision for efficient management of the minutiae of parochial business with the expression of the consensus of opinion in the parish necessary to support and sustain the work of these boards. But the system was a hybrid one: it was the product of evolution and aggregation, with ad hoc boards progressively added to existing bodies without any systematic restatement by parliamentary statute of the functions and powers of the elements it contained, so that confusion and inaction were often the unfortunate results of attempts under the system to remedy problems of parochial administration. Furthermore, it did not exist in a vacuum: there were classes and groups in society to whom it did not accord equal influence, and many who could not, on grounds of religion and politics, participate fully in its operation.

[6] Croydon Parish Church Magazine, May 1901.
[7] An assumption made by the Webbs, 'In crowded urban districts, with shifting populations and sharp economic religious or political cleavages the task of creating, out of the disjointed legal framework of parish government, an efficient instrument of democratic government, appeared . . . absolutely insuperable': B. and S. Webb, Parish and county, p. 104, and echoed by K. B. Smellie, A History of Local Government (3rd edn, London 1957), p. 13.

There were defects in the system itself which arose from the structure of its constituent boards and from the manner in which these boards had been set up, namely to cater for a particular problem rather than to supervise a general area of local administration. First was the problem of confused jurisdiction. In a growing urban area like Croydon issues could be thrown up which were not clearly the responsibility of any particular authority in the parish. In 1836 and 1837, for example, complaints about the state of the footpath in the High Street were taken up by the Improvement Commissioners, passed on to the Board of Surveyors of the Highways, who passed them back to the Improvement Commissioners, claiming that they had no funds available and that the Commissioners would have to raise a General Purpose Rate through the vestry; however, a vestry meeting held eventually on 14 December 1837 adjourned the question indefinitely, presumably reluctant to sanction an increase in local taxation.[8] It had taken a year and a half to reach this stage, only to procure no firm decision on the issue. The atmosphere of uncertainty and confusion produced by the failure to place the system on a firm, organised statutory basis is well illustrated by the experience of Thomas Frost, the radical journalist, who in 1848 applied to use the Town Hall for a meeting of Chartists (an application subsequently refused by the magistrates):

> There was a doubt, however, as to the authority in whom the control of that building was legally vested, the senior overseer informing me that he did not possess it, and standing aghast at the suggestion of a medical gentleman who came up while we were discussing the question, that the town-crier and bill-poster, being also the head constable under the old parochial system, was the right man to apply to.[9]

In fact, the real authorities in the matter, to judge by their readiness on other occasions to let out the Town Hall for public meetings, were a body which neither Frost, the senior overseer, nor the medical gentleman, seem to have thought of – the Trustees of the Waste Lands.[10]

Second, there were limitations to the powers of the ad hoc boards, the result both of their constituting statutes and of the way in which they were consequently thrown back upon a vestry dominated by

---

[8] Minutes of the Improvement Commissioners for the Parish of Croydon, entries for 1836 and 1837, *passim*.

[9] T. Frost, *Forty Years Recollections; Literary and Political* (London 1880), p. 130.

[10] Waste Land Trustees, Rough Minutes, 1801–68, e.g. 21 Aug. 1848, when they let out the magistrates' room in the Town Hall for use by the Croydon Building Society.

landlords and wealthy ratepayers. A typical difficulty was that faced by the Improvement Commissioners, whose powers in some areas, such as street-lighting and the provision of accommodation for assize judges, were strictly and clearly defined; yet their statute left only a very vague, general provison for 'other parochial purposes and improvements in the parish' as agreed upon by a vestry meeting.[11] When, in the 1830s, complaints about the deteriorating condition of Croydon's primitive sewerage and drainage system became more vociferous, overstrained as it was by the growing volume and density of housing in the town, the Commissioners first had to establish where the responsibility lay (whether with them or with the Board of Surveyors of the Highways), and then whether they had the power to act, even with the vestry's sanction. At first they denied responsibility and passed complaints onto the Board of Surveyors;[12] then they undertook to clean a certain public cesspool, the large Scarbrook pond, at their own expense, then rescinded the resolution as their clerk considered the action would not be legal under the terms of their parliamentary act;[13] and in 1844 the Board again decided it had no power in the matter.[14] The Board's confusion over its powers and reluctance to act in the matter of sanitary provision was almost certainly related to the knowledge that the vestry would not sanction a rate to finance an ambitious programme of sanitary reorganisation in the parish; a badly-needed extension to the over-crowded churchyard for example was resisted in 1846 and 1847 by the vestry, and only carried eventually by a narrow vote of 531 to 497 in a poll of the parish.[15]

This points in turn to a third and perennial problem of the parochial system of administration: sheer lack of will to effect any lasting parochial improvement on the part of those landowners and professional men who composed the ad hoc boards and took up parochial offices for the most part in this period. In the first decade of the Improvement Commissioners' existence meetings were frequently adjourned because too few Commissioners turned up for them (there were twenty Commissioners, and five formed a quorum); in late 1830 and early 1831, for example, no less than nine successive meetings were adjourned for this reason.[16] The same problem dogged

[11] An Act for Lighting, Watching, and Improving the Town of Croydon, in the County of Surrey . . . and for other purposes relating thereto (10. Geo. IV, Session 1829).
[12] Improvement Commissioners, for example, 4 May 1842.
[13] *Ibid.*, entries for 3, 17 Aug. 1842.
[14] *Ibid.*, entry for 25 Jul. 1844.
[15] Croydon Parish Vestry Minutes, entries for 14 Apr. 1846; 6 Apr. 1847.
[16] Improvement Commissioners, entries for 9 Nov. 1830 to 23 Jan. 1831.

the Board of Surveyors and the Trustees of the Waste Lands in the 1830s.[17] Only in the early to mid-1840s does there seem to have emerged a class of local residents, still Anglican and Conservative in the main like their predecessors, who were sufficiently interested in the management of local affairs to turn up regularly to meetings and to initiate or advocate positive schemes of improvement. Significantly, most of these men were not landowners, farmers or directly engaged in agricultural occupations, though some were, and many of them were comparatively new residents in Croydon. They were men like Dr Edward Westall, for example, who came to Croydon in the late 1830s from a northern industrial town. He gradually developed his practice in Croydon and, in the 1840s, using the experience he had gained from the north, began to advocate improved sanitary measures in Croydon, eventually getting himself elected onto the Board of Improvement Commissioners in 1848 where he pressed for the adoption of the Public Health Act in the town; he sat on the local Board of Health for the first ten years of its existence.[18]

Furthermore, there were often allegations about the operation of the parochial system which implied that it was being manipulated and distorted to the advantage of certain groups within the parish. Leaving aside the strictly religious and political conflicts which the system produced, and which demand separate treatment, these allegations principally involved the manipulation of meetings and the aims and motives of officials and representatives. It was, for example, within the power of the chairman of the vestry, usually the vicar, to direct the outcome of a meeting to some extent by refusing to put a motion.[19] A trick employed quite often by churchwardens who feared uproar in a meeting was to advertise a vestry only for the minimum required time and with inadequate publicity; this resulted in allegations of 'hole-in-corner' meetings being used to push through unpopular motions. A church rate of 2d. in the pound was unanimously passed by such a meeting in 1865, only about thirty or forty parishioners being present because of the lack of publicity.[20] Plurality of office-holding came in for criticism: John Drummond, the vestry clerk, was criticised in 1860 for being clerk to the magistrates as well, so that, it was alleged, 'He advises the chairman of the vestry to make bad laws, and then advises the magistrates to

[17] See, for example, Minutes of the Board of Surveyors of the Highways, entries for June to Aug. 1836 and Apr. to Aug. 1837, and Minutes of the Trustees of the Waste Lands, entries for Jan. to Aug. 1836 and June 1837 to Oct. 1838.
[18] Obituary, *C Chron*, 15 June 1878.
[19] See p. 32.
[20] *C Chron*, 24 June 1865.

carry out those laws.'[21] Had his critic, Herbert Skeats, wanted to say so, he could have pointed out that Drummond was also clerk to the Trustees of the Waste Lands, and the solicitor to (and a Trustee of) the Whitgift Charitable Foundation, one of the largest property owners in the parish; furthermore, John's brother William was chairman of the Local Board of Health, secretary to the Croydon Commercial Gas and Coke Company, and clerk to the Whitgift Foundation – in fact, between them, the Drummond brothers almost had Croydon in their pocket.[22] It is not surprising, then, that allegations of self-interest and conflicting duties were frequent: William Drummond often found himself in the embarrassing position of having to defend, explain or refrain from attacking the actions of the Whitgift Charity on the Local Board of Health.[23] Allegations of actual corruption were rare and much harder to substantiate, unlike criticisms of the inefficiency of parochial officers, though few were subjected to as humiliating a treatment as the beadle who, in 1864, was called to account by Cuthbert Johnson, the then chairman of the Board of Health, for being unfit to carry out his duties because he was lazy and 'too fat'.[24]

However, the greatest weakness of the parochial system of government was one which largely seems to have escaped the notice of Croydon residents until the Liberal and Nonconformist campaign to reform it got under way in the 1860s and 1870s, and that was its unrepresentative character. The property-weighted local franchise tied in very well with early and mid-Victorian conceptions of the connection between political intelligence and the ownership of property, but it also served to throw the inadequacies of these ideas into sharp relief. There could be no surer indictment of the theory than the behaviour of men of property who, to avoid rate increases, got themselves elected onto local boards and once there failed to carry out the reforms the town badly needed. Even when, in the 1840s, a new kind of businessman began to settle in large numbers in Croydon and to take an active part in parish affairs, their interest was potentially no greater than that of tradesmen and professional men of the town centre, many of whom, however active in political, charitable and religious movements in the town, could never hope to

[21] *Ibid.*, 1 Dec. 1860.
[22] For John Drummond, see obituary in Ward, *Croydon in the Past*; for his brother William, see committee and local board lists in *Gray's* and *Warren's Croydon Directories*, 1851–1869.
[23] For example, *C Ad*, 25 Oct. 1873, for a meeting of the Board at which Drummond pressed for acceptance of an offer of £175 made by the Charity for enlargement of a sewer on land owned by the Charity at Addiscombe.
[24] *C Chron*, 19 Nov. 1864.

command the same weight on the polling sheet as their social superiors. Furthermore, the electoral inadequacy of the system was worsened by the class roots of religious allegiance, for the property vote could invariably be wielded to the advantage of Anglicanism. The parochial system in mid-century was a microcosm of the weakness of the mid-Victorian parliamentary system, a property-based franchise which was bound to become top-heavy with the rapid growth of the urban middle and lower middle class. In mid-century this was still not generally perceived to be a weakness; indeed, in its practical operation in Croydon in the late 1840s the solidarity of the ruling elite in the town, socially, politically and religiously, was actually reinforced by the property vote. What turned the property vote into a weakness, a focus of attack, was the expansion of social groups in the town who could not directly benefit from it.

The Liberal-Nonconformist attack

The parochial system of administration operated in Croydon at best fitfully by the 1830s; in the 1840s its ability to deal with the business of the town was stretched to the limit. The crisis in the 1840s was clearly related to Croydon's urban growth because it centred on deteriorating sanitary conditions caused by the overuse and breakdown of a 'system' (though it was hardly that) of sewerage and drainage which depended upon natural resources, a water supply and an 'outflow'. Problems did not trigger responses in the straight-forward pattern of cause and effect beloved by some historians: the older, long-resident members of the town elite were relatively indifferent to the problem of the town's health and sanitary condition, and the real impetus for change came from new residents, a number of whom (like Dr Westall, and Cuthbert Johnson, first chairman of the Local Board of Health)[25] had gained experience in sanitary matters elsewhere and were clearly interested in the intellectual aspects of the sanitary debate. Yet sufficient ratepayers' signatures were obtained to get Croydon on the list of the first fifteen towns to adopt the Public Health Act of 1848, opinion in the town and outlying districts fuelled by the cholera epidemic of 1848. The new Local Board of Health possessed much more extensive rating and statutory powers than its predecessors, the Improvement Commis-sioners and the Board of Surveyors of the Highways; its personnel were, for the most part, either men who had not served on local bodies before or who had been the more progressive Improvement

---

[25] Obituary, *ibid.*, 9 May 1878.

Commissioners in the mid- to late 1840s.[26] However, the Board became enmeshed, along with the other parochial authorities, in what was to become a concerted campaign to reform the structure of local government in the parish, a campaign which, as it gathered momentum, developed into a wide-ranging political campaign as well, led by Nonconformists and Liberals.

The origin of the Nonconformists' attack on the parochial system lay in the campaign they mounted to abolish church rates in Croydon. Before the 1850s, Disssent would not have been strong enough in numbers in the parish seriously to challenge Anglican supremacy: there were no disputed rates before 1853, although in July 1851 a rate was amended from 2d. to 1d. in the pound.[27] Usually Quakers had refused to pay the rate, but the churchwardens had customarily treated them and others who refused to pay leniently, passively allowing the law to take its course, permitting non-payment for two or three years at a time, and then using a low estimate of expenses in subsequent court cases to enforce payment.[28] The system had worked well, apparently averting conflict and scarcely diminishing the churchwardens' revenue, but it was an arrangement Dissenters can only have accepted from a position of weakness.

With the growth of the town in the 1850s, however, a challenge to the voting of church rates in the vestry became an annual event, 1856 being the only year in that decade after 1852 in which a rate was passed without opposition. Almost without exception every year showed that Dissenters could raise enough support in the vestry meeting to defeat a rate, but that they lost heavily in the inevitable subsequent poll of the parish, usually polling a third as many votes as Anglicans. In the early years the principal opposers of rates in the vestry were well-established townsmen, and some of them from the late 1840s even began to take an active part in parochial administration: one Edward Russell, for example, had even been an Improvement Commissioner in the late 1830s and 1840s, although as such he was an exception, and then took up places in the 1850s on the Trustees of the Waste Lands and the Local Board of Health.[29] A distinct change occurred in the late 1850s, however, as more militant Dissenters moved to Croydon and took up the church rates battle; for a few years, from 1859 to 1862, a small knot of Nonconformists in the parish, all of them newly-resident, led the abolition movement in Croydon. Its most prominent members were H. S. Skeats, Edward

---

[26] See pp. 125-6.

[27] Croydon Parish Vestry Minutes, 18 Jul. 1851.

[28] C Chron, 8 Sep. 1860.

[29] Minutes of the Improvement Commissioners and Minutes of the Trustees of the Waste Lands, passim; C Chron, 10 May 1862.

Miall's son-in-law, the Rev W. G. Barrett, a Congregationalist minister, and J. W. Buckley, a prominent Congregational layman, all of them politically Liberal and from the most militant denomination of Political Nonconformity, the Congregationalists.[30] The bitter wrangling in these years over church rates produced a protracted case in the Queen's Bench Court in late 1860, a case the parish officers eventually won;[31] yet the polls remained solidly Anglican. The most surprising result was that of November 1860, before the Queen's Bench case had been settled, and therefore when local interest in the issue could have been expected to have been high: Dissenters could only poll seventy-eight votes against a rate, in opposition to an Anglican vote of 481.[32] The 'utmost apathy' in the anti-church rate camp the *Croydon Chronicle* claimed this result displayed was probably a reaction against the stance taken by militant Dissenters:[33] in a parish where the churchwardens were able to claim that relatively friendly relations had prevailed until the recent arrival of Nonconformists determined to oppose actively a rate, it was easy to stigmatise the newcomers as disruptive intruders, and this is what they did. When Edward Miall himself moved briefly into the area in 1861 and appeared at the vestry to oppose a rate, his interest only served to strengthen the force of this allegation. A local, long-resident Dissenter who, at the same meeting, claimed he would not oppose a rate because he was not ashamed to confess he was a Dissenter, was warmly applauded; again the poll, assisted by the property vote, swung firmly in favour of Anglicanism.[34] The result of the Queen's Bench case, declared in mid-1861, and the defeat of resistance led by as prominent a Dissenter as Edward Miall, took the confidence out of the Nonconformist campaign; Miall soon moved away, and in 1862, though they opposed a rate in the vestry, Nonconformists failed to press for a poll of the parish.[35]

In the mid 1860s it seemed that Nonconformist agitation, therefore, had completely died down. No opposition to church rate was thereafter mounted, and it appeared that Anglicans had successfully defended their ability to levy a form of compulsory taxation which was anathema to Dissenters. Moreover, some of the leaders of the anti-church rate campaign seem to have withdrawn

---

[30] See in particular the account of a vestry Meeting in *C Chron*, 3 Sep. 1859 and the account of a case of prosecution for non-payment of church rate in the magistrates' court, *ibid.*, 8 Sep. 1860.

[31] *Ibid.*, 1 June 1861.

[32] Croydon Parish Vestry Minutes, 27 Nov. 1860.

[33] *C Chron*, 1 Dec. 1860.

[34] *Ibid.*, 21 Dec. 1861.

[35] Croydon Parish Vestry Minutes, 14 Oct. 1862.

from active participation in the town's affairs: Skeats, for example, does not seem to have been a member of the committee of any charitable, social or political organisation in the area, and certainly did not take part in any local government authority. Yet the defeat of the Nonconformists over the immediate issue of church rates proved to be something of a pyrrhic victory for Anglicans, for just as they had been able to cast some of the leading Nonconformist agitators in the light of troublemakers, so they had been forced to concede the moral force of Dissenters' arguments: the vicar at the vestry of 1861 had claimed that personally he would welcome the abolition of church rates by Parliament, and many Anglicans had begun to advocate the levy of a voluntary rate.[36] Undoubtedly this had imparted some sense of achievement to the Nonconformists. Nowhere could this be seen more clearly than when a meeting was called, after the Parish Church had been destroyed by fire early in January 1867, to oppose the proposed church rate to pay for rebuilding: the vicar, at a vestry held the following day, renounced the church rate proposal and opted for a voluntary subscription instead.[37]

The significance of the 1867 meeting does not end with this apparent Nonconformist victory, however, because it forms a link between the earlier phase of agitation, centred around church rate, and the second, more prolonged phase of the attack on the parochial system of government. This lasted from about the late 1860s to the early 1880s, and culminated in the incorporation of Croydon. It was a period which, at least in terms of local political life, may be labelled the 'rise of the Liberal party'; the strictly religious agitation of the church rate controversy was gradually widened into a wholesale attack on the existing system of local government in Croydon, though it took most of the 1870s to bring the different strands of the attack together. This was because the Liberal party in Croydon was a party with a wide basis of social support: tradesmen and small manufacturers of the town centre certainly constituted one of the most powerful groups within it, but it also drew on the support of gentlemen, professional men and even some landowners.[38] So, whilst the property vote and the existing structure of local government still

---

[36] *C Chron*, 21 Dec. 1861; 'A Looker On', for example, after the poll in 1859 simultaneously criticised opponents of the rate and advocated its replacement by a voluntary levy: *ibid.*, 3 Sep. 1859.

[37] *Ibid.*, 19 Jan. 1867.

[38] Notable figures in Croydon Liberalism in the 1860s and 1870s included men such as Theodore Lloyd, Anglican stockbroker (obituary, *ibid.*, 24 Jan. 1880), J. M. Eastty, Anglican 'gentleman' and landowner (obituary, *ibid.*, 12 Jan. 1878), and the banker Thomas Leedham Robinson (references assembled from *C Ad* and *C Chron*).

tended to favour Anglican Conservatism, Liberals and Nonconformists were able to participate in local government in ever-increasing
numbers during the 1870s. The gradual development of the
Nonconformist-Liberal critique of local government was marked by a
fitful process of hostility and accommodation, criticism and participation. Liberals and Nonconformists found themselves acquiring
influence at the same time as they were complaining of exclusion
from parochial life. Their rise owed much to the growth of those
classes most likely to vote for them, and to the gradual weakening of
the power of the property vote this entailed. Particularly significant,
however, is the fact that it also owed much to the emergence of a
Nonconformist-Liberal elite, a relatively small group of men who
dominated the town's affairs for most of the remaining years of the
century and who were at the centre of each of the various movements
which eventually coalesced in the pro-incorporation movement.[39]
Many of these men were present at the meeting to oppose a church
rate in 1867:[40] all of the Anglicans and Nonconformists present at the
meeting were political Liberals, and the rise to influence of many of
them can be traced to institutions and movements in the town which
also showed a close affiliation with Liberalism, from the various
attempts to establish a Working Man's Club in the town in the 1860s,
for example, to benefit societies and some charitable and missionary
societies.[41]

The outright attack on the parochial system of government which
emerged from this Liberal upsurge in the mid-1870s proved to be
only a half-way stage on the way to incorporation, but it was a highly
significant stage in its effect on the political status of religion in
Croydon. It was the outcome of a seemingly tangential campaign to
reform charitable endowments in the parish; apart from the very
large Whitgift Foundation, by the 1860s Croydon had at least
seventeen endowed charities for the support of the poor, elderly and
sick, although the funds of most of these were very small; one of
them, Tenison's, supported a school, and two of them maintained
almshouses.[42] They were an integral part of the parochial system:
their properties were for the benefit of the inhabitants of the parish,

---

[39] See pp. 147–52.
[40] *C Chron*, 19 Jan. 1867.
[41] On the Working Man's Club, *ibid.*, 30 Jan. 1864 and 24 June 1865; on the Starr-
Bowkett Benefit Building Society, *ibid.*, 2 Sep. 1865 ; on the War Victims Fund, C Ad,
24 Dec. 1870; on the Emigration Aid Society, *ibid.*, 1 Apr. 1871; other societies and
movements in the town could be cited.
[42] 'Charities of the Parish of Croydon', an extract from 13th Report of the Charity
Commissioners, 22 Jan. 1825; Charity Commissioners, *Scheme for the Administration of
the Croydon Charities of Henry Smith and others* (London 1892) and *Scheme for the
Administration of the Almshouse Charity of Elis David* (London 1893).

their trustees were mostly appointed by the vestry, the vicar and churchwardens were ex officio trustees of many of them, and the vestry had the power of supervision of them.[43] Their management exhibited some of the worst features of the parochial system: many of them had seemingly disappeared by mid-century or had been forgotten, no clear reformed guidelines had been established for the distribution of income and relief which had been allocated under charters and statutes now many years out of date, and their trustees often seemed wholly unaware of their responsibilities and defensive about the execution of their duties.[44]

In the ensuing controversies the parish officers showed a remarkable ignorance about the real state of many of the charities. The vicar of Croydon in 1856, in consultation with the archbishop and the Whitgift governors, produced a new scheme of management for the Whitgift Foundation, with the aim of establishing a middle class, 'grammar' school, and it was the painfully slow implementation of this scheme which reawakened interest in the issue of parochial charities in the 1860s. A newly-resident, retired actuary, Michael Saward, Liberal and Anglican, in 1866 began to correspond with the Whitgift Governors about the scheme and its delay; in 1868 he organised a public meeting to discuss the matter, a committee was appointed and an appeal to the Charity Commissioners to investigate launched.[45] From then on, the implications of Saward's interest began to widen. A correspondent to the *Croydon Chronicle* suggested that the Elys Davy charity should be investigated as well;[46] Saward himself requested a list of parochial charities from the vestry clerk, and then found omissions in the list he was given;[47] then, in 1871 at the Easter vestry, he and other Liberals pointed out apparently defunct charities and carried a motion calling on the Charity Commissioners to investigate;[48] an investigation was held, but no scheme drawn up immediately.[49] All of this occurred against a background of continuing allegations about the inefficiency of the Whitgift Governors. In 1874, at the Easter vestry, Saward produced a requisition calling for all the parochial charities except the Whitgift

[43] See the summary of constitutions and properties of Croydon parish charities in *C Chron*, 11 Sep. 1869.

[44] See criticism of their administration in Croydon Parish Vestry Minutes, entries for 1821 and 1822, *passim*; also in *C Ad*, and *C Chron*, numerous entries throughout the 1860s and 1870s, but esp. *C Chron*, 5 Sep. 1868; 11 Sep. 1869; 11 June 1870, and *C Ad*, 23 Apr. 1870; 15 Apr. 1871.

[45] F. H. G. Percy, *A History of Whitgift School* (Croydon 1976), pp. 154–64, 166.

[46] *C Chron*, 5 Sep. 1868.

[47] *Ibid.*, 11 Sep. 1868; 11 June 1870.

[48] *C Ad*, 15 Apr. 1871.

[49] *C Chron*, 27 May 1871.

Foundation to be united under one elected board of management. Of the sixteen signatories, all chosen because they were affluent, influential townsmen, the political opinions of twelve are known: ten were Liberals, and one of the two Conservatives was known for Nonconformist-Liberal sympathies on other issues, though himself an Anglican.[50] The motion was carried by a considerable majority. Saward died suddenly in 1874, but although he had made the reform of parochial charities and law something of a personal bandwagon, the issues themselves had been taken up by other Liberals and Nonconformists in the town. His actions received open support from men like F. M. Coldwells, J. S. Balfour, H. Moore and W. T. Malleson, leaders of the campaign for incorporation and prominent in other progressive movements in Croydon, and it was they who continued the agitation he had begun, a long, complicated process which did not end until the 1890s when comprehensive schemes of management for the Croydon charities were executed.[51] Liberals and Nonconformists were interested in the popular control of parochial institutions and funds; by implication, therefore, the attempt to reform parochial charities involved a re-examination of the constitution and operation of the whole structure of the parochial system.

This in fact was how Saward's thinking about the parochial system had developed. He had begun with a criticism of one institution, the Whitgift Foundation, and then extended it to include other parochial charities. Presumably on religious grounds he had supported in 1869 pressure led by some leading members of the congregation of the Parish Church to make all the sittings in the new, rebuilt church free and unappropriated, a movement which had resulted in an agreement in 1869 binding the churchwardens to free seats as the proprietors died or left the district.[52] He had then, in 1872, taken up the issue again at the Easter vestry, when it became apparent that one of the churchwardens had broken the compact.[53] At all of these stages he had experienced opposition and sometimes chicanery on the part of the parish officers. The logical culmination of the development of his critique came in 1874, when he organised what amounted to a concerted attack at the Easter Vestry on what he regarded as the abuse of virtually every office in the parochial system.[54] Two weeks

[50] *C Ad*, 11 April 1874.
[51] See the composition of the Committee to investigate the Whitgift Charity in 1878, for example (*C Ad*, 27 Apr. 1878); on the appointment of Trustees, see Croydon Parish Church Vestry Minutes, entries for 3 Apr. 1877; 4 Apr. 1893; see also Charity Commissioners, Scheme for the Croydon Charities.
[52] *C Chron*, 28 Aug. 1869.
[53] *C Ad*, 6 Apr. 1872.
[54] *Ibid.*, 11 Apr. 1874.

before the vestry he published a long article in the local newspapers outlining his criticisms of the system as it now existed in Croydon, the gist of which was that the parish had originally been an entirely secular organ of administration, and that unwarranted intrusions of ecclesiastical offices and power into the parish had occurred. He denied that the vicar, for example, had any right to preside at the vestry, claimed that the vestry clerk's duties were entirely secular and that his was an annual, not a permanent, appointment, and that the churchwardens were temporary officers who should be appointed only by the vestry and not by the vicar.[55] Supported by local Liberals and Nonconformists, he raised each of these points at the subsequent vestry; few of them in fact were carried – the Conservative majority still held in the vestry – but he and his supporters received some reward for their efforts by carrying the election of a rival candidate for churchwarden to the Conservative party's nominee.[56]

The 1874 vestry proved to be the first and last occasion on which Liberals and Nonconformists mounted an all-out attack on the parochial system: they never raised the issue with such force again, probably not from lack of will or from failure to believe that they could succeed, but because by the mid-1870s they were already looking towards other institutions in the parish as the real focus of local power. Nevertheless the campaign had shown that Liberals' and Nonconformists' hostility to the parochial system was not based solely on objections to the levy of church rates, for the abolition of compulsory church rates in 1868 had merely served to concentrate Dissenting agitation on the underlying structures of power which had enabled the rate to be levied locally in the first place.

'An Engine of Ecclesiastical Oppression': the parochial system discredited

Michael Saward was a celebrated figure in Liberalism in Croydon in the early 1870s; he was president of the town's Liberal Association, and a prominent speaker on the platform of many Liberal meetings.[57] Yet in some ways he was an isolated figure. Like many of his fellow townsmen, he had grasped the central importance in local affairs of the curious tangle of custom and statute which formed the parochial

[55] *Ibid.*, 11 Apr. 1874.
[56] *C Chron*, 28 Mar. 1874; *C Ad*, 11 Apr. 1874.
[57] Obituary, *ibid.*, 5 Sep. 1874.

system; unlike most of them he had not perceived that the system had outlived its usefulness. He had not renounced faith in the vestry as a genuine basis for local democratic government; he believed the system should be reformed. Like that of his fellow townsman, John Corbet Anderson, a local historian also active in the campaign to reform the Whitgift Charity, his Liberalism was founded upon a romantic interpretation of English history which saw liberty as an Anglo-Saxon property crushed by centuries of Norman and Roman Catholic rule, the recent past as a progressive rediscovery of part of that libertarian tradition. He lamented the apathy of his contemporaries, claiming that they thought: 'It is too much trouble to us to exercise those Saxon institutions that made England great, glorious, and free. They take up time, and time is money.'[58] Corbet Anderson, who used history with a vengeance when he read Archbishop Whitgift's Will to a crowded meeting in the Public Hall to show the modern governors' departure from its spirit,[59] cast the Anglican Church in the same light, a free institution once submerged beneath tyranny: 'The Anglo-Saxon Church and the English princes, however, never yielded a servile obedience to the See of Rome. Yet vital religion everywhere was suffocated beneath the thick folds of superstition and ignorance.'[60]

Anderson, like Saward, was an Anglican; for both of them, and indeed for many other Anglican Liberals in Croydon, the Church of England with all its faults was the 'National' church; they did not back disestablishment. Because of its middle class, suburban residential character, Croydon probably produced a higher proportion of Anglican Liberals than were to be found in many other Victorian towns; nevertheless the backbone of the Liberal cause in the area, as elsewhere, tended to be Nonconformists, many of them tradesmen. Nonconformists remained the largest, most vociferous group of critics of the parochial system; they supported Saward at every step, and after his death continued to attend vestry meetings and get their nominees elected to the trusteeships of parochial charities; in 1879 they carried the campaign a stage further by securing the appointment of a vestry committee (composed almost entirely of Liberals) to investigate the Whitgift and other parochial charities.[61] Though it was led by an Anglican from the late 1860s, the campaign was as much a Nonconformist as a Liberal one.

[58] C Chron, 31 Mar. 1877.
[59] Ibid.
[60] J. C. Anderson, A Short Chronicle Concerning the Parish of Croydon (Croydon 1882), p. 29.
[61] C Ad, 19 Apr. 1879.

Yet Nonconformists could not see the parochial system in the same light as Saward and Anderson; to them it was closely associated with an ecclesiastical system they detested, and though they were prepared to attend vestries and support measures of reform of the system for the immediate purposes of local control, in the long run they were much more interested in institutions of government which would ultimately take effective power in the parish out of the hands of the parochial authorities. The parochial system in their eyes was a discredited method of government: not only did they associate it with corrupt, ineffecient administration, but they regarded it as machinery for ecclesiastical domination. Consequently for them it was beyond reform. When, early in 1870, it seemed as if Forster's proposed Education Bill would put the election of School Boards in the hands of vestries, the response of Croydon Nonconformists was to urge that the elections should be by direct ballot of the 'entire people'; as Frederick Sargood, a leading Congregationalist and vice-president of the Liberal Association, said, 'all vestries are supposed to represent the entire body of ratepayers, but what more can be opposed to fact? I ask you, gentlemen, from your past experience, what do you know of parish vestries except as engines of ecclesiastical oppression?' ['hear, hear'].[62] For a large, growing proportion of Croydon's population, the parochial system by the 1870s had lost its credibility as an organ of local government.

Nowhere can this be seen more clearly than in the falling popularity of the Easter Dinner. This was, in the 1840s and 1850s, the festive highmark of the parochial year; parochial officers, leading clergy and members of other boards in the parish would attend a feast held regularly at the Greyhound Inn after every Easter vestry meeting; the toasts were traditional, the Queen, the archbishop of Canterbury, the Army and Navy, the Volunteers, the vicar,and other parochial authorities; needless to say, virtually all those attending were Anglican Conservatives, the dominant shade of opinion in the parish at this period. Few Nonconformists, for example, could have assented to the vicar's toast to the churchwardens at the 1861 dinner: 'Churchwardens were a very respectable, honourable set of men, and their works, or the works over which they presided, proclaimed their usefulness.'[63] In the mid-1860s attendances began to fall off, so even for the dominant group in the parish the tradition began to lose its appeal;[64] by 1871 some Liberals were attending, though not in

[62] *Ibid.*, 19 Mar. 1870.
[63] *C Chron*, 6 Apr. 1861.
[64] *Ibid.*, 27 Apr. 1867.

numbers proportionate to their influence in the parish, and only as they took up official posts and membership of public boards.[65] Nonconformist clergy never attended, and for some Liberals attendance would in any case have been embarassing on matters of principle: Quakers, for example, would not have assented with ease to the toasts to the armed forces. By the late 1870s the local newspapers were only reporting the dinners briefly, and it is clear that the decline in attendance had continued; as the *Croydon Chronicle* said, 'neither professional men nor tradesmen seem inclined to perpetuate a good old custom'.[66] Members of what was by then fast becoming the dominant political group in the parish could not enter into the spirit of the dinner with enthusiasm; their attitude could be summed up more neatly in what Michael Saward had said several years previously: 'There seems to be something in parish affairs which is excessively repulsive to respectable men.'[67] In 1878 no dinner was held, and thereafter the custom ceased altogether.

In the view of Nonconformists, the parochial system of government was no longer one which could pretend to be neutral. To Anglican Liberals, it was largely a question of political reform, separating what they perceived to be political insitutions from their ecclesiastical accretions; to Nonconformist Liberals the whole system was discredited and should be discarded. Religion in the 1840s and 1850s in Croydon had been intimately bound up with civil administration; the effect of the gradual growth of Liberalism and Nonconformity in the parish had been to cast the system in an ever more divisive light. The demand which emerged for a reform of the system was no less than a demand for the separation of civil and religious government. The implications then of the Nonconformist challenge to Anglicanism were that religion and politics, at least where they concerned local affairs, had their own independent spheres of action. This in turn helps to explain why the attack on the parochial system never developed into an all-out onslaught; by the 1870s Liberal concern to reform the institutions by which local control was exercised had turned to the extra-parochial institutions of government in the parish, the Local Board of Health and the School Board, and the vestry was coming to seem a less important institution altogether. Whilst Anglican and Conservative opposition in the vestry remained obdurate, Liberals were already pinning their hopes for overturning the status quo in the parish on alternative movements.

[65] *C Ad*, 15 Apr. 1871.
[66] *C Chron*, 7 Apr. 1877.
[67] *Ibid.*, 6 Apr. 1872.

Mid-century: town leadership

At the outset of Victoria's reign, the principal local offices and townsmen were drawn from a compact group of Anglican Conservatives, many of whom derived their wealth from landownership and agriculture-related trades. Parochial offices could be monopolised by particular families, and the same individuals served frequently in many capacities. The church wardens were invariably recruited from the body of men who formed the membership of the public boards: not a single warden from the 1820s to the 1840s did not serve on any other public board at some time before or after his wardenship.[68] The Penfold family occupied most of the main parochial clerical offices from the 1820s to the early 1850s: George Penfold, for example, in the late 1830s and 1840s was vestry clerk, clerk to the Improvement Commissioners, and employed as solicitor by the Board of Highways; he was also to become the first clerk of the Local Board of Health, and clerk to the Justices and to the County Court.[69]

The way in which the compactness of this elite was a matter not just of participation in structures but of an association of political and religious opinion as well, and of occupational and social origin, can be illustrated from a close analysis of the Local Board of Health and of its most important predecessor, the Board of Improvement Commissioners.[70] Such an analysis also serves to highlight the gradual fracture of this compactness with the rise of Nonconformity and Liberalism from the 1870s. Of the twenty gentlemen elected as Improvement Commissioners at the Board's inception in 1829, at least nine were landowners, and another three were involved in the agricultural trade. In two cases the occupation is unknown; the others were tradesmen of the town centre, though some again (like John Harman, a Liberal) were linked indirectly to the agricultural interest. All known religious affiliations seem to have been Anglican; most were probably Conservative (although most political opinions were unknown), though John Maberley, MP for Abingdon, as a Whig with considerable landed estates in the vicinity of Croydon would fit in well with early nineteenth century conceptions of a landed base for Whiggery.[71] Within a few years most of the landowning members of

[68] Cross references from Croydon Parish Vestry Minutes to Minutes of Boards of Improvement Commisisoners, Select Vestry, Surveyors of Highways, Guardians and Waste Land Trustees.
[69] Details from Minutes of Improvement Commissioners and Board of Surveyors of the Highways, and from Vestry Minutes; also *Gray's Croydon Directory*, 1851.
[70] Appendix 4, tables 1–3.
[71] For sources for these and for following assertions, see list of source material for appendix 4.

the Board had dropped out and been replaced by tradesmen and professional men based in the town centre. However, the agricultural interest retained considerable representation through agriculture-related trades. In 1839, for example, there were four grain merchants on the Board, one butcher, two saddlers, one farmer and three landowners who may have relied on rent from agricultural land for their income. The religious and political composition of the Board remained overwhelmingly Anglican and Conservative.

The personnel of the Board of Health at its institution in 1849 did not show a dramatic change in composition: six out of twelve of the members of the new Board had been Improvement Commissioners anyway, and with one exception, the Quaker Richard Sterry, all were Anglican. The occupational composition of the Board registered a further change away from the agricultural interest with four of the members professional men (two doctors and two solicitors), three of them High Street tradesmen, one an oil merchant (Richard Sterry), one occupation unknown (a 'gentleman'), and only two known to have farming interests. This remained approximately the balance of opinion and occupation on the Board for twenty years, with a slight increase in Liberal representation in the 1860s to three by 1869, two Quakers and one Anglican. The 'commuting interest' achieved representation to a limited degree with figures like Charles Coleby Morland, Quaker umbrella manufacturer, but Morland, often able to spend his days in Croydon, was hardly typical of the commuting, city-employed middle class settling in large numbers in Croydon in the 1850s and 1860s. In the main, therefore, the Board consisted of professionals and tradesmen who were Anglican and Conservative. This town elite was still a relatively compact one, with many familial and business connections and active participation by many of its members in other social and political movements in the town. The most striking example is Alfred Carpenter, Anglican Liberal doctor, whose presence in some representative or official capacity can be traced through at least twenty-four different movements in Croydon – political, religious, philanthropic and social.[72] The scale of Carpenter's activity was unusual, but other members of the Board were almost as busy: Thomas Farley, Anglican Conservative farmer, for example, was also vice-chairman of the Board of Guardians, a charitable Trustee, manager of the Industrial Schools at Anerley,

---

[72] For Carpenter's political activity: *C Chron*, 30 Jan. 1864; 11 Apr., 3 Oct. 1885; for his philanthropic work: *ibid.*, 8 Oct. 1864; 3 Nov. 1866; 25 Dec. 1869 and *C Ad*, 28 June 1879; for temperance work: *C Chron*, 26 Nov. 1864, and *C Ad*, 1886 *passim* (on a Temperance Congress in Croydon); this list provides only a few of the more important references.

vice-president of the Literary and Scientific Institution and a prominent supporter of Anglican church activity.[73]

The closeness of the Board members began to break up in the 1870s. Its overall occupational balance stayed much the same, although separate representation for Norwood (six members out of eighteen from 1874) increased the number of commuting mercantile and commercial representatives, and the Norwood group – with its constant appeals for separate treatment and separate rating levels – fractured the unity of the Board in the 1870s. The activity of the Ratepayers' Association from 1876 propelled onto the Board a number of members, some Conservative, some Liberal, who had previously had little direct connection with the existing town elite. Although the Board remained very much Anglican, Nonconformist members increased to at least four by 1879, and Liberal members to at least eight. By 1879, in fact, the composition of the Board had come to reflect more closely what might have been expected of it from traditional pictures of social and political alignments in the Victorian era, with a decline in the Conservative trading interest and the rise of a Liberal one, and the emergence of a professional and commuting Conservative interest. Instead of one closely knit group, there were several competing but overlapping groups: the Norwood members (mainly Conservative and Anglican), Liberal tradesmen, Conservative professionals of the 'old' Board, Ratepayers' candidates (who, however, functioned entirely as independent members once elected), and Conservatives.

Insofar as Nonconformists fitted into the town elite in mid-century at all, they tended to reinforce the picture of a small network of influential, affluent townsmen and ministers working together. But of course the situation was not a static one: by the 1830s and 1840s the social base of Anglican power had already diversified from the agricultural interest to an amalgam of trading, professional and agricultural interests, a process carried further in the 1860s and 1870s with the appearance of the Anglican, Conservative residential class in the town leadership, albeit on a small scale. The political colour of this leadership was changing too, by the late 1860s and 1870s, as the Liberal upsurge in Croydon gained momentum and propelled more of its supporters into the hitherto closed governing circle of the town. Nonconformists and Liberals, drawing strength increasingly from the expansion of trading and manufacturing occupations in the town, had no doubts in the controversies of the 1850s through to the 1870s over the parochial system of government that they were dealing with

[73] Minutes of the Board of Guardians of the Croydon Union, *passim*; *C Chron*, 5 Dec. 1876; 22 Apr. 1865; Ward, *Croydon in the Past*, obituary, p. 137.

a small group, a clique, which it was of course in their interest to stigmatise as unrepresentative of the trend of opinion in the parish. Thus the abandonment of the parochial system and the dismantling of the property-based franchise which had sustained Anglican Conservatism in power locally (when continuing social change had undermined its proportional weight in the population at large) had implications for town leadership as well as the actual structure of local government. It meant that the system of government which came to replace it had to be one which abandoned formal connections with religious activism, if it was to be seen to represent all interests in the town.

6

The Limits of Voluntarism

The voluntarist argument

The rise of collective action in municipal affairs in the late nineteenth century was a response to a general, contemporary perception that urbanisation had brought with it social problems which could only be addressed on that level. However, it was also a successor to a particular period of urbanisation which showed the shortcomings and eventual failure of alternative proposals for reform, namely those which can be subsumed under the title 'voluntarist'. Church action was an integral part of the voluntarist response to urbanisation; if moral authority could not be found for all areas of life in the self-limiting State in the mid-nineteenth century, where else could it reside but in organised religion? The 'blueprint' which lay behind mid-Victorian philanthropic and social activity was one defined not so much by material needs as by a moral and religious vision of mankind.

Even those movements which owed little to clerical initiative and did not operate under the umbrella of a particular denomination were often overtly religious in their aims, and attracted clerical participation on a significant scale. A Labourers' Dwellings Improvement Society, founded in 1866 along lines similar to other housing reform societies in England in the period as a combination of philanthropy and joint-stock enterprise, in its prospectus typically deduced moral conclusions from material conditions:

> The painfully low condition, both physical and moral, of some districts of Croydon, has excited the warm interest of the friends of the poor. . .This evil tends largely to lower their moral tone and counteracts all the efforts that are made to improve their condition, or to introduce amongst them the saving truths of religion.[1]

The failure of voluntarist action, its failure to achieve the high ambitions its proponents claimed for it, not its failure to meet some more limited aims, therefore implied the failure of the moral authority of religion, because it made plain the insufficiency of

[1] Cited in Cox, 'Urban Development and Redevelopment', p. 179.

religious motivation alone to resolve the social problems of the Victorian town. In the process it left the door wide open for municipal authorities to step in, and even though churchmen often welcomed municipal action on the grounds that it could remove problems of poverty and ill-health which they believed to be material obstacles to the evangelisation of the population at large, in doing so they were confirming a reduction in the social role of their own churches.

If, in a fundamental sense, religion defined the moral vision which underlay the voluntarist argument as it was conceived by most townsmen and philanthropists in the mid-nineteenth century, its relationship towards voluntarist action was also bound by other related considerations. In the first place, voluntarism tended to accord greater importance to clergymen and ministers, religious professionals, across the whole range of parochial affairs than was later to be the case when they were partially edged out by municipal leaders. In setting a premium on the moral and religious aims of their various ventures, the supporters of such movements implicitly exalted the perceived universal role and status of religious experts. Not only were clergymen and ministers ready and willing to take an active role, but their participation was actively canvassed. Hence the anxiety with which Nonconformists regarded the lack of interest of the clergy of the Church of England in the work of the London City Mission;[2] hence also the predominance of ministers of religion on the committee of the Charitable Society established in 1869 in Croydon.[3] Hence, too, the frustration of early temperance reformers at the aloofness of some clergymen in the town: 'A Dissenting Minister who was present expressed his approbation of what he had heard (at a total abstinence meeting), and invited the audience to show their approbation also. Had he invited them to sign the pledge, himself setting the example, he would have acted more consistently.'[4] At the same time, since voluntarism relied above all on moral influence for its success, it also gave prominence to the town elite, men who in mid-century were still closely involved in church activity in any case. The success of voluntarist action was almost held to depend on the numbers of influential gentlemen who actively supported a particular cause. Alfred Burton Cowdell, an Anglican evangelical philanthropist, sought to emphasise the financial stability of the Labourers' Dwellings Improvement Society by pointing out that: 'It must be remembered that the committee generally were representative men, belonging to other committees, and therefore they brought the weight

[2] *C Chron*, 31 Oct. 1857.
[3] *C Ad*, 8 Jan. 1870.
[4] *The Metropolitan Temperance Intelligencer and Journal*, 6 May 1843.

of other influences with them, and gave confidence to this movement.'[5] In this way existing ties between churches and voluntary movements were reinforced by the close participation in both of leading local worthies.

The prevalence of belief in voluntarism should not obscure the fact that the collective arguments which were eventually to replace it, though unpopular or controversial and as yet restricted in their application, were nevertheless already present in parochial affairs. As early as 1829 the inadequacy of individual action in Croydon in some parochial matters had been recognised in the preamble to the Improvement Act, 'whereas the said Town hath never been Lighted or Watched, except in a very partial manner by private individuals'.[6] Thirty years later, in the course of one of the many disputes at the Board of Health over the liability of Norwood residents to pay for the Board's services, the then chairman, local lawyer William Drummond, enunciated what could almost be regarded as the classic statement of the scope and principle of parochial responsibility:

> The inhabitants of the whole of the parish of Croydon are bound together by certain interests affecting them as parishioners, and the welfare and the burdens of one part of the parish are materially affected by the welfare and burdens of each other. You cannot on any one occasion dismember a parish because it would seem better for one particular part of it for one particular parochial purpose, to be dissevered.[7]

Drummond was of course arguing against a particular interest and not for an extension of parochial responsibility as such, though he and others in a few years were to use the same argument in favour of public swimming baths and recreation grounds.[8] There was, then, nothing novel in the arguments used from the 1880s to support the gradual extension of municipal activity; what was novel was the way in which they were being applied in areas such as education and housing where previously voluntary action had been regarded as the best hope for effective, remedial action.

In the middle decades of the century the town leadership entertained a view of local government which restricted its operation to a handful of functions, giving free rein to churches and other voluntary organisations to advance their own particular remedies. As

[5] *C. Chron.*, 2 February 1867.
[6] An Act for Lighting, Watching and Improving the town of Croydon, in the County of Surrey . . . and for other purposes relating thereto (10. Geo. IV, Session 1829).
[7] *C Chron*, 24 Nov. 1860.
[8] *Ibid.*, 12 Sep. 1863; 10 Feb. 1864; 30 Dec. 1865; 10 Oct. 1868.

a consequence of similar qualms about centralised, compulsory action, it was also a period in which central government lodged the initiative in various fields of social action in local authorities by measures of permissive legislation. The guiding principle was to make available means for achieving certain ends to those communities which (it was hoped) would thereby show themselves to be sufficiently morally responsible.[9] However, the result, as in the issues of burial grounds, public baths and, later, public libraries, was to encourage protracted and sometimes bitter local controversy over the issue of expense. The scope for voluntarist action was thus very wide. In the following two sections the gradual failure of the voluntarist response and its implications for the churches are examined in relation to specific philanthropic ventures, and the situation of the churches in mid-century as voluntarist organisations themselves is studied in greater detail.

Voluntary action

There were strong practical as well as ideological reasons for the close inter-relationship between organised religion and philanthropy. Churches were a natural base for philanthropic work; they could provide information and expertise in certain specific fields – district visitors, for example, supplied the Charitable Society with information about the poor they visited,[10] and similarly could help to put the Rescue and Preventive Association (formed in 1883 to combat prostitution in the town) in touch with 'fallen' women and girls[11] – and they also provided the religious counselling which philanthropic organisations saw as part of their work, through the readiness of clergymen to participate in the organisations and to preach on their behalf. Ideally they could function, too, as fund-raising units for philanthropic work, through donations to charities solicited from individuals or through collections made specifically for a certain cause; through the institution of annual 'hospital' sermons in Croydon churches, for example, the Croydon general hospital fund could by 1879 raise nearly a quarter of its annual income, which in that year totalled £2,500.[12] Yet with all the advantages of resources

---

[9] According to J. M. Prest one of the purposes of permissive legislation was to dispense with the need for each town to sponsor its own private Bill on specific matters: *Liberty and Locality: Parliament, permissive legislation, and ratepayers' democracies in the mid-nineteenth century* (Oxford 1990), p. 9.
[10] *C Ad*, 8 Jan. 1870.
[11] Croydon Rescue and Preventive Association, Annual Report 1883–4.
[12] Croydon General Hospital, 12th Annual Report, 1878–9.

and moral support which churches were able to provide, there were limits to what voluntary, philanthropic causes were ultimately able to achieve. These were imposed firstly by ideological considerations and secondly by material ones.

Philanthropy was the point of contact between churches and the life of the poor in the town; its function was both to maintain the centrality of church action in urban life and to activate the ranks of a church's supporters. Yet sooner or later such activity, however well-intended, came up against a barrier created by the class perceptions of its own proponents. In the mid-1860s, for example, a Labourers' Dwellings Improvement Society was founded in the town as a limited liability company, its aims being to purchase, lease or acquire lands and buildings in Croydon in order to erect improved housing for the working class.[13] The Society was lay-run and its founding members were all prominent local professional men, landowners, merchants and tradesmen; in religious terms its composition was mixed, yet with an Anglican and evangelical predominance. Its principles of operation were overtly religious, as stated in its prospectus and in a stipulation in its Articles of Association that the committee 'should . . . have the discretion to set apart, without remuneration, a portion of the buildings for moral and Christian instruction, free from denominational distinctions'.[14] Its aspirations were grand but its achievements limited; at a cost of over £5,000 the 'Shaftesbury Buildings' were erected in Elis David Road for some two hundred tenants, yet the rents it was necessary to charge to keep the society afloat were too high to attract the social groups for whom the buildings were intended, and by 1877 the Society was in liquidation.[15] But in any case the Society's activity was hampered by its members' own inability to tolerate amongst its tenants the very kinds of behaviour they had set out to reform through offering housing and religious instruction. Some hint that this would be the case could perhaps have been suspected from the vicar of Croydon's assertion at the foundation stone-laying ceremony that: 'The inmates of these dwellings would be taken from the most industrious and moral of the poorer classes.'[16] When Ambrose Noble, a hawker and tenant of the Shaftesbury Buildings, was charged with being drunk and incapable, Sir Thomas Edridge, magistrate and founder member of the Society, asked him how long he had lived there; Noble replied a year and a

---

[13] Cox, 'Urban Development and Redevelopment', p. 180; *C Chron*, 10 Feb. 1866.
[14] Cox, 'Urban Development and Redevelopment', p. 179; *C Chron*, 10 Feb. 1866. Cox used original papers of the Society deposited at C Ref Lib; these have since been lost.
[15] *C Chron*, 24 Feb. 1877.
[16] *Ibid.*, 13 Apr. 1867.

half; Edridge announced: 'Then tell the Superintendent from me that you must find fresh lodgings. We can't have drunken people there.'[17] Nor, apparently, could they have debtors.[18]

Despite the comprehensiveness of their aspirations, exactly the same limitations faced those voluntarist initiatives which were directly linked with church activism. A. W. Jephson, later a priest in various working class inner London parishes and a writer for the Christian Social Union, arrived at the Parish Church as a curate in 1876 and stayed for five years. He initiated an ambitious programme of visiting and teaching amongst the lodging houses and 'slums' of the market area in the centre of the town, eventually building up an organisation involving some 120 assistants, visitors and teachers.[19] He established a mission hall with the homely name of 'Welcome Hall', and his aim was no less than 'to improve the moral and intellectual conditions of the toilers in the by-ways of life'.[20] Yet his efforts were hampered by just the same kind of moral aspirations which helped to strangle the Labourers' Dwellings Society. He opened a religious lodging-house, the Glowworm, but it was never popular: 'I had to suppress evil language – and that was more than most of the people could stand or understand . . . We always had our complement of lodgers, but they were of a slightly higher type than those in the surrounding houses.'[21] In fact he charged a relatively high fee at the Glowworm, 6d. per night, with the explicit intention of keeping away the roughs and tramps, who would otherwise throng to the Glowworm, and whose 'unsavoury presence is not desired'.[22] His attempts to run a school for the children of the district, 'to separate these boys from their former idle and vicious associates', ran into similar problems, and he was constantly short of funds.[23] Like the committee members of the Labourers' Dwellings Society (many of whom subsequently entered municipal politics) Jephson came to realise that municipal action could be the only effective remedy for the problems posed by decaying areas such as Old Town and the market; later he wrote a handbook for the Christian Social Union in which Corporation and Church were treated as two entirely separate agencies, the responsibility of the Corporation for welfare admitted, and Christian action perceived only as a supplement to effective local

[17] C Ad, 22 Mar. 1884.
[18] C Chron, 14 Oct. 1876.
[19] A. W. Jephson, My Work in London (London 1910), pp. 6–10.
[20] C Chron, 24 Aug. 1878.
[21] Jephson, My Work, p. 9.
[22] C Chron., 24 Aug. 1878.
[23] Ibid., and 3 Jan. 1880.

political initiative.[24] He was also to become an ardent supporter of the 'progressives' on the London County Council and a member of the Fabian Society.[25]

Accompanying the problem of perception, or rather of misconception, was the related and very pressing one of financial resources. All philanthropic organisations, as voluntary bodies, suffered from problems of scale: they were only able, using voluntary finance, to achieve a certain degree of success in a small way because they had to operate mostly with part-time helpers and relied absolutely on subscriptions to their funds. The readiness of subscribers to give money could only be pushed to a certain point, and it was that point which ultimately determined the scope of the particular organisation's activity. It was a problem related to that of perception, because the financial buoyancy of a charity was inevitably directly related to its perceived value amongst those who contributed by far the greatest proportion of subscriptions, the middle class. Thus the general hospital, established on voluntary lines in 1866 and supported by subscriptions, was always able to command regular and generous donations, because it offered a service that was of immediate and obvious benefit: by 1890, for example, individual subscriptions constituted a third of its total income of £3,368, a very large income for a philanthropic venture,[26] and twenty years later the proportion had not changed.[27] The general hospital is perhaps the only convincing example of a philanthropic venture in the town in the mid and late nineteenth century which can be regarded as a success in material terms; yet even though the hospital was in fact partly self-sustaining, via paid treatment, its annual accounts make it evident that it kept going on this scale very much because of irregular forms of income, principally bequests, legacies and occasional donations. In 1904, for example, over a third of the total income of the hospital was derived from such sources, and this was not an exceptionally high proportion.[28] Despite its continuing success, its finances were never established on a firm basis. By the 1880s and 1890s other charities were clearly experiencing serious financial problems. The Croydon Gordon Boys' Home, for example, founded independently by an Anglican layman in 1885 and taken over by the Church of England Waifs and Strays Society in 1891, was already experiencing financial shortages by that date, with a falling-off in subscriptions recorded in

---

[24] A. W. Jephson, *Municipal Work from a Christian Standpoint* (London 1912).
[25] Thompson, *Socialists, Liberals and Labour*, pp. 96, 140.
[26] Croydon General Hospital, 24th Annual Report, 1890–1.
[27] *Ibid.*, 43rd Annual Report, 1909–10.
[28] *Ibid.*, 38th Annual Report, 1904–5.

the annual report.[29] The founder and secretary denied that financial considerations had led to the merger, and claimed that the real cause was his overwork, although significantly he added 'I also feel that it now requires someone of a better social standing and education to steer it along.'[30] Yet the takeover was the saving of the home, for by the 1900s the parent society was regularly bailing out the home with grants to cover its deficits.[31] No such central body existed to help the Rescue and Preventive Association, which, after initial enthusiastic efforts in the 1880s, was also in financial difficulties by the early 1890s, and forced to resort to the expedient of holding concerts and bazaars to supplement subscriptions;[32] the 14th annual report, for 1896–7, revealed that the vicar of Croydon and the gentlemen on the Auxiliary Committee had sent out 1,000 letters appealing for help, but that only £10 had been received in response.[33] The Association's financial position remained shaky throughout the 1900s; its report for 1904–5 carried a note of exasperation when it pointed out that 'In a place as large as Croydon we should be able to secure a sufficient number of annual subscribers to place the Association on a sound financial basis.' Again it was having to fall back on extraordinary expedients such as fêtes.[34]

A. W. Jephson's progress through disillusionment with voluntarist remedies to wholehearted endorsement of collective action was not a typical one, and it is significant that it was in the slums of Inner London that his radical sympathies developed and not in suburban Croydon. In general in late century most Croydon clergymen continued to pour their energies into voluntarist approaches to problems of poverty and welfare. It is worth examining the temperance movement in some detail, for it is perhaps the best example of a voluntarist movement which was openly harnessed to religious principles. Initially begun as an independent movement and gradually 'taken over' by religious organisations and the religiously active, it quickly reached a low ceiling of effectiveness. Like 'mutual improvement', temperance was not intrinsically a religious cause, yet drunkenness was believed by many clergymen to pose one of the greatest obstacles to the work of evangelisation. When the Rev O. B. Byers was asked by his bishop in 1876 if there was any special impediment to his work at Christ Church, he replied simply

[29] Croydon Gordon Boys' Home, 6th Annual Report, 1890–1.
[30] G. J. Murdoch, *The Reasons for the Transfer of the Croydon Gordon Boys' Home to the Church of England Society for Providing Homes for Waifs and Strays* (Croydon 1891).
[31] Croydon Gordon Boys' Home, Annual Reports for 1900s, *passim*.
[32] Croydon Rescue and Preventive Association, 10th Annual Report, 1892–3.
[33] *Ibid.*, 14th Annual Report, 1896–7.
[34] *Ibid.*, 22nd Annual Report, 1904–5.

'intemperance among the lower classes'.[35] As the Rev A. Hannay, pastor of West Croydon chapel, said to the autumnal assembly of the Congregational Union in 1869: 'It is because we have found the drinking habits of the people a hindrance to the progress of the Gospel among them, that we have been shut up to the practice and preaching of abstinence.'[36] In its early stages, as elsewhere in England, the temperance movement was nevertheless only loosely linked to religious activitism; it was from about the 1850s, as the town began to expand rapidly and the movement began to seem a viable, even necessary solution to the problem of the urban poor, that churches began to intrude seriously upon the campaign for abstinence, founding Bands of Hope and temperance societies of their own, and clergymen and prominent laymen participating closely in the running of temperance organisations. Even so, Anglicanism officially held aloof until with a burst of enthusiasm in 1876 a branch of the Church of England Temperance Society was formed, with the encouragement of the archbishop of Canterbury.[37] From this date Anglican activism was constant. A further step in the direction of close association between religion and temperance was taken in 1882 when, supported strongly by pro-temperance townsmen and ministers, a Blue Ribbon Gospel Temperance mission was established in Croydon.[38] The Croydon Temperance Union had been formed in 1880 on the grounds that an undenominational temperance society was needed in the town, but this did not preclude participation by clergymen and ministers.[39] It was the Gospel temperance mission, in fact, which in the 1880s became the largest single temperance society in the town, taking over permanently a skating rink in Park Lane and then, in the wake of the development of the area in the early 1890s, building its own Temperance Hall in Mint Walk where it held weekly services.[40]

The religious associations of temperance were very strong, and yet there is no evidence of any success in promoting temperance on the scale advocates hoped for, and much evidence to suggest strictly limited achievements. There was no fall in the number of cases of drunkenness brought before the magistrates' bench; in 1882, after more than forty years of temperance activity in Croydon, the chairman of the bench complained that cases of drunkenness and disorderly behaviour were becoming too frequent in the town.[41] Nor

[35] Visitation returns, 1876.
[36] *Congregational Year Book*, 1869, p. 78.
[37] *C Ad*, 29 Jan. 1876.
[38] *C Chron*, 30 Sep. 1882.
[39] *C Ad*, 3 Jan. 1880.
[40] *Ward's Croydon Directory*, 1900.
[41] *C Ad*, 14 Oct. 1882.

was any serious impact made on the scale of the drink trade; between 1851 and 1900 the number of public houses, beer houses and drink retailers more than trebled from seventy-four to 255, a figure outstripped by population growth but which understates the situation as it does not reflect the expansion of individual beerhouses as they gradually became established as fully-fledged pubs.[42] At a meeting of the Parish Church branch of the Church of England Temperance Society in 1896 the vicar of Croydon urged further effort on Anglicans, and in doing so revealed that he considered the situation in Croydon a poor one:

> He was quite sure that if they had full enlightenment and full instruction as to the real state of things in Croydon, they would know that there was need for the work of that great society on behalf of which they were met together that evening . . . They could never set this matter right by Act of Parliament, it must be done by Christ's disciples.[43]

Furthermore, if the temperance movement faced similar constraints to other voluntarist causes and was liable to the same cycle of expectation and disappointment, so it was also a cause fraught with potential embarrassment for the churches. Unlike other voluntarist causes it was one which divided middle class society, and could even set congregations against clergy, for the commitment of clergy and ministers to the cause of temperance was often not shared by all their congregations. One correspondent to the *Croydon Chronicle* protested in 1882 at Dr Carpenter's support for Sunday closing legislation, an attempt which, he claimed, aimed 'to deprive by law a large number of their countrymen of their right to enjoy themselves in a respectable and sober way'.[44] In fact Alfred Carpenter was burnt in effigy behind the Town Hall two years later on 5 November by labourers and 'roughs' incensed at critical comments he had made about publicans.[45] In 1871 the Rev William Clarkson stirred up angry comments when he criticised the intemperate language of some advocates of teetotalism in his sermon at George Street Congregational Chapel.[46] The resentment of the drink trade at temperance activity must have increased as the movement gained increasing 'respectability' (and

---

[42] Figures extracted from *Gray's* and *Ward's Croydon Directories*, 1851–1859, 1874–1914; see J.N. Morris, 'The temperance movement in Victorian Croydon', *Proc CNHSS*, xvii (1984), 200.
[43] *C Ad*, 18 Jan. 1896.
[44] *C Chron*, 6 May 1882.
[45] *C Ad*, 15 Nov. 1884.
[46] *C Chron*, 1 Apr. 1871.

patronage by clergy and some leading townsmen) from the 1870s, and this finally surfaced in the founding of a branch of the Licensed Victuallers' and Beerseller's Protection Society in 1883.[47] It was by no means a society of low social standing either; Sir Thomas Edridge, chairman of the bench, supported it and its first chairman was councillor Bruce Johnston, who focused on the anti-teetotal purpose of the society at its first annual dinner: 'This society was formed about nine months ago in Croydon to supply a want which was very much felt – a want of protection of themselves and interests from the intemperate language of the teetotal well-paid lecturers.'[48] As an economic interest-group and not a voluntarist platform, the Licensed Victuallers' society no doubt had relatively little numerical support compared with the temperance movement; its power lay rather in its popularity with some members of the town elite, particularly those who followed a Conservative line in politics. For this reason it was an awkward obstacle for churchmen committed to the cause of temperance, and one that was likely to alienate some of those who composed the core of church membership.

Philanthropic activity in which the churches were closely involved – in 1905, for example, nine out of seventeen members of the General Committee of the Rescue and Preventive Association were ministers of various denominations[49] – was consequently impeded by the ideas of its middle class activists and supporters, and yet seriously limited in the extent to which it could rely on these supporters for financial assistance. These pressures particularly began to take their toll from the 1880s, as the churches themselves began to face financial difficulties; the scale of the problems these organisations set out to tackle continued to grow, and the readiness of the middle class to subscribe to such causes slackened. Voluntarist activity did not disappear – it was too closely woven into the attitudes of the period – yet there were already severe limits to what it could achieve. Its relative lack of success opened up gaps which ultimately only concerted municipal action could fill.

A comparison of the Croydon Guild of Help with the Croydon Charitable Society shows this process particularly well. At the inception of the Charitable Society at a meeting in the Town Hall in December 1869 a committee of twenty was formed. Eight of these were clergymen, including the chairman who was the vicar of Croydon: four were Anglicans, two Congregationalists, one a

---

[47] *Ward's Croydon Directory*, 1884.

[48] *C Ad*, 1 Mar. 1884.

[49] Croydon Rescue and Preventive Association, 23rd Annual Report, 1905–6.

Wesleyan, and one a Roman Catholic.[50] Of the twelve laymen, ten at least were Anglicans. Equally significantly, all these laymen were closely involved in other movements and societies in the town; the committee therefore illustrates well the close co-operation between clergy and the town leadership in mid-century. Their aims were ambitious: to collect information on cases of distress, to unite and co-ordinate the work of the multiplicity of relief organisations in the town, and thus to discriminate between the 'deserving' and 'undeserving' poor to eliminate altogether the award of relief to the undeserving, and to lower the poor rate. Sir Thomas Edridge, chairman of the magistrates' bench and member of the committee, called the plan to co-ordinate charitable work so that relief would come from one source the 'essence' of the scheme.[51] From the very beginning, the society faced some hostility from the local press and from some members of the Board of Poor Law Guardians.[52] It was not able to co-ordinate local charitable work because some relief agencies would not cooperate, and it thus became in effect just one relief organisation among many. The Anglican domination of the Committee remained; although it continued to attract the service of town councillors into the 1900s, nevertheless by this period its annual reports indicate that it was losing subscribers, often running at an annual loss, facing high running costs, and certainly having to reduce the amount of relief it was able to give.[53]

The falling-away of support for the Charitable Society was probably linked to the foundation of the Guild of Help in 1907. At its formation this seemed to be almost a replica of the older organisation: so close indeed did its aims appear that its first president expressly acknowledged that there was a danger of superseding the work of the Charitable Society. He stressed that its prinicipal aim too was co-ordination of activity: 'Now it is evident to us already that our great function . . . is that of a Clearing House, on the one hand as regards the Charitable, and on the other as regards the poor and distressed.'[54] Again, what it was actually able to achieve was far below what it set out to do: it could not raise enough volunteers to work as district visitors, and rather than supervising or absorbing the work of existing agencies, was often forced to leave the field entirely to them.[55] What is striking about the Guild is that it was almost entirely a councillor-run organisation: the local clergy absented themselves from the first

[50] *C Chron*, 25 Dec. 1869.
[51] *Ibid.*
[52] *Ibid.*, 1 Jan. 1870; *C Ad*, 19 Feb. 1870.
[53] Croydon Charitable Society, Annual Reports, 1896–1914, *passim*.
[54] Croydon Guild of Help, leaflet no. 1, Jan. 1908.
[55] *Ibid.*, magazine, Nov. 1911.

public meeting and took no active part thereafter.[56] Whereas the chairman of the Charitable Society was always the vicar of Croydon, the president of the Guild was always the mayor; and nearly all the active members of the Guild were at some time councillors or aldermen. It carried no religious overtones and fitted much more closely into 'secularised' conceptions of local municipal life than into the ideology of the churches, for its first stated object was defined as 'To deepen the sense of civic responsibility, and to promote through personal service, a neighbourly feeling among all classes of the community.'[57]

If municipal enterprise was to take upon itself newer and wider functions in the late nineteenth and early twentieth centuries, it had to be shown that the existing voluntarist methods had failed. Yet the churches had been intimately involved with them, and they were based on particular assumptions about the moral and religious nature of mankind. The failure of voluntarism, then, would hit the churches hard in two ways. Firstly, it would remove (or at least restrict) positive incentives of benefits and social amelioration which buttressed the Victorian Church's attempts to appeal to the poor and the 'lower classes'. Secondly it would undermine the ability of the church to cast itself as the indispensable social and moral binding force which the classes which principally attended and supported it hoped it would be. The limitations of voluntarism were the other side of the coin to pressures and demands for increased municipal responsibility, and the precursor to them; they were also a pointer to the way in which the social role of the churches in the late Victorian period was gradually being whittled down to a narrower, more circumscribed definition of spiritual endeavour.

Voluntarism, religion and lay activism

In the mid-nineteenth century the moral vision intrinsic to many voluntary movements meant that the close involvement of the churches and the religiously-minded was inevitable. Man was depicted as moral being, whose religious and moral capabilities were restricted by material conditions. These in turn were determined by the absence or the inadequate exercise of moral qualities in individuals and not in the 'world outside.' A noted Croydon engineer

---

[56] C Chron, 2 Feb. 1907.
[57] Croydon Guild of Help, magazine, 1910–1914, passim; Ward's Croydon Directories, 1908–1914.

and philanthropist, John Grantham, who was active in the Labourers' Dwellings Society, the YMCA and the British and Foreign Bible Society, wrote a series of letters to the *Croydon Chronicle* in 1870 and 1871 on the condition of the labouring poor which epitomised this argument: 'The origin of all suffering is to be traced to moral causes. Had man's nature remained upright, as created, there could have been no more sorrow.' On this he based his appeal for the effective organisation of 'Christian philanthropy'.[58]

However, the churches were not only an influence upon voluntarist action; they were in a sense themselves part of the voluntarist response to social problems. They relied very largely upon voluntary finance: this was true even of Anglican churches, since church rate could not be used to finance the building of new churches or to support charitable agencies. They also relied upon moral arguments to persuade people to attend church and to take up the services they offered, and not of course upon legal compulsion. They were subject to the same pressures and constraints as other philanthropic ventures, and in the long run this was bound to mould perception of their relative success or failure. One other feature which they shared with philanthropy and which requires analysis in some detail was the tendency in mid-century to ascribe particular importance in the running of churches to influential local leaders: the local 'elite' both sought involvement in church affairs as a necessary aspect of their perceived responsibilities, and were themselves courted by the churches for their influence and money.

The influences which drew local worthies into active association with the work of the churches in the mid-nineteenth century were particularly strong ones. In a period before intellectual controversy had seriously begun to dent the religious sensibilities of the educated middle class, the recent memory of social and political upheaval served to strengthen faith in the saving 'social grace' of the Christian message. Even in an urbanising, middle class town such as Croydon well into the late nineteenth century the threat of riot and disorder was never absent.[59] Popular celebrations of Guy Fawkes night regularly turned into pitched battles with the police in the centre of the town, until the town authorities in the late 1870s and 1880s began to recognise the demands for some sort of celebration and granted the use of Duppas Hill, outside the town, as a bonfire site.[60] The suppression of the Croydon fair in 1867–8 produced crowd action on

[58] *C Chron*, 7 Jan. 1871.
[59] See J. N. Morris, 'A disappearing crowd? Collective action in late nineteenth century Croydon', *Southern History*, xi (1989), 90–113.
[60] *C Ad*, 20 Oct. 1877.

a similarly violent, uproarious scale, with the police station attacked and the windows of magistrates' houses smashed.[61] On the local level there seemed to be very strong reasons for the local elite groups to support the work of the churches: religious regeneration was assumed to bring with it a series of social virtues which would make Croydon a more pleasant place in which to live. As Lieutenant Colonel Rowlandson said of the work of the City Mission in Croydon: 'It acted as a preventive police in arresting crime. It did Her Majesty's work, and was, therefore, patriotic.'[62]

Religion did more, however, than buttress the desire for the maintenance of law and order and for the creation of a morally pure town. It was also closely associated with the whole pattern of culture of the classes from which influential local figures were drawn. The sense of the intimacy of middle class family life into which religion fitted so closely was captured by a biographer of John Pelton, Anglican grocer, Liberal and Alderman, one of the leaders of the pro-incorporation movement. Pelton was a strict sabbatarian, and regarded the playing of any sport or the use of any tool on Sunday as a 'flagrant breach' of the Fourth Commandment; instead he spent the day reading religious works:

> He liked best reading aloud to his family, sitting in a circle around him, one of his favourite religious books, including 'Lecturers to Young Men', some of which he had heard delivered in Exeter Hall during his city days. He read them without any trace of stammering or hesitation, having acquired the art, so his wife said, of conducting family prayers.[63]

The middle classes gave practical expression to the cultural importance of religion in their lives by the active interest they took in church life, sitting on church building committees, subscribing to church and charitable funds, and taking up the available lay offices in their churches.

In turn churches were dependent upon lay interest to sustain the scale of their activities; in Croydon above all the reliance of churches upon local worthies was particularly conditioned by the exigencies of finance. Central church funds could rarely provide more than a modest contribution to the amounts required for the lengthy business of church building. Anglicanism to a limited extent benefitted from

---

[61] *C Chron*, 12 Mar. 1868.
[62] *Ibid.*, 12 Mar. 1859.
[63] Anon., 'Alderman John Pelton: memoir', C Ref Lib (c. 1920), p. 7; the intimate detail of this script would suggest that the author was in fact John Pelton's son, John Ollis Pelton, a local historian.

its social prestige amongst the landed and monied interests, and from its property and endowments, although the burden placed upon central funds by the parochial system was considerable, and its commitment to parochial subdivision deprived it of the flexibility Nonconformists could show in tailoring building programmes to match the location of their principal sources of financial support. The Ecclesiastical Commissioners and the archbishop invariably bargained over requests for financial assistance, in order to place as great a burden as could be borne upon wealthy local supporters.[64] Even the ambitious, systematic scheme of church building developed at the instigation of Archbishop Temple in 1897–8 required some £13,000 to be raised locally before central funds would be applied.[65] The situation was usually worse for Nonconformists. Some central Nonconformist funds existed for the larger denominations – such as the London Chapel Building Society for Congregationalists, for example – but in most cases they were forced to rely on voluntary subscriptions. Once built, chapels could be burdened with debt for years. Holmesdale Road Baptist Church, for example, was built in 1885–6 at a cost of £5,700, only £3,700 of which had been raised (by voluntary subscription) by the time it was opened; a programme of extension of the building begun in 1899 further burdened the church financially and the accumulated debt was still being paid off in 1906.[66] At Enmore Road Congregational Church it took eight years to pay off the £3,000 cost of the prefabricated iron building erected in 1873.[67] Obviously the scale of debt was influenced by the locale of the church and the kind of support it was able to fall back on: George Street Congregational Church, for example, was able to sustain a much more ambitious re-building programme than most because, as the 'parish church' of Congregationalism in Croydon, and in the town centre, it attracted a disproportionately high number of affluent Congregationalists, and in turn (the reverse side of the vicious circle in which so many churches were caught) was usually able to attract preachers of a quality and standing who could keep such congregations.[68] Churches such as that at Holmesdale Road, built in a less impressive, less prestigious location at South Norwood, could not command the same support. With the lack of central funding, churches could sometimes fall back on leading denominational men

---

[64] See, for example, White, *Short History of St Augustine's*, p. 18, for a case where the Commissioners linked provision of an endowment to a condition that the congregation should provide themselves at least 500 sittings at St Augustine's.
[65] *C Ad*, 18 June 1898.
[66] Stockwell, *The Baptist Churches*, pp. 143–7.
[67] Enmore Road Congregational Church, Church Meeting Minutes, 31 Aug. 1881.
[68] Cleal and Crippen, *Story of Congregationalism*, pp. 37–42.

for financial help, such as Samuel Morley for Congregationalists or C. H. Spurgeon for Baptists (Spurgeon's brother was minister at West Croydon Tabernacle). It was said by the historian of West Croydon Tabernacle of Jeremiah Colman (of Colman's mustard) that: 'Year after year, he paid off any deficit in the Church accounts, and . . . in one year of exceptional prosperity the Church had a balance of 1d. on the right side: the Treasurer felt it only fair that this should be handed over to Mr. Colman.'[69] Yet, more often than not, churches turned to wealthy members of their own congregations to give a lead in donating money. A Mr Nettlefold baled out the Unitarian Mission, Dennett Hall, in 1888 when he paid a lump sum of £500 for life membership of the mission, on condition that a suitable building be begun immediately; five leading gentlemen of the congregation immediately followed suit with loans of £50 each.[70]

Once built, the maintenance of the church fabric and its extension as the congregation increased placed constant financial pressure on church supporters. 'No Habitual Grumbler' complained to the *Croydon Chronicle* in 1869 that the vicar and churchwardens of the Parish Church were under the control of the 'moneyocracy'.[71] Successful financial management became essential to the running of a church or chapel. Influential laymen were also necessary to the running of church organisations; their wives and daughters provided teachers, leaders and organisers for Sunday schools, district visiting programmes, Bands of Hope and charities. Moreover, in Croydon at least (and indubitably elsewhere) the authority of central church bodies, and the direction they could give to local patterns of church activity, were very weak. Anglicanism's lack of an effective system of church discipline gave a clergyman, once appointed, a very secure position in his parish against the interference of his clerical superiors. However, financial and organisational considerations meant he was dependent upon his congregations, so although he was irremoveable, the scope and extent of his activities were subject to some congregational control. Local lay influence was built into the highly decentralised church systems of Baptists, Presbyterians, Primitive Methodists and Congregationalists, through cadres of church councils, elders and deacons. The local congregations or their representatives themselves issued invitations to the ministers they had chosen, could regulate their ministers' activities considerably during their tenure of office, and could force a minister's resignation. Virtually all

[69] Anon., *One Hundred Years on the Bridge: West Croydon Baptist Church 1869–1969* (Croydon 1969), p. 10.
[70] Croydon Domestic Mission (Dennett Hall), Minutes, 15 Feb. 1888.
[71] *C Chron*, 11 Sep. 1869.

the mid- and late nineteenth century pastors at George Street Congregational Church were for one reason or another forced out by their congregations in this way.[72]

Church building committees in this period illustrate very well a desire by the sponsors of a would-be church to enlist the support of leading townsmen (for their names and influence as much as for their money), and a willingness by those townsmen to respond. The picture is a sharper one for Anglicanism, given the predominant political and religious colouring of the town elite in this period. The committee formed to supervise the building of St Matthew's in 1865 consisted of nineteen gentlemen, headed by the vicar, most of them active in other movements in the town: six of them were members of the Local Board of Health, two others magistrates, another three holders of various parochial offices at various times, and most of the others well-known for extensive charitable work.[73] The committee formed to purchase the 'dissenting' church of St Paul's, Addiscombe, for use as the permanent church of St Mary Magdalene in 1874, composed of eleven gentlemen (with two clergymen), included the solicitor and two members of the Board of Health, two future members of the School Board and the Council, and several other gentlemen influential in the town, such as Theodore Lloyd, wealthy Liberal stockbroker and magistrate.[74] On a lesser scale a similar conclusion emerges from a consideration of Nonconformist building committees. The aim was clearly to draw in the town elite as far as possible, as at West Croydon Baptist Tabernacle, where the committee of six gentlemen included Joshua Allder, Liberal, tradesman and later Alderman, and Charles Messent, a leading figure in the Literary and Scientific Institution and the Volunteer Fire Brigade.[75]

The corollary of giving men of property a wealth-related franchise was to give them the same measure of informal influence in local affairs. The leaders of most philanthropic, social and political movements in early and mid-Victorian England aimed to transform their causes into mass movements by means of moral suasion. But they also sought particularly to capture men of influence for their causes, in the belief that deferential relationships between lower and higher classes were so strong that the real balance of opinion must ultimately lie in what the propertied thought. This certainly was the belief of the founder of the Croydon Volunteer Fire Brigade, a self-

[72] Raymer, *The Congregational Church, passim.*
[73] *C Chron*, 24 June 1865.
[74] *Ibid.*, 18 Jul. 1874.
[75] Anon., *One Hundred Years*, pp. 6–7.

proclaimed 'humble individual': 'I may, perhaps, be allowed to add, that had this movement been started by a gentleman of position, it would have been carried to a successful issue, at a much earlier period'.[76] The active interest of 'gentlemen' was requested and obtained for the first Working Man's Club in Croydon,[77] for the Labourers' Dwellings Improvement Society,[78] and for the Literary and Scientific Institution;[79] political committees sought to enrol the names of as many gentlemen as possible, the lists of committees running often into a hundred or more names.[80] As such the elitist connotations of much of the thinking of the leaders of mid-Victorian movements owed something to a sincere belief in the practical relevance of religion – his faith 'was the fountain from whence flowed the copious stream of his good deeds' it was said of the auctioneer and philanthropist John Blake[81] – but they were also part and parcel of early and mid-Victorian social and political thought. They naturally assigned an exalted role to religion as the vanguard of moral reform. The challenge to the property vote, launched locally in the arguments for incorporation and nationally in parliamentary reform, did not in itself carry immediate consequences for the status of the churches, but by seeking to give all political (defined by ownership and occupancy, not yet by natural right) men an equal voice in local affairs, it eroded the formal influence churches had been able to accord to the elites. Arguments for the ownership of pews, for example, began to lose their force, and the deference which had sustained elite presence in church offices began to recede.

[76] C Chron, 19 Nov. 1864.
[77] Ibid., 30 Jan. 1864.
[78] Ibid., 2 Feb. 1867.
[79] Ibid., 16 June 1860.
[80] See, for example, C Ad and C Chron, issues for Jan. 1874, passim.
[81] Anon., 'A Tribute to the Memory of the Late Mr. John Blake of Croydon', Surrey Standard, 28 Feb. 1852.

7

The Corporation

The campaign for incorporation

Discontent over local government in Croydon by the late 1870s was definitely crystallising around a common aim: the incorporation of the town. Though it was not a change which appealed directly and principally because it would bring a rupture with the older Anglican-dominated structure of local administration, this was one of its attractions and was to be a direct consequence. The creation of a single, powerful representative local governing body, which in all but the most formal sense was entirely secular, thus carried great significance for the practical status and operation of organised religion in the area, particularly in the late nineteenth century context of the gradual extension of municipal responsibility.

Judging by the personnel involved, it would seem that the incorporation movement developed from three initially separate movements. The first of these, the campaign to reform parochial endowments and the parochial system, has already been described at some length. The issue continued to be of interest long after the charter of incorporation had been granted and was never entirely subsumed under the campaign for incorporation, because until the final schemes were produced in 1893 the parochial charities remained separate from the Council, with trustees still appointed by the vestry. However, the same group of Liberals who had supported Saward's initiatives were prominent in the campaign for incorporation: it was a key means by which the power of the vestry could be circumvented. Francis Moses Coldwells, for example, a Liberal, Nonconformist tradesman who became one of the leaders of the pro-incorporation movement, got himself elected as trustee of various parochial charities in the 1880s and pushed for their reform.[1] In the schemes of 1893 a certain measure of control devolved upon the Council, which selected representative trustees for the charities.[2] The movement had been the first in which Nonconformists and Liberals had actively

---

[1] Anon., 'Frances Moses Coldwells 1827–1895', typescript (c. 1920), C Ref Lib.
[2] Charity Commissioners, *Scheme for the Croydon Charities*, and *Scheme for the Charity of Elis David*.

identified themselves with reform of local government in the area; it had given them some experience of political activism and had served to strengthen their influence in parochial affairs.

The second and by far the most important element in the movement for incorporation, however, was the gradual development of criticism of the Local Board of Health. By the late 1850s the success of the Board's early sanitary measures was clearly reflected in a falling rate of mortality due to epidemic diseases in the parish, and by the reputation the town quickly acquired as a 'model' town for improved sanitary measures.[3] Yet the potential contradiction which always existed in Victorian improving towns between the demand for the provision of efficient services and the pressure from middle class residents for lower rates, which could lead, for example, in the hands of 'economists' to the complete abandonment of schemes of improvement, as happened at Birmingham in the late 1850s,[4] frequently hampered the work of the Board. Like Birmingham, Croydon refused to appoint a medical officer of health, resisted efforts to procure a stipendiary magistrate for Croydon, and quarrelled with three of its successive engineers, partly over their salaries.[5] The proponents of 'economy' who sometimes got themselves elected onto the Board in the 1850s and 1860s, however, were unable to prevent altogether the gradual extension of the Board's work. By 1867 the Board was in financial difficulties: a statement of its financial condition showed an excess of accumulated expenditure on permanent works over *borrowed* capital of £3,500.[6] The high rates the Board was consequently forced to levy, together with its financial instability, led to further charges of incompetence: the *Croydon Chronicle*, for example, blamed irregularities in the water supply on the 'slovenly manner [in which] the business of the parish has been carried on – where the signing of cheques has been deemed the only thing necessary for the welfare of the inhabitants'.[7] A Ratepayers' Protection Association was formed by leading townsmen in April 1867 to fight the elections; two ratepayers' nominees were returned out of four candidates.[8] A public inquiry, held by Thomas Taylor of the Home Office in response to pressure by the Association, called for

[3] E. Westall, *On the Advantages to be derived from the Adoption of the 'Local Government Act' as exemplified in Croydon* (address to South-Eastern Branch of the BMA, Croydon 1865).
[4] Briggs, *Victorian Cities*, pp. 210–12.
[5] Minutes of the Croydon Local Board of Health; on medical officer of health, see meetings in Aug. and Sep. 1865 and throughout 1872–4; on stipendiary magistrate, *passim*, but Jan. 1870 in particular; on a particularly bitter dispute with their engineer, meetings in Aug. to Nov. 1863.
[6] Latham, *Permanent Sanitary Works*, p. 71.
[7] *C Chron*, 17 Aug. 1867.
[8] *Ibid.*, 16 Mar. 1867; 27 Apr. 1868.

strict economy in the Board's management and placed a straitjacket on its activity by making it impossible for the Board to raise loans in future without a full inquiry on each and every occasion.[9] Consequently the work of the Board in the 1870s was limited in scope, and certainly not extensive enough to meet the ambitions of local pro-improvement men. Furthermore, it became increasingly apparent in the 1860s and 1870s that the structure and size of the Board were inadequate for the growing volume of business; in the 1870s it was forced to abandon full discussion at open board in favour of a committee system;[10] with only sixteen members, however, the seven committees in existence by the late 1870s were themselves over-worked and too small.[11] In 1879 one Norwood member complained that committee business had sometimes been transacted when only one member had been present.[12] It was apparent by the late 1870s that the Board was becoming unworkable as an instrument of parochial government, its powers restricted, resources overstretched and membership insufficient.

In any case Liberals and Nonconformists regarded the Board with some suspicion. Elected on the property-weighted franchise, its membership was, with a few exceptions, generally recruited from the Anglican, Conservative elite of the town. The *Croydon Advertiser*, for example, opposed the candidature of S. L. Rymer on the grounds that, 'he is too consistent a follower of the party represented by the Vestry Clerk to be acceptable to the general body of ratepayers, and we do not like to see the Secretary of the Conservative Association put on a Board in which there is already too great a proportion of the Tory element'.[13] Those few Liberals who sat on the Board in the 1860s were 'respectable' members of the town elite: their most prominent member, Alfred Carpenter, an Anglican who was medical adviser to successive archbishops, was hardly typical of mainstream Liberalism in Croydon.[14] The number of known Liberal members on the Board rose to seven by the late 1870s, with another probable one too.[15] Yet it was the Liberals who, in the mid- and late 1870s, threw their weight behind mounting public criticism of the Board. In late 1875 and early 1876 a typhoid epidemic caused a crisis of confidence in the Board.[16] A new Ratepayers' Sanitary and Protection

---

[9] *Ibid.*, 6 June 1868.
[10] *C Ad*, 30 Apr. 1870.
[11] Elborough, *Croydon*, p. 14.
[12] *C Chron*, 8 Mar. 1879.
[13] *C Ad*, 19 Mar. 1870.
[14] For Carpenter's activity in Croydon, see p. 125.
[15] Appendix 4, table 2.
[16] Dr Buchanan, *Report on an Epidemic of Enteric Fever at Croydon in 1875* (Croydon 1876).

Association was formed (the 1867 association had lapsed some time in 1868) to monitor its actions; leading Croydon Liberals became its main proponents.[17] The first provisional committee chose J. S. Balfour to preside; Balfour was fast becoming the most distinguished man in Croydon, on the basis of what was later shown to be a massive fortune acquired by fraudulent means through his Liberator Building Society; Liberal and Congregationalist, he was president of the Liberal and Radical Association, treasurer of the Croydon Nonconformist Committee, and a member of the School Board.[18] After securing the return of several of their nominees at the 1877 elections for the Board, in 1879 the Association stepped up its campaign by pressing for the division of the Board into wards, with an increase in the number of members. The Board, urged to adopt the proposal by Liberal members, indicated it would do so only if the general opinion of the parish could be seen to be in its favour.[19] In fact, at the subsequent public inquiry, the Ratepayers' Association's arguments were rejected, probably because, as the *Croydon Chronicle* pointed out, its case was very badly prepared.[20] It was at this point that the Association began to consider openly the possibility of incorporation. They began by taking up the related issue of parliamentary representation, and Frederick Foss and J. H. Mitchener, two leading local Liberals, persuaded the 1879 Easter vestry to appoint a committee to consider the issue.[21] It was not until a year later, in December 1880, that the members of the Association called a public meeting to form an organisation to press for incorporation, and from then on it was Liberals and Nonconformists who called the meetings, filled most of the posts of responsibility, and were the most active speakers.[22]

The movement for incorporation sprang directly out of criticism of the Local Board of Health, but it was fuelled by the agitation over parochial charities, and by a third element. This was the tramways company. In 1877 four local tradesmen formed themselves into a company to promote a tramway in Croydon, with J. S. Balfour at their head; the four, F. M. Coldwells, J. Pelton, J. Allder and D. B. Miller, were all to become pro-incorporation activists, and councillors or aldermen in the 1880s; only Miller was a Conservative,

[17] *C Ad*, 25 Dec. 1875.
[18] Details of Balfour's participation in political and social movements in Croydon assembled from *C Chron* and *C Ad*, *passim*; for an account of Balfour's business dealings, see G. Sparrow, *The Great Swindlers* (London 1959).
[19] *C Ad*, 19 June 1878.
[20] *C Chron*, 12 Apr. 1879.
[21] *C Ad*, 19 Apr. 1879.
[22] *Ibid.*, 4 Dec. 1880.

one of a handful who allied themselves to Liberal progressive movements in Croydon and who in doing so were very much out of step with contemporaries of a similar political persuasion. The Company's solicitor, W. H. Hebb, became the secretary of the pro-borough committee, and other tradesmen with whom the company had business dealings, such as John Thrift, Baptist and Liberal, were supporters of incorporation.[23] The connections between the personnel were so close that one of the points frequently raised at the incorporation inquiry by the anti-borough party was that the pro-borough party was merely an expression of the economic interests of the tramways company. As one witness, the Norwood resident Robert Hovenden, said: 'His opinion was that if there had been no tramways there would have been no agitation for a borough. He believed that the tramways were not a paying concern, and that it was wished to get a borough in order that the corporation might take over the liabilities.'[24] The tramways company, operating successful lines by 1881, did in fact have a sound motive for supporting incorporation, and it was one they took pains to conceal from the inquiry. The High Street was so narrow that it was impossible to run tram lines along it. Thus, the Croydon system was effectively cut in two, with a route running in the south of the town, along the Brighton Road, and a number of routes in the north, but no direct link between them.[25] The Local Board of Health had been unable to widen the High Street, partly from lack of will, as an attempt in 1864 had shown, and partly because it had no powers of compulsory purchase. With its unstable financial record in the 1860s and 1870s it would certainly never have been able to secure the parliamentary act necessary to acquire these powers.[26] Only a corporation, which would start afresh with a clean financial record, with increased powers, and therefore with a greater chance of gaining compulsory powers of purchase, would be able to tackle the question of High Street improvement.

To describe the origins of the pro-incorporation movement is not to describe why incorporation took place: some examination of the possible motives of the pro- and anti-incorporation parties is necessary. It is easier to do this for the opponents of incorporation, as

---

[23] Baddeley, *Tramways*, pp. 10–13; see also the report of the first ordinary meeting of the Company, in *C Ad*, 28 Sep. 1878.
[24] Elborough, *Croydon*, p. 83.
[25] Baddeley, *Tramways*, p. 14.
[26] Lack of compulsory powers of purchase was a serious limitation to many of the Board's activities: in 1858, for example, the chairman of the Board had stated this as the prime reason for the Board's difficulties in finding a suitable site for a new parochial burial ground: *C Chron*, 20 Nov. 1858.

the pro-borough party had to cast themselves in as comprehensive a light as possible: they had to show that the change they desired was one favoured by all sections and classes in Croydon, and not a partisan proposal, because they failed to gain the open support of the existing public authorities in the town. For the same reason, the pro-borough witnesses at the inquiry refused to construct their arguments in terms of a direct attack on the Local Board of Health, though the weakness of that body was in fact a very powerful argument in favour of incorporation. Instead they merely claimed that the Board was too small for the burden of work it carried.[27] Most local political movements in the Victorian period are difficult to analyse, and the pro-incorporation group is no different: such movements, no matter how partisan in origin, covered themselves with a fog of rhetoric about unity; they stigmatised opposition as factious, divisive and 'troublesome', and sought to place a notional 'community' (usually articulated in words like 'the feeling of the town' or 'the interests of the people') above the policies of political parties, ignoring the fact that what constituted the 'community' was not an ideal which could be separated altogether from the political philosophies of parties and religious and other groups. The stated 'no politics' policy of the Board of Health, the School Board, and later the Council (and, initially, elections to the Council) concealed very deep party alignments.

The anti-borough party were very quick to point out the fact, openly admitted, that the pro-borough party were actively supported by the town's tradesmen.[28] At least five of eleven members of the executive committee of the pro-incorporation association were High Street or North End tradesmen, and four of them had close connections with the tramway company.[29] These men would certainly have had powerful economic motives: apart from the tramways issue, tradesmen would stand to benefit from town improvement (particularly High Street widening and the part-demolition of the old market area which this would entail) because of the increased attractiveness of Croydon as a retail centre which this could bring. In 1878 High Street traders had petitioned the Board of Health to pave the street to improve its condition. They had been told they would have to pay for

[27] Elborough, *Croydon*, pp. 10–11; the counsel for the Petitioners for the Charter openly admitted at the enquiry that the movement in 1879 to have the Local Board of Health divided into nine wards with 54 members had failed because it was believed that it was intended as a direct attack on the work of the Board.
[28] *C Chron*, 22 May 1880.
[29] The five were Joshua Allder, Charles Hussey, D. B. Miller, John Thrift, and George Williams: C Ad, 4 Dec. 1880.

it themselves, so they had no reason to admire the Board.[30] The conscious mixing of political and religious groups on the borough committee and in the witnesses it summoned at the inquiry tends to obscure the strong tendency of Liberals and Nonconformists to side with the pro-borough camp, but this can be seen from the virtual absence of both of these groups from the batch of twenty-eight witnesses summoned by the anti-borough party: only four identifiable Liberals were summoned, and two of these were Anglicans.[31] All the Conservatives summoned by the anti-borough committee as witnesses were Anglican. The close affiliation between Nonconformity and Liberalism in the town in this period would help to explain Nonconformist support for Liberal progressive movements in the town, against the relative solidarity until the 1870s of the political elite's Conservative and Anglican bias. Yet there were clear 'political' motives as well. On both ideological and opportunistic grounds, Liberals based a large part of their case for incorporation on their opposition to the property-weighted franchise.[32] In Conservative-dominated Croydon, Liberals who believed in a one man-one vote system also stood to gain from it electorally: leading Conservatives who supported the pro-borough movement, though exceptional in doing so, seem to have been professional men or tradesmen with businesses in the town centre, and not commuters.[33] The three arguments principally employed by the borough committee at the 1881 inquiry, do not comprehend the undoubtedly wide range of motives of those who supported it; they claimed, firstly, that the Local Board of Health was inadequate for the growing volume of business it had to deal with; secondly, that the property vote under which the Board was elected was inequitable and effectively excluded a large proportion of the ratepayers from representation; and, thirdly, that the mayor and municipal officers a corporation would require would bring prestige to the town and revitalise the apparent slackening in its public life.[34]

The opposition to incorporation produced a far less consistent case at the inquiry. They were not able seriously to question the array of statistics cited by the pro-borough group which challenged the ability

---

[0] *C Chron*, 11 Oct. 1879.
[1] Elborough, *Croydon*, cross-referenced with lists of the supporting committees for the 1872, 1874 and 1880 elections (extracted from the *C Chron* and *C Ad*), and with known religious affiliations, also extracted from the local press.
[2] Elborough, *Croydon*, p. 11.
[3] See witnesses summoned by the borough committee, *ibid.*, cross-referenced with occupational details in *Ward's Croydon Directories* for the 1870s and early 1880s.
[4] Elborough, *Croydon*, pp. 7–12.

of the Local Board of Health to carry out its business. Instead, they chose to base their case on a defence of the property franchise, and on speculation which even they admitted they could not substantiate about the probable effects of incorporation on the level of the rates.[35] If the anti-Local Board activists had presented their case shoddily in 1879, it was now the other way round. Some witnesses for the anti-borough camp must have been downright embarrassing; the Rev James Archer Spurgeon was one such, unusual in being one of the few Liberal Nonconformists to oppose incorporation:

> He [Spurgeon] did not know what the Local Board spent in salaries, but he believed the expense for officers would be greater under a corporation. He presumed there would be a number of beadles to attend upon the mayor, and this would, of course, mean an extra expense.
> Mr Clarke [Counsel for the borough committee] – Are you serious?
> Mr Spurgeon – Yes.
> Mr Clarke – You think the extra expense would be caused by the beadles?
> Mr Spurgeon – Yes.[36]

The anti-borough group also claimed, again without evidence, that incorporation would lead to the intrusion of party politics into town affairs, and then switched to an attack on the motives of the pro-borough group, pointing out its connections with the tramways company and its Liberal political colour.[37] Their witnesses were far more impressive than their arguments. The chairmen of all the existing public authorities in Croydon criticised the pro-borough group; other witnesses summoned were leading members of the town elite, many of whom had served on public bodies.[38] Yet in a sense – though this was not a point made by the pro-borough counsel – this merely served to confirm the contention of the pro-borough camp that the plural franchise had perpetuated the influence of a group of men who were out of step with the main trends of opinion in the parish. For these witnesses were overwhelmingly Conservative and Anglican; they were representative of the kind of opinion which had

35 *Ibid.*, pp. 55–8.
36 *Ibid.*, p. 70.
37 *Ibid.*, pp. 57–62; see particularly William Drummond's evidence on pp. 71–2.
38 All three chairmen, the Rev G. R. Roberts of the School Board, William Drummond of the Board of Health, and Sir Thomas Edridge of the magistrates' bench, were Anglicans and Conservatives: *ibid.*, pp. 57–90.

always governed Croydon in the past, but which, as the council elections of the 1880s were to show, no longer occupied so dominant a position.

The growth of municipal power

Incorporation in Croydon, originating as it did in Nonconformist criticisms of the parochial system and supported by a solid combination of Liberals, Nonconformists and dissatisfied Conservatives, was achieved in such a way as to ensure that no close connection could remain between the Established Church in the borough and the principal organ of local government. Even the means by which the Board of Health had been assimilated into the old parochial system, the property-weighted franchise, had disappeared, and the town's new political elite was different in political complexion and to some extent religious affiliation from its predecessor.[39] The product of intense religious and political rivalry, the new corporation was at the same time a powerful, prestigious agency of government, and attracted the interest of those who had originally opposed it. Conservatives did not refrain from standing at the first municipal elections, and two members of the Board of Health who had opposed incorporation succeeded in securing places as councillors on the new Croydon Council.[40] The creation of the Council and the way it worked affected the status of organised religion in Croydon in two ways: first, it took over the work of the Local Board of Health, extended the range of municipal activity and rapidly became the principal, effective organ of local government; second, in so doing it began to set firmer boundaries to what was to be regarded as the legitimate sphere of religious activity.

In expanding the responsibilities of local government in the area, the Council made itself the centre of municipal attention, and thus drew interest away from the churches. Though the Local Board of Health had gradually taken upon itself an extended range of activities, these all had the issue of public health at their source, and the Board could not – and would not – attempt to expand its work beyond limits defined by that. For example, it completely ignored an attempt led by the Unitarian minister in Croydon, the Rev R. R. Suffield, to get a rate-supported library instituted in the parish in 1871.[41] Thus there was a large area of parochial life which was

---

[39] Appendix 4, table 2.
[40] Commentary on the first borough elections, in *C Review*, Jul. 1883.
[41] *C Ad*, 29 Jan. 1876.

open to voluntary charitable and social activity, and in this the churches could play a considerable part, even to the extent of taking a lead in some movements for social amelioration. Moreover, in mid-century the Board had occasionally to contend with strong hostility to centralisation of the kind which, nationally, surfaced in the opposition to the General Board of Health and the work of Edwin Chadwick. A correspondent to the *Croydon Chronicle* in 1858, for example, criticised the Local Board's willingness to become the Local Burial Board with charge of cemeteries, asserting: 'are not Englishmen opposed to Government Centralisation – and if so, will they permit Parochial Centralisation, by giving the Local Board the sole control of every scheme for disposing of the rates raised, and to be raised, in this parish?'.[42] When Croydon tradesmen formed a volunteer fire brigade as a rival to the Board's brigade on the grounds that they wished to retain control of the movement themselves, one of the leading founders, E. Huntley, voiced the hope that it would inspire other independent movements.[43] Consequently the potential sphere of church activity, with the Board's authority so closely drawn, was very wide.

This was a situation which began to change dramatically towards the end of the century. The adoption of the Free Libraries Act in 1888, and the achievement of the Croydon Improvement Act in 1890 marked new developments in municipal action. From then on the responsibilities of the Council began to widen considerably. In 1894 the Parish Councils Act finally brought about the demise of the parochial system of government by conferring the remaining powers of the vestry on the Council; as the *Croydon Chronicle* somewhat excitedly said: 'The end of the Easter vestries has been reached, and one more historical custom has been sacrificed to the exigencies of our revolutionary times. The new Local Government Act will separate the Church from the parish work.'[44] In 1899 the Council purchased the Tramways Company, on the grounds 'That a Company's only aim is to make profit for its shareholders, whereas the Corporation will consider solely the public convenience and public health.'[45]

Further steps in the direction of united, collective responsibility for social services and welfare provision came in the early 1900s, with the initiation of large Council-funded schemes to provide working class housing, the building of a mental hospital for the Borough near the village of Warlingham, outside the borough boundaries, and the

[42] *C Chron*, 18 Dec. 1858.
[43] *Ibid.*, 19 Nov. 1864.
[44] *Ibid.*, 31 Mar. 1894.
[45] Borough of Croydon, Council Minutes and Incidental Papers, xvii, 5 June 1893.

abolition of the School Boards, fraught though this issue was with religious controversy. Some of these measures met with opposition in some form – particularly where it was feared that rate-rises would be the consequence – but although the turn-out at municipal elections was frequently low, the residential and lower middle class were never entirely alienated from the work of the Council;[46] by the mid-1900s ratepayers' associations were fielding candidates who usually supported municipal activity, despite grumbling about the level of local taxation. Arguments against centralisation heard in the 1850s and 1860s had disappeared. The underlying assumption of more extensive municipal activity was not a neo-socialist one; even at their peak before 1914 Labour could only achieve five councillors, and with most other candidates by that date standing on an anti-Labour ticket, they were hardly in a position to influence Council decisions directly.[47] It was, however, a collective one, namely that the Council was justified in taking on schemes which could benefit all (for example, tramways), or could solve specific problems of welfare (for example, housing). Churches were not in a position to compete seriously with increased municipal power. As the previous chapter sought to establish, wider Council responsibility was partly the result of the failure of voluntarist philanthropic and religious schemes. In turn, the relative success of the Council and the importance it was acquiring as its functions widened were bound to draw away from the churches those leading lay figures who, in mid-century, had seen in the churches and in voluntarist charitable agencies the principal means of urban regeneration.

The increasing functions and importance of an entirely secular, representative local authority necessarily had implications for the activity and status of the churches in Victorian urban society. This was especially true, given that their heightened prestige and perceived role in the middle decades of the century had committed them to a very wide range of auxiliary agencies designed to re-Christianise the urban populace. What was taking place by the end of the century amounted to a re-definition of religious activity, even to a re-definition of the 'religious' in the urban context, as it was reduced from an all-embracing term which expressed not a particular activity or quality but an entire culture (or, rather, what the dominant classes perceived as culture) to a specialist description of a particular way of life or approach to morality. As Stephen Yeo has recognised, in a

---

[46] The turnout in the 1890s and early 1900s was rarely above 50%; in the 1900s the appearance throughout the Borough of Labour candidates introduced renewed interest in the election results and frequently pushed the turnout over the 50% mark: Croydon Borough Election Results, C Ref Lib.

[47] Tichelar, 'Labour Politics in Croydon', pp. 1–4.

period which saw the rise of agencies designed to appeal specifically to a new concept of 'leisure', as opposed to 'work', the churches found themselves drawn into competition with 'leisure' activities.[48] The same dualism could be seen in 'religion' and 'politics', or in the local sense in 'municipal government' and 'church life'. This was a process, as argued earlier, which the churches themselves were assisting in the late nineteenth century by seeking to draw further into church life the existing community of believers, and increasingly abandoning the aggressive, informal or schismatic, outward-looking methods of mid-century.

Local government in turn was effectively delimiting church activity by staking out for itself areas of local administration and welfare. In some of these fields – gas, sanitary reform, town improvement, tramways – the role of the churches had been marginal or non-existent. Here, then, the assumption of responsibility by the local authority tended to enhance the prestige and functional importance of the secular organ of government relative to the prestige of the churches, but not directly at the cost of it. There were other areas, however, in which the churches had been involved where the passing of the initiative to local government (I mean extra-parochial government) involved a direct reduction in the activity of churches, and was sometimes the result of the churches' failure; in these instances church activity was effectively discredited.

In Croydon three issues in particular bore this out. The first, the question of burial grounds, harks back principally to the Board of Health. The second, the adoption of the Free Libraries Act in Croydon, illustrates the Council assuming a responsibility for a service churches had provided on voluntarist lines, with the active support of religious leaders and yet ultimately to their cost. The third is the issue of education, and because of the long-running nature of this dispute cannot be more than a brief discussion of the relevant points. The burial of the dead had always been regarded as a prerogative of religious groups, and yet it was a question which, with the threat of overcrowded grounds in rapidly urbanising areas, was bound to raise anxiety about public health and the dangers of epidemic disease. Churches were in a difficulty over the matter: often burial fees made a significant contribution to their income, and yet they were not in a position to sustain the capital requirements of the large, extended cemeteries which had to be built for urbanising areas. They could not at the same time keep control of all burials and make sufficient provision for the entire population. It was a problem which particularly beset the Anglican church, bound as it was by tradition

[48] Yeo, *Religion and Voluntary Organisations*, esp. ch. 11.

and originally by law to the burial of Dissenters as well as Anglicans, though it also affected those Nonconformist churches which established their own small churchyards.[49] In such a situation open conflict was likely to arise between a church which wished to retain its control of burials, and residents fearful of a health hazard. Opposition to an extension of the crowded Parish Church ground in 1846 and 1847 came about principally because of the dampness of the burial ground, and the consequent fear of disease.[50] Similar tensions and conflicts surfaced in a bitter dispute at All Saints, Norwood, in the late 1860s: within forty years of the churchyard's opening in 1829, some 3,025 corpses had been buried in an area designed to hold only 1,368; overcrowding and the dampness of the ground led to fears of disease and complaints from nearby residents, including a churchwarden of All Saints, and to the appointment of a Commissioner empowered by the Home Office to conduct an enquiry.[51] The *Norwood News* referred to the vicar's 'childish obstructiveness' in the matter;[52] his opposition to closure collapsed only when another local resident offered £10 towards a fund to make up for the loss of burial fees the vicar would suffer and was followed by others. The cramped conditions of All Saints and other churchyards in the parish had already led the Board of Health, acting as a Burial Board, to build the first 'municipal' cemetery in the area. Opened in 1861, this was divided into separate plots for Anglican, Nonconformist and Catholic burials. It became known as the Queen's Road Cemetery, and was by the 1870s by far and away the principal site for burials in the parish.[53] Its management was entirely in the hands of the Board of Health, and subsequently Croydon Council, which paid its keepers and gardeners and collected burial fees, though a proportion of these still went to the vicar of Croydon.[54] Apart from those in family vaults, burials in Croydon churchyards had all but ceased by the 1880s, and provision for them had passed entirely to the local authorities.

Burial of the dead had been a regular feature of church activity, and an important point of contact between the Established Church

[49] In Croydon the Society of Friends maintained their own burial ground at their Meeting House in Park Lane: Ward, *Croydon in the Past*, p. 5.
[50] Croydon Parish Vestry Meeting Minutes, 14 Apr. 1846; 6 Apr. 1847; *Surrey Standard*, 24 Mar. 1849.
[51] Details from Warwick, *Phoenix Suburb*, pp. 84–90.
[52] *Norwood News*, 10 Apr. 1869.
[53] Minutes of Croydon Burial Board (the Local Board of Health), 1861, *passim*; for a description of the ceremony of consecration of the cemetery, see *C Chron*, 20 Jul. 1861; by 1869 it was estimated that there was sufficient room in the original ground for only another two and a half years, and plans were initiated for its extension: *C Chron*, 30 Oct. 1869.
[54] *Ibid.*, 22 June 1861.

and the community at large. The provision of libraries was a voluntarist cause adopted by some churches, and yet it was another area in which local authorities 'took over'. It was an issue which brought out very sharply the increasing divergence between the perceived legitimate spheres of religious and political action: religious arguments to justify clerical involvement in what was beginning to be seen as a non-religious matter provoked something of a backlash from congregations and some members of the local elite. The vicar of Croydon, the Rev J. M. Braithwaite, and W. T. Malleson, a member of the School Board and an influential Unitarian, led the campaign to adopt the Public Libraries Act from 1886. In 1886 and 1887 they managed to secure a poll on the issue, but on both occasions were defeated.[55] In April 1888 they again announced in the local press their intention of pressing the issue, claiming that a Free Library was 'in these times a necessity of civilisation'.[56] A stinging letter in reply from H. G. Bremner, a Park Hill resident and persistent critic of Corporation extravagance, homed in on the vicar in particular: 'I think a Vicar might be better occupied than in championing burning public questions which are certain to stir up bitter strife amongst his parishioners.'[57] In the School Board elections at the end of May, Malleson and W. H. Bishop, another supporter of the Free Libraries, were unexpectedly defeated; the Rev C. J. Street, pastor of the Unitarian church and supporter of Free Libraries, came bottom of the list of those who were elected, closely followed by R. S. Dick, another supporter, and Braithwaite.[58] The local municipal leaders who were most active as laymen in church congregations on this issue tended to side with the vicar, and yet allegations of self-interest were made against them by correspondents in the press.[59] One of the five large public meetings in October organised by the committee directing the campaign, a meeting held in the working and lower middle class area of Thornton Heath, was interrupted by vociferous support for a speaker from the floor who tried to move a motion rejecting Free Libraries altogether.[60] The vicar pressed the issue through his Parish Magazine, and through his sermon preached before the newly-elected Mayor and Council on 11 November, a week before the poll.[61]

[55] *C Ad*, 6 Mar. 1886; 26 Mar. 1887.
[56] *C Chron*, 28 Apr. 1888.
[57] *Ibid.*, 5 May 1888.
[58] *C Ad*, 25 May 1888.
[59] For example, 'A Large Ratepayer', *C Chron*, 23 June 1888.
[60] *C Ad*, 27 Oct. 1888.
[61] *C Chron*, 17 Nov. 1888.

The results of the subsequent poll showed a victory for Free Libraries, but the majority of 1,746 was not a large one in a total poll of 11,000 ratepayers, and this turnout was a very high figure (about 90 per cent) in comparison with the under 50 per cent figure habitually recorded in municipal elections.[62] The *Croydon Guardian* disputed the poll's legality, but an attempt by Bremner, S. G. Edridge (a councillor) and a group of other wealthy ratepayers to press this point in an action in Chancery was dismissed.[63] Not only was the involvement of religious leaders in the movement criticised by those who did not wish to see a 1d. in the £ rate imposed, but the assumption of responsibility by the Council reduced the importance of church provision of reading facilities. The parochial library, usually a small collection of religious tracts and books, was no match for the public libraries established throughout the Borough in the 1890s. In 1898 the vicar of St Mary Magadalene informed the Archbishop that he kept a parish library, but that it had been 'rendered useless' by the public library.[64] Croydon Free Christian Church had emphasised its possession of a free library as one of its attractions in the 1870s, but by the early 1890s had ceased to do so.[65] By 1907 Anglican visitation questionnaires no longer even required to know if a church supported a library or not.[66]

The issue of education is much more complicated. In some cases the School Board took over in part or in entirety the running of what had been church schools previously; its Princess Road schools, for example, started life as an infants' school run by the Primitive Methodists, and then supported by financial assistance from the wealthy Anglican Evangelical ship-owner, Thomas Edridge.[67] In others the gradual improvement and sophistication of educational regulations and inspection which took place in the last decades of the nineteenth century, principally through the agency of the School Boards, also affected the running of church schools. The ability to compel attendance, for example, was used by Father David, the Roman Catholic priest on the School Board in 1871, as one of his main arguments for the payment of denominational fees.[68] The Board itself was subject to controversies and tensions of a religious character which, surfacing triennially at the elections, frequently led to

---

[62] *C Ad.*, 24 Nov. 1888.
[63] Borough of Croydon, Council Minutes and Incidental Papers, vii, 21 Jan. 1889 (full council), 29 Jan. 1889 (Legal Committee), 2 May 1889 ((Financial Committee).
[64] Visitation returns, 1898, St Mary Magdalene, Addiscombe.
[65] *C Chron*, 14 Feb. 1880.
[66] Visitation returns, 1907.
[67] *C Ad*, 1 Apr. 1871.
[68] *C Chron*, 25 Nov. 1871.

criticism from local residents. Religion was increasingly inadequate, more divisive as a basis for popular education. In any case the gradual development of secondary and further education late in the century was also taking the initiative out of the hands of the churches. The Polytechnic, for example, was originally founded as an offshoot of the Scarbrook Road mission hall by a curate of the Parish Church in 1888 and named the Pitlake Technical Institute, but under the Technical Instruction Act of 1890 it was 'taken over' by the Corporation, who funded it, placed a number of councillors and aldermen on the Committee of Governors, and commissioned plans for a new building.[69] By this means the borough's only institution for further education passed directly from religious to municipal control.

By 1902 the churches were still the only powerful secondary agency in the provision of educational facilities, but they were lagging well behind the School Board. The abolition of the School Boards by the Education Act of that year had a number of effects. At one sweep it removed education from the arena of religious controversy, by subordinating it to an indirectly appointed Committee of Education dominated by council members; there were no longer elections specifically for the educational authority which could be fought on a religious basis. In this way it cut away at once much remaining religious interest in municipal affairs. When the Ruri-decanal Conference in 1904 lamented the absence of open church involvement in municipal affairs, it was principally education they had in mind; what is significant is that the resolution they framed calling upon church councils to put forward church candidates at municipal elections was almost completely ignored.[70] Co-option of non-councillor members of the Committee by the Council itself dramatically reduced the number of clerical members on the education authority, from an average of five on the School Board in the late 1890s to never more than two on the Council's Education Committee in the 1900s, and only one by 1910.[71] The abolition of the School Boards probably consolidated educational administration as well, and churches became more subject to local authority supervision than they had been under the Board: at the Parish Church in 1904, for example, it was the recommendation of an inspector sent by Croydon Education Committee which forced the church to take on the costly task of rebuilding its cramped, dilapidated National School buildings.[72]

[69] H.A. Warren, 'A history of technical education with special reference to the borough of Croydon', *Proc CNHSS*, xv (1976), 134–6.
[70] Holy Trinity Parish Magazine, Mar. 1904.
[71] *Ward's Croydon Directories*, 1874–1914.
[72] St James's Parish Magazine, June 1904.

In the areas cited – burial grounds, public libraries, and education – the local authorities, principally the Corporation, were pushing back the boundaries of church action; in certain other, more minor matters, the Council was also stepping on the toes of religious organisations. In 1885, for example, councillors were in trouble with Salvationists and Primitive Methodists because of a recent by-law restricting open-air parading and preaching. The Primitives appointed their superintendent to interview the town clerk, though nothing is known of the outcome.[73] Nearly twenty years later the Council aroused religious controversy again by permitting pleasure bands to perform on Sunday in recreation grounds.[74] What is at first sight striking about the Corporation, is that, despite everything, it remained overtly at least a 'religious' body, in that every year, after the municipal elections and the choice of the new mayor, the whole Corporation attended church. The tradition was established for the morning service to be at whatever local church, Anglican or Nonconformist, the mayor himself regularly attended, and for the afternoon service to be at the Parish Church. Clergymen and ministers were consequently required to deliver sermons upon themes associated with the duties of the Corporation.

Just how far apart Corporation and Church really were, however, becomes apparent from a closer study of the remaining 'Corporation' sermons, either published separately or reproduced in the local newspapers. They could be interpreted as evidence of a new religious sense of civic duty, an apotheosis of municipal responsibility, but this would ignore two crucial points. The first is that these were entirely artificial occasions. The services demanded some appropriate comment by the preachers on the work of the Corporation; the sermons were not spontaneous or gratuitous expressions of a deeply-held belief, but produced 'to order', and there is no evidence to support the view that on any other occasion preachers were ready to formulate a general religious basis for citizenship. The second point is that, after the 1880s, the content of the sermons in any case was entirely vague, and consisted of little more than weak comparisons between Christian and municipal life, or appeals to the council members to be aware of Christian duty. When the Rev Charles Lee preached on 'citizenship' at Christ Church in 1893, he could only conclude a discourse on the nature of 'God's City' with two distantly connected statements: 'And so, brethren, the disgrace and shame of the Commonwealth of God is the unbelief, the inconsistency and the sin of its members. Every citizen of this borough who goes abroad, or carries on his business or his pleasure away from home, carries the honour of this town with him.'[75] Preachers shied away from using religious insights to comment upon municipal issues. Canon White-Thomson also preached on 'citizenship' at the Parish Church in 1909, yet in effect he gave up the attempt to define it by reserving the conception entirely to an immaterial, transcendant plane: 'What, then, is the true meaning of an occasion like the present, interesting and important as it is in itself, but to acknowledge publicly that our citizenship is in Heaven, that all earthly authority and government is the type and shadow of heavenly things, that "the powers that be are ordained of God"?'[76] The extension of municipal authority and the politicised nature of municipal activity so defined the relationship of religion to the Corporation that the links clergymen and ministers drew could be no more than of the vaguest. The Corporation was not a religious institution, and it contained within it men of as wide a range of political and religious opinion as could be found in any town in England at this period. Consequently preachers had to remember that they could be addressing Liberals, Conservatives, even Labourites, and Nonconformists, Catholics and Anglicans amongst the members of the Council. In this context, the religious conception of 'civic duty' could only be one which carefully avoided an open pronouncement of opinion on municipal affairs. The most a preacher could do was appeal to a sense of unity, just as the Rev W. J. Jupp, preaching on the 'nobility of service', did at the Free Christian Church in 1907: 'If only a poor preacher could persuade men, he would plead with all sections and parties and churches in this borough to unite in combined action against the evils that are doing us all such serious wrong.'[77]

Municipal leadership, religion and the residential middle class

The municipal background to religious activity in Croydon in the late nineteenth century was a more heterogeneous one than had been the case in mid-century. The social base of the Council did not differ

[75] Rev C. Lee, *Citizenship* (Croydon 1893), p. 4.
[76] Canon L. J. White-Thompson, *Citizenship; a sermon preached before the Mayor and Corporation in the Parish Church, Croydon on Sunday 14th November 1909* (Croydon 1909), p. 5.
[77] W. J. Jupp, *The Nobility of Service* (Croydon 1907), p. 11.

significantly from that of the Board of Health:[78] local trading and professional interests predominated, and the 'commuting interest' represented only a small proportion of Council members up to the First World War. The religious colour of the Council was mixed, with Anglicanism tending to prevail over Nonconformity, but with religion scarcely an important factor in Council politics until the abolition of the School Board in 1902, when a Council motion to condemn Balfour's Act eventually passed by a narrow margin; in this instance, however, even religion did not play an all-determining part, as several Anglican Liberals supported the motion.[79] In any case, the very process which this section seeks to establish – the gradual separation of municipal from religious activism – makes it difficult to trace the religious affiliations of many councillors in the 1890s and 1900s, as fewer served on church committees or as church officers. It was in the political complexion of the municipal elite that change particularly occurred. Liberal control persisted until the early 1900s, though it is not known when a 'turning point' was reached.[80] Just as the Conservatives were gaining control, however, another change was occurring which was to make the old, covert party struggle of Conservatives versus Liberals irrelevant – the rise of the Labour Party. Labour had had one representative on the School Board from 1892, and had to wait until 1902 for their first municipal success; by 1906, at the peak of their pre-war strength in Croydon, they had five members on the Council. In fact from 1909 the movement declined locally, caught between the aspirations of the middle class progressives and socialists who produced many of its activists in the 1900s, and the local trade union movement which, artisan and small-production based, was much more accommodating towards Lib-Labism. By 1914 the number of Labour councillors had dropped to three.[81] Before the First World War Labour councillors were hardly in a position to form an influential part of the municipal elite. Their candidatures, however, did have the effect in the 1900s of galvanising the residential middle class into taking what, in local political terms, was an unusual course. Labour candidates were the first to stand in municipal elections on overt party tickets; by the mid-1900s their appearance had prompted the adoption of candidates by local

[78] Appendix 4, table 3.
[79] *C Ad*, 1 Nov. 1902.
[80] See tabulated election results compiled by the C Ref Lib.; unfortunately not all candidates' political affiliations are known, and the rise of ratepayers' associations in the 1900s, with their endorsal of candidates for Council elections, further complicates the matter.
[81] Tichelar, 'Labour Politics in Croydon', pp. 1–5.

ratepayers' associations determined to combat 'municipal social-ism'.[82] Conservatives and Liberals co-operated in this: by 1905 all non-Labour candidates were endorsed as ratepayers' candidates by the local associations, including respected figures in Croydon Liberalism like Henry Keatley Moore, son of one of the original pro-incorporation enthusiasts.[83] The strength of Labour in Croydon in the mid-1900s, which has been described as a product of the alliance of trade union organisation and suburban, intellectual progressive socialism,[84] consequently produced a typical 'suburban' response, a federation of Conservatives and Liberals explicitly concerned with resisting socialism.

Effectively excluded from municipal politics by the Council's concentration on non-religious issues (with the exception of the abolition of the School Board), and gradually squeezed out by the Council in some areas of activity, the hesitancy of clergymen to make pronouncements on municipal issues in the 1890s was confirmed by the controversies over the rise of Labour in the 1900s. Quite apart from this, however, the attractions of municipal responsibility and the scale of municipal business were drawing the municipal leadership further into municipal activity and away from an active role in the churches. Only a few exceptionally prestigious churches in the area retained the active support – defined by participation as leaders of church organisations and in church offices – of the municipal elite on a significant scale: the Parish Church, George Street Congregational Church and West Croydon Baptist Tabernacle. Elsewhere church offices and lay responsibility fell increasingly into the hands of the 'respectable' middle class who had no direct connection with municipal politics and who began therefore to form a separate lay elite within congregations. The original church building committee of the ritualist church of St Augustine's, formed in 1880, had included a chairman of the School Board, the Rev G. Roberts, Croydon's second mayor, John Cooper, and John Berney, a prominent local architect who filled several parochial offices in mid-century.[85] Nearly twenty years later, in 1898, when a committee of five gentlemen and seven ladies was formed to supervise the church's completion fund, none of the gentlemen were prominent townsmen, and neither, for that matter, were any of the ladies related or married to prominent townsmen.[86] By the 1900s none of the active laymen whose names I have been able to trace at St James and at St John the Evangelist,

[82] Council election results, C Ref Lib.
[83] Moore was elected for the relatively affluent East Ward in 1902: *ibid*.
[84] Tichelar, 'Labour Politics in Croydon', p. 7.
[85] Minutes of the Church Building Committee of St Augustine's, 1880–1914.
[86] Minute Book of the Church Completion Fund, St Augustine's, 1898.

Upper Norwood were municipal leaders.[87] Likewise, with the exception of some candidates chosen at the Parish Church, none of the representatives chosen at various Anglican churches for the Ruri-Decanal Conference whose names I have been able to trace were prominent townsmen.[88] The diaconate and elders of Nonconformist churches by the 1900s were only rarely containing active, prominent townsmen. At the affluent, middle class Presbyterian church of St Paul's in South Croydon, for example, of the twelve elders and nineteen deacons of the church between its inception in 1901 and 1914, none were leading municipal figures and none served on the Council.[89] The same was true of many chapels built in suburban districts outside the town centre – at the Baptist Church at Woodside,[90] at Brighton Road Baptist Church,[91] and at Enmore Road Congregational Church, for example.[92] This is not, of course, to say that the municipal leadership was ceasing to attend church or ceasing to take an interest in religion – there is no direct evidence to support such a view – but it is to say that it was ceasing to play an active role in running churches, and was choosing to concentrate their time and attention on municipal matters.

It is not possible to indicate a precise turning point in the process by which Croydon's municipal leaders gradually drew apart from religious activism; the development of church organisations, described in chapter three, and the parallel inception and development of municipal action suggest that the 1880s marked the real beginning of the change, though its effects were still working themselves out in the 1900s. A figure like Sir Frederick Edridge is a sign of continuing complexities at the Parish Church. In 1887, the year his father died, he gave up his office as churchwarden at the Parish Church and took over his father's position as chairman of the magistrate's bench; two years later he joined the Council, was elected mayor the following year, and held that office on another four occasions thereafter; he continued to act as one of the most prestigious Anglicans in Croydon, sitting on various ad hoc church committees in the 1890s, and later again taking up the active responsibilities of the churchwardenship.[93]

---

[87] St James Vestry Minutes, ii (1899–1957); St John the Evangelist Vestry Minutes, 1876–1926, and Church Council Minutes 1905–20.
[88] This assertion is based on names assembled from parish magazines.
[89] 'The Pauline', magazine of St Paul's Presbyterian Church, 1901–14, *passim*.
[90] Woodside Baptist Church Meeting Minutes, i, 1899–1904; ii, 1904–8; iii, 1908–28.
[91] Brighton Road Baptist Church Meeting Minutes, ii, 1900–15.
[92] Enmore Road Congregational Church, Church Meeting Minutes, iii, 1902–4; iv, 1904–8; v, 1912–3.
[93] Details assembled from *C Chron* and *C Ad*, *passim*; for Edridge's membership of the archbishop's 1897 committee to investigate the spiritual needs of Croydon, see esp.

However Edridge was exceptional. The withdrawal of councillors and other municipal leaders from church activity, gradual as it was, may have had an impact on churches in the form of dwindling financial resources, but it is extremely difficult to positively prove such an assertion. What it did mean was that, locally at least, religion was ceasing to occupy the central position of prestige and power it had held in mid-century. Failure to hold on to the active loyalty of those influential in town politics and municipal affairs meant that, in the last resort, churches were ceasing to convince the town elite that they were necessary and effective organs of local control. They were losing status and role to the Corporation.

If the town elite in mid-century tended to provide churchwardens, committee members, deacons and elders for the churches in Croydon, it was the residential middle class that provided the backbone of Anglican and Nonconformist congregations. It was this class which the *Croydon Chronicle* had in mind when, in 1860, it said of Croydon: 'It is rapidly becoming a huge dormitory for the merchant princes of London.'[94] Yet the residential middle class itself was subject to the same process of specialisation which was tending, by late century, to pull apart municipal leaders and religious activists; the potential urban constituency of the churches was consequently becoming increasingly fractured, and whilst there was as yet no positive withdrawal from church life by the middle class, the churches were becoming increasingly isolated and forced to adapt to an ever more specialised role in urban society.

The typical bodies through which the local aspirations of the residential middle class were expressed by the end of the nineteenth century were ratepayers' associations. These were a different kind of organisation from the short-lived Croydon associations established in 1867 and again in 1876 to monitor the actions of the Board of Health, which had drawn very much upon the support of disaffected members of the town elite and had not sought to express the opinion of a particular locality,[95] for they were strictly local, yet broader in their aims and support. Their origin almost certainly lay in the developing dissatisfaction of suburban settlements with the quality of service provided by the town authorities from the late 1850s.[96] The local associations of the 1880s and 1890s, the ancestors of the permanent

C Chron, 8 May 1897; see also J. Dixon (ed.), *The Church in the Community: a record of the life and work of Croydon Parish Church* (Croydon 1971), p. 34.
[94] *C Chron*, 9 June 1860.
[95] See pp. 148–50.
[96] The most vociferous of these settlements was Norwood; for example, for the support of Norwood residents for the separation of the suburb from Croydon and its formation as an independent rating authority, see *C Chron*, 30 May 1858.

associations established throughout Croydon by 1914, were relatively short-lived too, generally thrown up by specific issues such as the Free Libraries campaign or the movement to redevelop the town centre.[97] A proposal by the Metropolitan Asylums Board to build a convalescent fever hospital at Norwood in 1893, for example, frightened residents concerned about their own health and the value of property in the area sufficiently to bring a concerted campaign of opposition from the Upper Norwood Ratepayers' Association, the Thornton Heath Ratepayers' Association, and a South Norwood Ratepayers' Association.[98] Yet in 1902, ten years later, local papers reported residents at South Norwood holding a public meeting to form a Ratepayers' Association, as if one had never existed.[99] Some idea of the aims of these local associations – predecessors of the web of highly organised residential associations Peter Saunders found in Croydon in the 1970s[100] – can be gained from the rules of the permanent association formed on the residential estate of Addiscombe in 1896, which typically defined its objects as 'To secure energetic advocacy of the views of the ratepayers upon the County Council, Board of Guardians, and School Board. To foster and promote public opinion on affairs generally affecting the district.'[101] The final, permanent establishment of ratepayers' associations in every part of the Borough came in the 1900s; the result was to make effective electioneering on sensitive issues possible. By the mid-1900s these associations were openly endorsing non-Labour candidates for the Council; in 1903, for example, the Central Ward Ratepayers' Association adopted Councillor Price and Mr David Waller as their candidates in open opposition to the Labour party and, as Councillor Pelton argued, on the grounds that 'In the Central Ward the majority were traders, and they desired that those who represented them should be traders and sympathise with them.'[102] Although the associations were often headed by councillors, and of course it made sense for would-be councillors to be seen to be responsive to their aims, their defensive, localised nature made close co-operation difficult and, from the point of view of the councillor, undesirable.

---

[97] Cox, 'Urban Development and Redevelopment', p. 240; it seems likely, for example, that the Thornton Heath Ratepayers' Association was formed around the time of the Free Libraries campaign, probably in direct oposition to it: Ward's *Croydon Directory*, 1889.

[98] Memoranda and petitions of residents at Upper Norwood, South Norwood and Thornton Heath: 'Grange Wood' folder at C Ref Lib.

[99] *C Ad*, 19 Nov. 1902.

[100] P. Saunders, *Urban Politics: a sociological interpretation* (London 1979), pp. 239–44.

[101] Rules of the Addiscombe Ratepayers' Association, George Clinch papers, C Ref Lib.

[102] *C Ad*, 10 Oct. 1903.

They never became, and were never meant to be, machines for the systematic achievement of progressive municipal reform.

Underlying the formation and activity of the ratepayers' associations was a quite distinct suburban middle class view of municipal affairs which was a far cry from the municipal progressivism of many of the members of the municipal elite in this period, and which could act as a brake on council activity, as it did over the issue of Free Libraries. The key was local taxation: the near-contradictory demands of suburban residents for efficient services with low rates could only be resolved (at least in theory) by a council highly efficient in its organisation and operation; consequently rises in the rates occasioned by programmes of municipal activity (which in themselves often had substantial ratepayers' support) led to allegations of extravagance and sometimes corruption on the part of the Council. The South Croydon Ratepayers' Association's annual dinner in 1902 presented the amusing spectacle of a string of speakers calling for special services (including a swimming bath, a library and a branch of the Polytechnic) for the ward, promptly followed by enthusiastic applause for a call to keep the rates down, when Alderman Taylor introduced the sober reflection that: 'Croydon was a scattered borough, and no doubt the outlying districts would like to have many things, but these meant the Corporation undertaking very large expenses. The loans were going up, and it would be impossible, he was afraid, to keep the rates at the present amount.'[103]

The dual aspect of suburban sensitivity over municipal issues – the desire, on the one hand, to keep rates low, balanced on the other by criticism of inadequate services and poor sanitary conditions – can be traced through the struggle over burial grounds, the movement to establish public baths in Croydon in the 1860s, the controversy over recreation grounds, the incorporation campaign, the Free Libraries' campaign and the Croydon Improvement Bill, surfacing above all in the 1900s with the opposition to 'municipal socialism'. It conditioned a scepticism of corporation action, thus emphasising the gap between members of the town elite and the residential middle class. It also had the effect of pulling middle class interest away from the churches as effective local organs of social and political action, as in some of these disputes – burial grounds, libraries, education – church action itself seemed to be tainted by partisan interest, and ratepayers' associations, aside from their anti-Labour stance, were as yet non-party political and non-religious organisations. The only case I have been able to discover of a church actively proposing a candidate for a municipal election in the 1900s occurred in 1907, when St John the

---

[103] *Ibid.*, 20 Dec. 1902.

Evangelist, at the prompting of Croydon Church Defence Committee, put forward Stanley Jones for Upper Norwood ward: it is perhaps of some significance that Jones was not adopted as a candidate by the Ratepayers' Association and, in the event, did not stand at all.[104] It is the essence of a suburb that those who live there do not work there; in giving institutional expression to the relative lack of interest of the residential middle class in the local affairs of a borough in which they passed only part of their time, and by concentrating on the specific issues of services and rates, the ratepayers' associations seemed to confirm the separation of municipal from religious issues. Religious organisations, with their notion that religion was the motivating force for effective social action, a belief to which a proportionately diminishing number of residents could actively subscribe, were left stranded.

[104] St John the Evangelist, Church Council Minutes, 22 Nov. 1907.

8

Conclusion: A Crisis in the Church?

The essence of the argument of this book concerns the appropriation and manipulation of power by middle class groups in the Victorian town, and relies on the assumption that, in mid-century, the political ambitions of the middle class were intimately connected with their religious beliefs, which formed the base of their social and moral conceptions of the world. The sectarian basis of local politics this implied has become widely accepted as a feature of Victorian urban life, from small country towns to large industrial conurbations.[1] To my knowledge it has not been argued that religion was the sole determinant of political loyalties, but rather that religion was one important influence upon political behaviour and, in this sense, was part of a matrix which also included economic interest, national identity and class loyalty. If there were distinctive features in Croydon's history which sharpened the relationship between religion and municipal life identified in this book, then the timescale and perhaps the outcome of these local, sectarian struggles would have been different elsewhere. Nevertheless the same essential processes were at work elsewhere: the discrediting of religion as a basis of local, united political action; the perceived failure of philanthropic endeavour; the dislodging of religion from its central, functional role in society; the rise of alternative agencies, particularly reformed local government; and the gradual emergence of a more limited social role for the churches. This is true even of towns which, by mid-century, had seemingly non-religious governing authorities, for here religion remained a controversial feature of local social and political life.[2] Croydon's religious history was not markedly different from that of other London boroughs.[3] Due to its historic connections with

---

[1] For example, B. H. Harrison and B. Trinder, *Drink and Sobriety in an Early Victorian County Town: Banbury 1830–1860*, EHR Special Supplement 4 (1969); P. T. Phillips, *The Sectarian Spirit: sectarianism, society and politics in Victorian cotton towns* (Toronto 1982); also D. Fraser, *Urban Politics in Victorian England* (Leicester 1976); oral evidence for sectarianism is examined in McLeod, 'New Perspectives'.

[2] Vincent argued that the impact of religion on political behaviour actually increased significantly in the middle decades of the century: J. R. Vincent, *The Formation of the British Liberal Party, 1857–68* (London 1966; pelican edn. 1972), pp. 21–2.

[3] For a collection of essays on the recent religious history of a number of southern towns, see *Southern History*, iii (1981), esp. B. I. Coleman, 'Southern England in the

the see of Canterbury and to extensive church ownership of land within its boundaries, Croydon was admittedly an area dominated by Anglicanism in the first half of the Victorian period, and this was reflected in the local battles over church rate. However its religious development in the course of the century was analogous to that of other parts of London, and certainly by the early 1900s its religious life was broadly in line with the picture for London as a whole.[4] Similarly, there is no evidence to suggest that the history of Croydon's middle class was significantly out of line with other urban and suburban areas. It had a reputation as an affluent commuter suburb in the second half of the century, but in fact it was entering a period of gradual social decline by the end of the nineteenth century; the peak of its affluence probably lay somewhere in the 1860s, later than that of an area such as Lambeth and earlier than that of an area such as Hampstead, for example.[5] Thus, despite the distinctive features of its social and religious life and its economy, Victorian Croydon was broadly assimilated into social and demographic trends for London as a whole.[6]

Incorporation certainly did polarise arguments and radically transform the local government of Croydon, because it offered Liberal-Nonconformists an opportunity of breaking the log-jam in local improvement, and in this way the situation in Croydon may have been especially acute. However some of the individual stages of the argument of this book may be coupled with references to the work of other historians to show how the essential elements did occur elsewhere. The incorporation movement in Croydon grew out of Nonconformist and Liberal criticism of church rates and the parochial system; the same kinds of campaign have been traced for mid-century in many other towns and cities in England, with the same implication that religion was discredited as a basis of social and political authority.[7] The rise of alternative institutions of government at the local level is similarly well charted elsewhere; Stephen Yeo's study of religious and voluntary organisations in Reading, for example, argued that municipal power was becoming the real fulcrum of social and political life in the area, though his argument might have carried even more force had he depicted the churches as

census of religious worship, 1851'; also W. N. Yates, 'The major Kentish Towns in the religious census of 1851', *Archaelogica Cantiana*, ciii (1986).
[4] Mudie Smith, *Religious Life*.
[5] J. Roebuck, *Urban Development in Nineteenth Century London: Lambeth, Battersea and Wandsworth 1838–1888* (Chichester 1979), ch. 8; Thompson, *Hampstead*, ch. 8.
[6] For example, P. J. Waller, *Town, City and Nation: England 1850–1914* (Oxford 1983), pp. 2–3, 165.
[7] Ward, *Religion and Society*; Inglis, *Churches and the Working Classes*; Fraser, *Urban Politics*.

one-time overseers of certain functions as well as 'private economic' interests: 'Gradually, however, functions which had been the preserve and focus of competitive fights between private economic interests came under municipal control, and the municipality increased its visibility by initiating rate-financed projects. A particular version of "community" came into being.'[8] There are, as yet, few studies of Victorian municipal ceremonial; however, Cannadine's study of the Colchester Oyster Feast identified the 1880s to 1913 as the peak period of the feast's pageantry and corporation munificence, and this accords well with the picture of local interest in municipal affairs identified in late Victorian Croydon.[9]

Though not on the whole so well documented, there are signs, moreover, that the connections I have made between the emergence and elaboration of municipal government in late Victorian Britain and the increasingly circumscribed, self-regarding role of the churches can be established elsewhere. Hugh McLeod, for example, has asserted of London that 'Now (by 1885) the association between religion and civic duty was beginning to weaken. The Churches were slowly returning towards a sectarian position.'[10] F. M. L. Thompson, in his study of the processes of suburban growth in Hampstead, was even more explicit, though he shunted the decisive change forwards into the twentieth century:

> [The] complete separation between the civil parish and the religious organisation of its inhabitants both made the divorce between secular and ecclesiastical aspects of parish administration unavoidable, and in the long run helped to make it possible for some kind of municipal existence and sense of community to grow through the work of the civil parish. In the short run, however, until at least the closing years of the nineteenth century, it was the ecclesiastical districts which reflected much more closely the social realities of an area with a number of local communities that happened to lie in a single administrative jurisdiction.[11]

Thompson's slightly later timescale – the turn of the century – is an illustration that the underlying processes of change were widespread, but that the pace of change was affected by local factors too, in this case the inclusion of Hampstead within the London County Council

[8] Yeo, 'Religion in Society', p. 79.
[9] D. Cannadine, 'The transformation of civic ritual in modern Britain: the Colchester Oyster Feast', *Past and Present*, xciv (1982).
[10] D. H. McLeod, 'Membership and Influence of the Churches in Metropolitan London, 1885–1914', unpubl. PhD thesis, Cambridge 1971, p. v.
[11] Thompson, *Hampstead*, p. 389.

and the high social status of the borough, with its consequent strong leaning towards Anglicanism. Quoted by Jeffrey Cox in his study of religious decline in Lambeth, the president of the Wesleyan Methodist Conference in 1890 pointed to a further feature of the argument I have advanced, namely the withdrawal of influential laity from church activism in the late nineteenth century and their increasing preoccupation with municipal affairs: 'In the early days of Methodism influential laymen used to preach . . . Amongst men of culture and social position the practice of preaching has declined. Such men prefer civic duties today, and when they occupy public position with dignity and honour, we rejoice with all our hearts; still we urge our educated young laymen to listen to the call of God.'[12] Cox, moreover, also establishes the link between the failure of voluntarist action promoted by the churches and the rise of alternative institutions of government which I have argued formed part of the context of the declining moral authority of the church at the turn of the century:

> The nineteenth century churches were very flexible in responding to demands for social services of all sorts, but their limited entrepreneurial success led them to assume far more responsibility than they could reasonably claim – for education, for supplemental poor relief, for entertainment, for individual character, for social cohesion. In the late nineteenth and the early twentieth century, many individuals decided that the churches were not up to the task, or what is more important, that their definition of the task had become irrelevant or nonsensical. In virtually every sphere of activity, the churches found that they were competing with a more specialised institution and they were generally (with some exceptions) eager to hand over responsibility to a more effective body.[13]

This quotation helps to pinpoint an important implication of the argument, namely the key importance of notions of the 'local' context of church action. Cox in fact does little more than draw a parallel between the 'failure' of voluntarist and church action and the rise of the welfare state, and assume a connection of some sort as churches were replaced in various fields by state action; he is impressed by the expansion of central state initiative but does not explain the connections between the trends he has described. The argument put forward in this book focuses instead on the rise of the 'local' state, or

[12] Cox, *Churches in a Secular Society*, p. 24.
[13] *Ibid.*, p. 182.

175

rather on changes in the composition and structure of local government, and argues for a connection with what was happening in the churches (aside from the general pressures of urbanisation which obviously had differentiated effects on various kinds of organisation, both secular and religious) by reference to the behaviour of those elite groups active in the churches and municipal life. The evidence for any positive impact on church life by central state initiatives before the First World War is very slender; the response of churches to the reforms of the post-1906 Liberal governments was cautious, neither strongly for nor against. At Christ Church, for example, the vicar alleged that the Insurance Act 'interfered with our liberty', but admitted that it was the duty of Christians to give their local backing to a law which 'teaches and enforces thrift'.[14] Few other churches seem to have commented on the change, and there is no evidence of any serious inroads upon church activity by these parliamentary initiatives before 1914. Quite simply the long-term implications of the legislation were probably not foreseen by Christians of all denominations in the area. The prestige and vitality of late Victorian municipal life owed something, then, to the non-interfering stance of central government; for this reason local political and religious disputes were of greater immediate significance for religion in the area than they would be today. The vicissitudes of the churches in nineteenth century Britain may be understood only in an analysis which takes account of specific local factors – and the contours of church action in a locality – as well as the intellectual and high political issues on which many historians have previously concentrated.

It needs to be stressed at this point that it is not argued here that the 'decline' of religion in late Victorian and Edwardian England is accountable solely or even largely in terms of the rise of reformed local government. It is recognised that there is, in any case, a difficulty in establishing precisely the pattern of causation underlying the changes described in this book. At one level, for example, it may be arguable that the failure of religious, philanthropic action prompted the middle class to take a greater interest in municipal reform, which in turn undermined the social role of the churches and engineered a crisis in religious organisations. On another level it is at least possible that a real decline in middle class interest in religion was caused by intellectual arguments over the truth of traditional Christianity, and that this in turn fuelled the gradual transfer of middle class interest elsewhere. The problem is most acute when trying to pinpoint the timing of these changes, for it is impossible to be certain at what point in the late nineteenth century changing

[14] Christ Church Parish Magazine, Aug. 1912.

intellectual fashions really began to impinge at the local level upon middle class churchgoers. Establishing a priority of causation with any degree of certainty is thus impossible. The patterns of causation were no doubt highly complex. What can be said is that, in addition to the threat of the intellectual and cultural changes identified by other historians, the churches were also vulnerable in the Victorian period because they carried so many of the aspirations of urban society: their perceived failure to put these aspirations into effect, and the attractiveness of the alternative method of local control, municipal government, drew local leaders away from active church involvement into a quite different, separate sphere of action.

The impact of urbanisation on organised religion remains a contentious issue in British historiography. Until recently, study of the subject appears to have been dominated by a broad consensus that the nineteenth century was a period of stasis and decline for the churches, a consensus which concealed considerable differences about the precise nature of the link between industrialisation, urbanisation and religion in Britain, and contained much uncertainty or confusion about the timing of change. C.G. Brown has launched a determined attack on what he has described as the 'pessimist' school of thought, namely the view that urbanisation necessarily and directly led to the secularisation of British society.[15] Brown's argument emphasises the evidence for increasing per capita church attendance for most of the nineteenth century, effectively denies any intrinsic linkage between urbanisation and secularisation, and pushes the visible evidence of secularisation back into the late nineteenth century, from about the 1880s; he refers approvingly to Jeffrey Cox's denial of decline before 1870, and in turn his work is cited approvingly by Robin Gill in his *Competing Convictions*.[16] The emphases of this book are broadly compatible with Brown's view: several alternative explanations of decline which seem to imply inevitability are rejected as total explanations, though not necessarily as partial ones, in favour of a view which sees decline as arising from specific local controversies; particular prominence is given to sectarian rivalry in these controversies; and, above all, the chronology of decline hinges on the late Victorian and Edwardian period. However there is some need for conceptual clarification. It is easy to attack notions of urbanisation, secularisation and decline if they are described in over-simplistic, monolithic terms, and certainly some of the proponents of the 'pessimist' school are guilty of doing that. Brown's understanding of decline appears to be one which focuses entirely on the visible

---

[15] C. G. Brown, 'Did urbanization secularize Britain?', *Urban History Yearbook* (1988).
[16] *Ibid.*, p. 1; Gill, *Competing Convictions*, p. 119.

evidence of religious commitment, church attendance, whereas I have tried to dissect some of the changes in function and status which accompanied decline; the roots of these changes clearly lie further back in the century. Brown, Cox and Gill all in their own way acknowledge that some form of 'secularisation' has occurred in modern Britain, but they have different ways of explaining it and, interestingly, slightly different timescales: Gill's data, drawn from rural parishes in which depopulation was occurring, naturally suggests decline from around the 1850s and 1860s, whereas Cox and Brown tend to see the last decades of the century as marking the change. While accepting, then, on his terms the force of Brown's revision of earlier ascriptions of religious decline to urbanisation per se, nevertheless these differences are themselves signs of a lack of consensus on what to put in their place. I use the phrase 'on his own terms' here, because it seems to me that if, by 'urbanisation', one means simply the concentration of population in cities, then it follows that a link between urbanisation and religious decline for most of the nineteenth century may be rejected. However, if the term is used both in a broader sense to denote the transformation of an entire society into one in which the majority of its people live in towns and cities, with all the social and economic changes that process entails, and in a historical sense (rather than a loose, sociological sense) to denote specific changes in Britain, then the link remains an important one, even though as an explanatory device it is not sufficient on its own.

The conflicts, trends and relationships described here were not a necessary aspect of some monolithic process which may be called 'urbanisation'. Certain of them – 'democratisation' and the prevalence of non-interventionist principles in central government policy, for example – were obviously such as to owe much to extra-local historical conditions, the 'British experience' of the nineteenth century, and in the form in which they were found in Britain would not be discovered elsewhere in the world anyway. The coincidence of such notions with a particular phase of national economic and demographic growth was not therefore a phenomenon which can with any confidence be used to describe general aspects of a relationship between religion and urban change. The argument does, nevertheless, carry general implications for 'secularisation' as it has occurred in Britain. It suggests that the indices of growth and decline habitually used to measure the performance of a church – attendance and membership – are insufficient and often misleading guides to the real status of organised religion: what has to be taken into account as well are the actual functions a church is performing, the demands for the provision of welfare services by churches, and whether there is

CONCLUSION

any shortfall between expectations and possibilities on either side. It also suggests that the roots of decline are not to be sought solely in changing patterns of belief as such, but in the relocation of the social role of the church to catering for a specialised category of citizenry, the religiously-susceptible, and that this process was in part a corollary of the forms of action adopted first by local government and later by central government to tackle social problems which were felt most acutely in urbanising areas. It also implies that these remedies were adopted ultimately because the widening of the franchise created a force, public opinion, which could in the last resort override most entrenched, partisan interests, and which therefore bypassed one of the most intractable problems of voluntarist action, namely the need of a minority to persuade a sufficient number of people to follow their cause. The interaction identified here occurred over a long period, yet there was a turning point in the 1880s, with parliamentary and local government reform, a renewal of interest in the problem of the urban poor and the consequent taking on by Nonconformist and Anglican churches of a series of missionary, charitable and administrative ventures. By the 1890s there were clear signs of a deepening sense of crisis in the church.

Despite the massive 'institutional revival' identified by some writers as one of the most important features of the religious history of Victorian England, by the 1900s a sense of failure was widespread amongst all the denominations.[17] In 1889 the vicar of Christ Church had complained that:

Wordly attractions and amusements, for such they are, are alluring the young away from God's house and worship. And when one realises that these young persons who now can with difficulty be persuaded to remain in a Sunday School or Bible Class at the age of thirteen or fourteen, but prefer riding about on Sunday on a Bicycle, or Tram, or Omnibus, will in a few years be the Parents of another generation, one's heart sinks at the thought of what our English Sabbath will become. I see it in all directions, among all classes, and I grieve to say among Churchgoers.[18]

He was sufficiently concerned to organise monthly prayer meetings on 'the crisis in the Church' in the following year for the whole of Croydon.[19] The vicar of St Mary Magdalene in the middle class district of Addiscombe was equally disillusioned, admitting that 'the

[17] Cox, *Churches in a Secular Society*, p. 273, and followed by Parsons and Moore, *Religion in Victorian Britain: Traditions*, pp. 5–12.
[18] Christ Church Parish Magazine, Oct. 1899.
[19] *Ibid.*, Feb. 1900.

spirit of the age is evidently against church attendance. There are fortunate exceptions here and there, but, speaking generally, there is a steady decline along the whole line'.[20] In 1903 the vicar of St Matthew's drew stark conclusions from the findings of the Mudie Smith religious census of London, and while he held it up as a challenge to Christians, he admitted that 'there is an inevitable, if gradual, lowering of the spiritual character where contact with definite religious influences has ceased'.[21] Nor was the perception of decline one restricted to Anglicans alone. At George Street Congregational Chapel, itself 'successful' in terms of the numbers it continued to attract before the First World War, the Rev Major Scott was also pessimistic about the 'spirit of the age', and asked his congregation the taxing question; 'What is the ideal attitude of the Church towards the spiritual travail of the age? Ought it to be one of antagonism or acquiescence?'[22] Nonconformist optimism was buoyed up in the mid-1900s by the Liberal victory of 1906 and the potential triumphs it seemed to offer for 'political Nonconformity', but by the end of the decade widespread pessimism was setting in. 'This quarterly meeting deeply laments the connexional decrease and is especially humbled as having contributed to it' was the resolution passed by the Quarterly Meeting of the Primitive Methodist circuit in September 1911.[23] South Norwood Baptist Church was ironically commenting by 1913 that those who attributed the poor attendance at Bible Classes in the summer to holidays seemed to think that 'some lucky fellows have very long holidays'.[24] By this time it was clear from words the Anglican Rev A. J. Easter addressed to his congregation at St Matthew's that this view of 'crisis' was a general one; he spoke of Elijah's grief when he felt that the cause of God had failed: 'Some of you here tonight know something of similar grief over what appears to be the decay of religion. As you watch the religious neglect which is sweeping like a flood through the young life of England, you may wonder whether Christianity is not doomed to extinction.'[25]

Despite the apparent wealth of testimony which exists in this period about the 'crisis' in the churches, the situation in fact was a more complex and variegated one than the bald statements of contemporaries seem to imply. The acid tests of a church's success, attendance and membership figures, are patchy and inconclusive, and sometimes suggest contrary conclusions. The evidence of Easter

[20] St Mary Magdalene Parish Magazine, May 1900.
[21] St Matthew's Parish Magazine, Jan. 1903.
[22] Rev W. Major Scott, *The George Street Congregational Church Pulpit*, Aug. 1912.
[23] Croydon Primitive Methodist Circuit, Quarterly Meeting Minutes, 4 Sep. 1911.
[24] South Norwood Holmesdale Road Baptist Church Magazine, Aug. 1913.
[25] Rev A. J. T. Easter, *God's Light Upon Earth's Problems: six sermons* (Croydon 1911), p. 12.

communicant figures shows that few Anglican churches were keeping pace with population growth in their districts from around the 1890s, if not earlier, though fewer still registered absolute decline in numbers before 1914. At Christ Church, for example, where the Rev O. B. Byers and his successor regularly complained about the falling away of the faithful, communicants' figures were still rising to 1912, as they were at St Stephen's, Norbury and at St Augustine's, South Croydon.[26] Certainly there is little positive evidence to suggest an absolute decline in attendances, although most (admittedly patchy) indices suggest a situation of slow growth or near-stasis throughout the 1900s. At St Michael and All Angels, for example, figures available for 1901 to 1906 suggest a 'decline' from a total annual figure of 10,420 acts of communion to 9,632, yet the figures in the intervening years fluctuated, with a high mark of 10,715 in 1904-5.[27] There is no evidence to suggest that High Churches fared any better or worse than Low Churches, though statements about the crisis of religion seem to have been typical of evangelical clergy above all: their pessimistic view might well have been affected by the success of the High Church in establishing itself as an accceptable religious tradition within the Church of England.

The picture – again working from inadequate figures – is only a little more clear-cut for Nonconformist churches. Certain churches were able to attract increasing membership right up to the First World War: these were the handful of prestigious Nonconformist churches, such as George Street Chapel for Congregationalists and West Croydon Tabernacle for Baptists, where the following built up by James Archer Spurgeon formed the solid basis of growth under his successor in the 1900s. The historian of George Street Chapel, indeed, called the years of Major Scott's pastorate before 1914 the 'zenith' of the chapel's prosperity.[28] T. I. Stockley's pastorate at West Croydon Tabernacle was similarly described as 'a period of reaping, and, in the immediate pre war years, of consolidating the gains of the early years of his ministry'.[29] Elsewhere in Croydon evidence on the whole suggests static or falling membership in the pre-war years. This was so at South Norwood Congregational Church, for example, where growth to the pre-war peak of 160 members in 1908 gave way to a steady decline to 120 by 1914.[30] It was also the case at Boston Road Baptist Mission Chapel, where the high-point of the church's

---

[26] Christ Church Parish Magazine, Annual Report for 1911 (1912); St Stephen's Parish Magazine, 1908-1914; St Augustine's Parish Magazine, 1900-1914, *passim*.
[27] St Michael and All Angels, 35th Annual Address and Statement of Accounts, 1906.
[28] Raymer, *The Congregational Church*, p. 33.
[29] Anon., *One Hundred Years*.
[30] Statistical chart in anon., *South Norwood Congregational Church*, p. 29.

history had been reached back in 1888.[31] Primitive Methodists entered a period of decline in 1911, national as well as local; Quakers seem to have done so well before, sometime in the 1870s.[32] Too few figures have been found for Wesleyan Methodists and Presbyterians to warrrant even tentative conclusions. The national figures collected by Currie, Gilbert and Horsley would suggest a 'turning point' for Baptists and Congregationalists around 1908–9, and this would tie in fairly well with impressionistic evidence relating to perceptions of decline from the late 1900s and the years immediately before 1914.[33]

The Croydon evidence, despite sketchy figures, does suggest several conclusions. The first is that all denominations were seriously falling behind population growth in the late Victorian period. One explanation of the apparent contradiction of conviction of decline with sustained gradual growth in some churches would be the simple fact that expansion was largely due to the children of existing church followers becoming themselves adult members.[34] Second, churches were only 'doing well' in terms of growth in this period where they commanded special prestige (and could attract impressive preachers), or where they were situated in areas where the population was expanding particularly quickly. Third, stagnation or decline was above all to be found in parts of Croydon where the population was increasing yet was changing in social composition, 'lowering' the status of the districts concerned to lower middle class and artisan, and in these areas Nonconformity was faring as badly as Anglicanism. The overall impression is of an ebb tide of church attendance, punctuated here and there by a few solid rocks of continued growth. Yet, as McLeod pointed out, even 'successful' churches probably achieved growth at the expense of surrounding churches.[35]

The ambiguity of the figures, however, belies the real pattern of decline, because they obscure the way in which the meaning of church attendance was changing. For a church to perceive decline in status, influence and attraction, it is not actually necessary for the congregation to contract at all, if the character of the commitment made by attenders is changing. This was what was happening in late Victorian urban society. In the crucial areas of manpower and money – tangible resources, in other words – decline was much more serious

[31] Anon., *Boston Road Mission*.
[32] See p. 41.
[33] Currie, Gilbert and Horsley, *Churches and Churchgoers*, pp. 147–51.
[34] See, for example, K. D. Brown's assertion that, in Nonconformity, 'Growth was increasingly a matter of natural increase from within the indigenous nonconformist community': *A Social History of the Nonconformist Ministry in England and Wales 1800–1930* (Oxford 1988), p. 53.
[35] McLeod, 'Membership and Influence', pp. 115–16.

than the attendance figures would seem to suggest, and these were areas in which the minister was especially likely to feel a sense of loss. In many Anglican parishes by the 1900s there were serious shortages of men and women willing to serve as district visitors and Sunday school teachers, for example. In 1906 the vicar of St James pointed out that ten districts in his parish were now without a visitor, and that this was especially serious since 'it is almost impossible for the clergy to begin to get into touch with a very large number of those to whom they should minister'.[36] Similar, serious shortages were regularly reported in the late 1890s and 1900s at Holy Trinity, St John's, Upper Norwood, Christ Church, St Luke's, Woodside and St Mary Magdalene, Addiscombe, to name but a few.[37] Even at St Augustine's, where the vicar was proud of the team of visitors he had built up, vacancies were regularly advertised from the mid-1900s.[38] Parochial finances faced similar problems. The number of communicants at St Augustine's doubled in ten years from 1902 to 1912, but the total yield of the offertories increased in the same period only by little over a third.[39] Most of the church charities and societies were in regular financial trouble at Christ Church in the 1900s; in 1905 the vicar was complaining that 'But for the SALE OF WORK it would be absolutely impossible to keep our present parochial machinery at work'.[40] Nonconformist churches were also in a serious position, and even more reliant upon the generosity of the congregation for maintenance than were, in the main, Anglican churches. Portland Road Primitive Methodist Church, for example, operating with an extremely slender budget which balanced annually around an average figure of about £50 from 1900, for every year after 1906 until 1918 except one recorded a deficit.[41] Even when attendance and membership figures were rising, ministers were not able to draw a proportionate increase in resources from their congregations.

There was a national dimension to the problem. The widespread belief of clergymen and ministers around the turn of the century that organised religion was undergoing a 'crisis' was influenced by national debates on the subject. Evangelicals, for example, could read the advance of liberal theology as a sign of decay. Yet the same argument would have been plausible earlier in the century, given the

---

[36] St James' Parish Magazine, Aug. 1906.
[37] Parish magazines of Holy Trinity, St John the Evangelist, Christ Church, St Luke's and St Mary Magdalene, *passim*.
[38] St Augustine's Parish Magazine, Jan. 1904 ff.
[39] *Ibid.*
[40] Christ Church Parish Magazine, 53rd Annual Report, 1905.
[41] Croydon Primitive Methodist Circuit, Portland Road Chapel, Treasurer's Accounts 1891–1922, *passim*.

intensity of doctrinal conflict and the acute fears of churches that they had 'lost' the working class, so it is clear that the context in which these debates were set had changed. The social groups on whom the churches had very much relied for practical and financial support were, by the end of the century, withdrawing from an active role in church life, and moving into municipal politics and other specialised agencies instead. The 'crisis' of the church, such as it was, was therefore as much as anything a product of the structural relocation of religion away from its assumed supremacy as the central active force in community affairs to a particular role earmarked as 'spiritual', decisively separated from other areas of local life. Before the First World War this change was hardly reflected in attendance figures: it was of enormous significance for the future of the churches, however, because it defined even more narrowly the parameters within which church action would be seen to be relevant, and gradually reduced the sources of material support available to churches. Alternative social, political and leisure facilities began to seem more important and more attractive than organised religion to an increasing proportion of the population.

In Croydon incorporation in 1883 put an end to the claims of Anglicanism to act as the focus of community loyalties. The Corporation naturally usurped the position of prestige in the town the Parish Church had once held. The new Town Hall, built as a result of the Improvement Act of 1890 and containing the Public Library, Law Courts, Council Chamber and offices and Corn Exchange, was a concrete expression of this; it was far and away the largest and most grandiose building in Croydon at the time, designed by a local architect and comprehending within its walls the principal administrative functions of the borough. The churches themselves began to look towards Council members to legitimise their social status by requesting their presence at ceremonies, at the opening of churches and church halls, at the opening of bazaars and such like. The mayor took over the status and authority previously possessed by the vicar of Croydon: he became the central figure of municipal life, combining political position with social prestige in a way which would only have been possible before incorporation had the vicar of Croydon been made ex officio chairman of the Local Board of Health.[42] The rising authority and prestige of the Corporation and its implications for church action may be seen in two final examples. The Croydon Distress Committee was formed under the Unemployed Workmen Act of 1905: with fourteen members nominated by the Council, ten by the Board of Guardians and six co-opted, councillors need not

---

[42] This is treated in more detail in Morris, 'Religion and Urban Change', pp. 373–7.

have had a majority say on the Committee, but in fact the Board of Guardians regularly chose several councillors amongst its nominees, giving the Council an effective majority voice; only one clergyman was ever co-opted onto it before the First World War.[43] An even more striking indication of the effect of reformed, local, municipal government on the status of organised religion in the years before the First World War was the response of voluntarist organisations, churches and the Council to the war. Parish magazines suggest a surprisingly unruffled picture of parochial life during the war, with few new relief funds and war charities established, and continuity with the pre-war pattern. Most of the relief committees established in the town during the war were directly inspired or founded by the municipal elite – the Croydon War Supplies Clearing House, for example, patronised by the mayor and mayoress and by alderman Edridge and his wife,[44] and a host of smaller committees such as the Mayor's Committee and War Fund Committee.[45]

The failure of voluntarist forms of action to remedy the social problems thrown up or exacerbated in the course of urbanisation paralleled the failure of the churches to achieve the programmes of moral and religious regeneration they had taken upon themselves in the mid-nineteenth century. The Victorian middle class attributed to religion in mid-century a vital, integrative function, perceived to be lacking in, for example, party politics: conflicts over problems of welfare and control were therefore bound to draw in the churches as purveyors of moral authority. At the same time such conflicts, given the high level of lay participation in church activity and the religious interest on the part of the middle class this signified, were also likely to promote sectarian and doctrinal conflict. Rather than being determined by centrally initiated and directed policies of church extension, the expansion of the urban church owed much more to a complicated mixture of deliberation, bitter doctrinal controversy, and the structural strengths or weaknesses of the various denominations, underlying which was the constant pressure of middle class interest in religion. Behind both the voluntarist solutions propounded in Victorian Britain for the remedy of social problems and the religious aspirations which sought to place the churches at the centre of national life, therefore, lay the same mesh of middle class activism: the result, given the prevailing hostility to centralisation, was that the responsibility for deciding upon courses of action lay ultimately in

---

[43] *Ward's Croydon Directories*, 1907–14, *passim*.
[44] H. K. Moore and W. C. Berwick Sayers (eds.), *Croydon and the Great War* (Croydon 1920), p. 175.
[45] *Ibid.*, esp. part five, pp. 163–208.

local hands just at the time when, in rapidly expanding towns like Croydon, these problems were becoming most acute.

When the initiative began to fall into the central state's hands from the 1900s onwards, the means selected for the local administration of welfare policies were those extra-religious governmental methods (pioneered by local government) which had proved most successful, and not the churches and their penumbra of voluntary charitable organisations. Sectarian rivalry became of lesser importance as the focus of local politics shifted decisively away from bodies in which the Anglican Church had a legal or assumed predominance, towards extra-religious, elective bodies. The Labour movement, outside traditional politico-religious affiliations, only served to further this marginalisation of the churches to political life. What the 'democratisation' of local government in Croydon through incorporation achieved therefore was the supersession of the Anglican oligarchy who had previously ruled the town by what was in effect a 'new municipal elite'.

Democratisation also provided the basis for the extension of municipal power, in ways which either directly or indirectly undermined the social appeal of the churches by intruding upon extra-religious functions they had taken upon themselves and by gradually restricting the sphere of church action. The secret of the success of local government action (and ultimately of the welfare state) lay in its combination of compulsory taxation with democratisation, raising the resources requisite to cope with urban social problems by means of a vote which, theoretically at least, gave representation to a wide range of groups in the community, and consequently negated objections raised under the parochial system that the opinions of the many had been overridden by the wealthy few. Under the new Corporation, religious squabbling was just as possible as before, and just as possible as political controversy – though in fact it was remarkable by its absence – but it could always be resolved by the ballot-paper, and there could be no allegations that the structure of the Corporation necessarily favoured any one political or religious faction. The very success of local government pulled the town's lay leadership further into municipal activity, severing many of the active ties which had bound them to the churches. It was an almost imperceptible change because it occurred gradually; it was the product of the increasing volume of business handled by the Council, but also of the increased prestige which, after incorporation, attached to participation in municipal life.

Local clergy and ministers were also drawn into a more specialised role. Both Anglican and Nonconformist churches sought to adapt to urban growth by increasing the range of services – welfare, educational, leisure – they provided for the population at large, and by developing and refining their systems of church government. They were, however, trying to extend activity or 'outreach' at a time when the social groups which they relied upon for support were themselves engaging in increasingly specialised areas of activity (whether work, leisure, political life or religion). Consequently they began to define their tasks themselves in a more specialised sense, failing to carry their influence beyond the areas which became defined as 'religious'. Exogenous growth gave way to endogenous growth. Schism, with the intense doctrinal conflict it implied, gave way to the 'denominational' front. Informal methods of church extension gave way to planned and minister-led growth. Domination or close involvement by the town's lay leadership declined as clergy and ministers became more powerful again within the denominations. The narrowing social basis of active church support and the gradual withdrawal of the town elite from church activity in turn reduced the resources of manpower and money available to the churches. Thus the situation in which the churches found themselves at the beginning of the twentieth century was a consequence of changes in the urban infrastructure which had also found expression in the emergence of reformed municipal government.

APPENDIXES

APPENDIX 1

Croydon: Demography 1801–1921

Table 1
Population of the parish of Croydon 1801–1921

Year	Population	% Increase
1801	5743	–
1811	7801	36%
1821	9254	17%
1831	12447	35%
1841	16712	34%
1851	20343	22%
1861	30240	49%
1871	55652	84%
1881	78953	42%
1891	102795	31%
1901	134037	31%
1911	170165	27%
1921	191375	13%

Source: *Croydon Natural History and Scientific Society, Regional Survey*, Atlas of Croydon and District, p. 81.

Table 2
Population of the parish of Croydon 1861–91, by 1861 districts

	1861	1871	1881	1891
All Saints, Norwood	4060	7854	13250	19767
Christ Church	4203	5909	7448	9283
St James	7590	17900	23578	27404
St John's, Shirley	642	683	697	639
St Peter's	2932	5541	8528	12335
St Mark	1489	5683	8188	10582
St John's, Croydon	9324	12082	17264	22627

Source: figures extracted from Census Reports, 1861–91.

APPENDIX 1

Table 3
Burgesses 1883–1913, by wards

	1883	1888	1893	1898	1903	1908	1913
Upper Norwood	1617	2119	2423	2800	3681	4233	4502
South Norwood	1768	2177	2546	2998	3888	4661	5000
West (& North, 1905)	3596	4374	5166	6105	7932	10040	11995
Central	1257	2484	2569	2855	2965	2904	2848
East	1294	1473	1537	2049	2640	3097	3978
South	1608	2150	2420	2848	3299	3496	3662
Total	11140	14773	16659	19655	24405	28431	31985

Source: *Ward's Commercial and General Directory for Croydon*, 1914, p. xlvii.

Table 4
Birthplace of 1851 heads of household

Place of birth	No. of 1851 heads of household	% of Total	
England:			
Parish of Croydon	859	23	
Not more than 5 miles from Croydon	287	8	51
5 to 10 miles from Croydon	763	20	
10 to 30 miles from Croydon	699	19	
30 to 75 miles from Croydon	459	12	
75 to 150 miles from Croydon	397	10	
Over 150 miles from Croydon	110	3	
Scotland & Wales	44	1	
Ireland	77	2	
Remainder of Europe	20	1	
Outside Europe	14	0	
Not Known	44	1	
Total	3773	100	
England – Total	3574	95	
Remainder of British Isles – Total	121	3	

Source: Cox, 'Urban Development and Redevelopment', p. 442.

192

Table 5
Social class and birthplace of 1851 heads of household
born between five and ten miles from the town

Three columns are devoted to the upper and middle classes and three columns to the working clases. The first column in each case gives the number of heads of household in Croydon in 1851 in those social classes; the second column expresses the first column as a percentage of Total (i); and the third column expresses the first column as a percentage of Total (ii).

Place	Upper and middle classes			Working class			Total (ii)
a) London	123	46	58	89	18	42	212
b) Suburbs of London	108	40	41	158	32	59	266
c) Rural Areas	37	14	13	248	50	87	285
Total (i) of (a), (b) and (c)	268	100		495	100		763

Note:
(a) refers to the City of London and its immediate environs.
(b) refers to the suburbs of London in 1851 and to other places between Croydon and London.
(c) refers to places east, west or south of Croydon.

Source: Cox, 'Urban Development and Redevelopment', p. 451.

Table 6
Places of birth of residents of Croydon county borough in 1911

Area	Male	%	Female	%
London	20464	26.37	25245	27.33
Croydon County Borough	28373	36.56	29158	31.57
Wimbledon Metropolitan Borough	170	0.22	191	0.21
Surrey	4223	5.44	5136	5.56
Kent	3894	5.02	5209	5.64
Sussex	2818	3.63	3346	3.62
Hampshire*				
Berkshire	605	0.78	808	0.87
South Midlands	4162	5.36	5517	5.97
Eastern Counties	3398	4.37	5417	5.86
South Western Counties	2074	2.67	3034	3.28
West Midland Counties	1360	1.75	2008	2.17
North Midland Counties	1157	1.49	868	0.94
North Western Counties	661	0.85	864	0.93
Yorkshire	590	0.76	760	0.82
Northern Counties	369	0.47	481	0.52
Wales	302	0.39	457	0.49
England (County not stated)	25	0.03	42	0.04
Other Parts British Empire	1230	1.59	1603	1.73
Ireland	505	0.65	811	0.88
Elsewhere	1229	1.59	1419	1.53
Totals	77609	100.00	92370	100.00

* Hampshire figures not entered in published summary.

Source: 1911 Census Report, County of Surrey (1914).

APPENDIX 2

Croydon: Occupations and Social Class 1861–1911

The sources for this and the following tables are the census reports for 1861, 1891 and 1911. Boundaries are consistent for 1891 and 1911, but not 1861, which used the Croydon Union as the unit of analysis; the 1861 figures are exaggerated, therefore, in the weight they give to agriculture in the town, since they include residents in the rural parishes neighbouring Croydon. For a description of a similar method of classification to that followed in this appendix, see the first appendix to G. Stedman Jones, *Outcast London* (1971), pp. 350–7.

The occupational classification is derived from the 1911 categories, with the 1861 and 1891 data re-classified accordingly. The categories used in the social classification are taken from the Registrar General's 1951 five-fold classification of social class, as follows:

Class 1: large employers, merchants, bankers, higher officials in shipping and insurance, property owners, and the liberal professions (civil service, church, bar, medicine, army, navy, science, fine arts, architecture, etc).

Class 2: small employers, small dealers, wholesalers, retailers, caterers, local government officials, teachers, entertainers, musicians, subordinate officers in insurance and church, clerical occupations.

Class 3: artisan crafts, skilled labour (mostly in construction and manufacture), lower class traders, higher class domestic service.

Class 4: semi-skilled or intermediate workers in transport, agriculture, wood, metals, textiles, soldiers, sailors (men), subordinate government and local government service, police.

Class 5: general unskilled labour, unskilled work in land and water transport, service and manufacture, municipal labour, street traders.

Table 1
Croydon 1861 census: occupational classification

Occupation	Males		Females	
	Numbers	%	Numbers	%
Agriculture	2221	19.16	177	1.23
Administration	265	2.29	14	0.10
Defence	262	2.26	–	–
Professional & teaching	610	5.26	171	1.19
Entertainment & sport	106	0.91	18	0.12
Commerce, finance etc	414	3.57	9	0.06
Clerical	208	1.79		
Retail & distribution	775	6.69	341	2.37
Personal service	638	5.50	3229	22.40
Transport, storage etc	846	7.30	10	0.07
Building industry	1440	12.42	–	–
Wood & furniture	324	2.80	24	0.17
Metal & engineering	237	2.04	1	0.01
Shipbuilding	9	0.08	1	0.01
Precision industry	124	1.07	1	0.01
Printing & paper	90	0.78	3	0.03
Leather & hides	85	0.73	2	0.02
Food & drink manufacture	411	3.55	93	0.65
Textile manufacture	67	0.58	18	0.12
Clothing trade	490	4.23	1483	10.29
Boot & shoe trade	241	2.08	132	0.92
Chemicals & allied trades	55	0.47		
Miscellaneous manufacture	145	1.25	158	1.10
Miscellaneous labour	1099	9.48	14	0.10
Total for working population	(11162)	(96.31)	(5899)	(40.77)
Others	428	3.69	8514	59.46
TOTAL	11590	100.00	14413	100.43

N.B. Any slight variation from 100.00% in the totals is accounted for by rounding of figures.

Table 2
Croydon 1891 census: occupational classification

Occupation	Males Numbers	%	Females Numbers	%
Agriculture	663	1.97	57	0.13
Administration	736	2.19	56	0.12
Defence	135	0.40	–	–
Professional & teaching	1587	4.71	2057	4.54
Entertainment & sport	370	1.10	211	0.47
Commerce, finance etc	1055	3.13	15	0.03
Clerical	2684	7.97	123	0.27
Retail & distribution	1991	5.91	688	1.52
Personal service	1893	5.62	10958	24.19
Transport, storage etc	2663	7.90	19	0.04
Building industry	3749	11.14	2	0.01
Wood & furniture	838	2.49	54	0.12
Metal & engineering	728	2.16	3	0.01
Shipbuilding	6	0.01	–	–
Precision industry	298	0.88	3	0.01
Printing & paper	443	1.32	31	0.07
Leather & hides	143	0.42	4	0.01
Food & drink manufacture	1165	3.46	6	0.01
Textile manufacture	145	0.43	352	0.78
Clothing trade	842	2.50	1885	4.16
Boot & shoe trade	655	1.94	44	0.10
Chemicals & allied trades	191	0.57	26	0.06
Miscellaneous manufacture	462	1.37	36	0.08
Miscellaneous labour	3124	9.28	133	0.29
Total for working population	(26566)	(78.91)	(16763)	(37.00)
Others	7101	21.09	28542	63.04
TOTAL	33667	100.41	45305	100.04

Table 3
Croydon 1911 census: occupational classification

Occupation	Males Numbers	%	Females Numbers	%
Agriculture	1790	3.00	117	0.16
Administration	2116	3.55	407	0.54
Defence	192	0.32	–	–
Professional & teaching	1844	3.09	1826	2.44
Entertainment & sport	896	1.50	475	0.63
Commerce, finance etc	1842	3.09	38	0.05
Clerical	6789	11.38	1141	1.52
Retail & distribution	6133	9.50	2866	3.82
Personal service	1725	2.89	12359	16.50
Transport, storage etc	5972	10.01	85	0.11
Building industry	7589	12.72	–	–
Wood & furniture	820	1.37	74	0.10
Metal & engineering	3003	5.03	47	0.06
Shipbuilding	–	–	–	–
Precision industry	562	0.94	15	0.02
Printing & paper	1234	2.07	128	0.17
Leather & hides	208	0.35	20	0.03
Food & drink manufacture	852	1.43	240	0.32
Textile manufacture	76	0.13	90	0.12
Clothing trade	811	1.36	2918	3.90
Boot & shoe trade	436	0.73	14	0.02
Chemicals & allied trades	345	0.58	101	0.13
Miscellaneous manufacture	191	0.32	–	–
Miscellaneous labour	3236	5.43	204	0.27
Total for working population	(48662)	(81.30)	(23165)	(30.91)
Others	11192	18.76	51728	69.12
TOTAL	59854	99.55	74893	100.03

Table 4
Croydon 1861–91: occupational classification: changes

	Males		Females	
Occupation	% change on 1861	Change in proport.	% change on 1861	Change in proport.
Agriculture	− 70.15	− 17.19	− 67.80	− 1.10
Administration	+ 177.74	− 0.10	+ 300.00	+ 0.02
Defence	− 48.47	− 1.86	−	−
Professional & teaching	+ 160.16	− 0.55	+ 1102.92	+ 3.35
Entertainment & sport	+ 249.06	+ 0.19	+ 1072.22	+ 0.35
Commerce, finance etc.	+ 154.83	− 0.44	+ 66.67	− 0.03
Clerical	+ 1190.38	+ 6.18	(0 in 1861)	+ 0.17
Retail & distribution	+ 156.90	− 0.78	+ 101.76	− 0.85
Personal service	+ 196.71	+ 0.12	+ 239.36	+ 1.79
Transport, storage etc.	+ 214.77	+ 0.60	+ 90.00	− 0.03
Building industry	+ 160.35	− 1.28	(0 in 1861)	+ 0.01
Wood & furniture	+ 158.64	− 0.31	+ 125.00	− 0.05
Metal & engineering	+ 207.17	+ 0.12	+ 200.00	Same
Shipbuilding	− 33.33	− 0.06	− 100.00	− 0.01
Precision industry	+ 140.32	− 0.19	+ 200.00	Same
Printing & paper	+ 392.22	+ 0.54	+ 933.33	+ 0.04
Leather & hides	+ ˙68.23	− 0.30	+ 100.00	− 0.01
Food & drink manufacture	+ 183.45	− 0.09	− 93.55	− 0.64
Textile manufacture	+ 116.41	− 0.15	+ 1855.56	+ 0.66
Clothing trade	+ 71.84	− 1.73	+ 27.11	− 6.13
Boot & shoe trade	+ 171.78	− 0.14	− 66.67	− 0.82
Chemicals & allied trades	+ 247.27	+ 0.10	(0 in 1861)	+ 0.06
Misc. manufacture	+ 218.62	+ 0.12	− 77.21	− 1.02
Misc. labour	+ 184.26	− 0.20	+ 850.00	+ 0.19
Total for working population	(+ 138.00)	(− 17.40)	(− 184.16)	− 3.77)
Others	+ 1559.11	+ 17.40	+ 233.25	+ 3.77
TOTAL	+ 190.48		+ 213.24	

N.B. In this and Tables 5, 6 and 10–12 'Change in proport.' refers to the increase or decrease of a particular occupational sector expressed as a proportion (percentage-wise) of the overall populations, male and female.

Table 5
Croydon 1891–1911: occupational classification: change

| | Males | | Females | |
Occupation	% change on 1891	Change in proport.	% change on 1891	Change in proport.
Agriculture	+ 169.98	+ 1.03	+ 105.26	+ 0.03
Administration	+ 187.50	+ 136.00	+ 626.79	+ 0.42
Defence	+ 42.22	− 0.08	−	−
Professional & teaching	+ 16.19	− 1.62	+ 11.23	− 2.10
Entertainment & sport	+ 142.16	+ 0.40	+ 125.12	+ 0.16
Commerce, finance etc	+ 74.60	− 0.04	+ 153.33	+ 0.02
Clerical	+ 152.94	+ 3.41	+ 827.64	+ 1.25
Retail & distribution	+ 208.04	+ 3.59	+ 316.57	+ 2.30
Personal service	− 8.87	− 2.73	+ 12.78	− 7.69
Transport, storage etc.	+ 124.26	+ 2.11	+ 347.37	+ 0.07
Building industry	+ 102.43	+ 1.58	− 100.00	− 0.01
Wood & furniture	− 2.15	− 1.12	+ 37.04	− 0.02
Metal & engineering	+ 312.50	+ 2.87	+ 1466.67	+ 0.05
Shipbuilding	− 100.00	− 0.02	−	−
Precision industry	+ 88.59	+ 0.06	+ 400.00	+ 0.01
Printing & paper	+ 178.55	+ 0.75	+ 312.90	+ 0.10
Leather & hides	− 45.45	− 0.07	+ 400.00	+ 0.02
Food & drink manufacture	− 26.87	+ 2.03	+ 3900.00	+ 0.31
Textile manufacture	− 47.59	− 0.30	− 74.43	− 0.66
Clothing trade	− 3.68	− 1.14	+ 54.80	− 0.26
Boot & shoe trade	− 33.43	− 1.21	− 68.18	− 0.08
Chemicals & allied trades	+ 80.63	+ 0.01	+ 288.46	+ 0.07
Misc. manufacture	− 58.66	− 1.05	− 100.00	− 0.08
Misc. labour	+ 3.58	− 3.58	+ 53.38	− 0.02
Total for working population	(+ 83.17)	(+ 2.39)	(+ 38.19)	(− 6.09)
Others	+ 57.61	− 2.39	+ 81.25	+ 6.09
TOTAL	+ 77.78		+ 61.31	

Table 6
Croydon 1861–1911: occupational classification: change

	Males		Females	
	% change on 1861	Change in proport.	% change on 1861	Change in proport.
Agriculture	− 19.41	− 16.16	− 33.99	− 1.07
Administration	+ 698.49	+ 1.26	+ 2807.14	+ 0.44
Defence	− 26.72	− 1.94	−	−
Professional & teaching	+ 202.29	− 2.17	+ 967.84	+ 1.25
Entertainment & sport	+ 745.28	+ 0.59	+ 2538.89	+ 0.51
Commerce, finance etc	+ 344.93	− 0.48	+ 322.22	− 0.01
Clerical	+ 3163.94	+ 9.59	(0 in 1861)	+ 1.52
Retail & distribution	+ 691.35	+ 2.81	+ 740.47	+ 1.45
Personal service	+ 170.38	− 2.61	+ 282.75	− 5.90
Transport, storage etc	+ 605.91	+ 2.71	+ 750.00	+ 0.04
Building industry	+ 427.01	+ 0.30	−	−
Wood & furniture	+ 153.09	− 1.43	+ 208.33	− 0.07
Metal & engineering	+ 1167.09	+ 2.99	+ 4600.00	+ 0.05
Shipbuilding	− 100.00	− 0.08	− 100.00	− 0.01
Precision industry	+ 353.23	− 0.13	+ 1400.00	+ 0.01
Printing & paper	+ 1271.11	+ 1.00	+ 4166.67	+ 0.14
Leather & hides	+ 144.71	− 0.38	+ 400.00	− 0.02
Food & drink manufacture	+ 107.30	− 2.12	+ 158.06	− 0.33
Textile manufacture	+ 13.43	− 0.45	+ 400.00	no change
Clothing trade	+ 65.51	− 2.87	+ 96.76	− 6.39
Boot & shoe trade	+ 90.91	− 1.35	− 89.91	− 0.90
Chemicals & allied trades	+ 527.27	+ 0.11	0 in 1861	+ 0.13
Misc. manufacture	+ 31.72	− 0.93	− 100.00	− 1.10
Misc. labour	+ 194.45	− 4.05	+ 1357.14	+ 0.17
Total for working population	(+ 335.96)	(− 15.01)	(+ 292.69)	(− 9.86)
Others	+ 2514.95	+ 15.01	+ 503.59	+ 9.86
TOTAL	+ 416.43		+ 419.92	

Table 7
Croydon 1861 census: social classification

Social class	Males		Females	
	Numbers	%	Numbers	%
Class 1	1274	10.99	522	3.62
Class 2	957	8.26	533	3.69
Class 3	2210	19.07	440	3.05
Class 4	5019*	43.30	3977	27.52
Class 5	1936	16.70	835	5.79
Working population				
Totals	11396	98.32	6307	43.74
Others	194	1.67	8106	56.25
Totals	11590	100.00	14413	100.00

* Class 4 is large because it includes agricultural labourers from the rural parishes around Croydon; removal of these (118 labourers plus 589 non-domestic gardeners) gives a figure of 3,312 (or 28.58% population), though some at least would have lived in Croydon Parish anyway.

Table 8
Croydon 1891 census: social classification

Social class	Males		Females	
	Numbers	%	Numbers	%
Class 1	2764	8.21	145	0.32
Class 2	5699	16.93	1967	4.34
Class 3	6247	18.55	1108	2.45
Class 4	8030	23.85	11822	26.09
Class 5	4391	13.04	1675	3.70
Working population				
Totals	27131	80.59	16717	36.90
Others	6536	19.41	28588	63.10
Totals	3667	100.00	45305	100.00

Table 9
Croydon 1911 census: social classification

	Males		Females	
Social Class	Numbers	%	Numbers	%
Class 1	4575	7.67	118	0.16
Class 2	7844	13.15	4698	6.27
Class 3	13623	22.84	4847	6.47
Class 4	14174	23.76	10605	14.16
Class 5	8234	13.81	2859	3.82
Working population				
Totals	48450	81.23	23127	30.88
Others	11192	18.76	51766	69.11
Totals	59642	99.99	74893	100.00

Table 10
Croydon 1861–91: social classification: changes

	Males		Females	
Class	% increase or decrease on 1861	increase or decrease on proport.	% increase or decrease on 1861	increase or decrease on proport.
Class 1	+ 116.95	− 2.78	− 72.22	− 3.30
Class 2	+ 495.05	+ 8.67	+ 269.04	+ 0.65
Class 3	+ 182.67	− 0.52	+ 151.82	− 0.60
Class 4	+ 59.99	− 19.45	+ 197.26	− 1.50
Class 5	+ 126.80	− 3.66	+ 100.60	− 2.09
Working population				
Totals	+ 138.07	− 17.73	+ 165.05	− 6.84
Others	+ 3269.07	+ 17.73	+ 252.67	+ 6.84
Totals	+ 190.48		+ 241.33	

Table 11
Croydon 1891–1911: social classification: changes

	Males		Females	
Class	% increase or decrease on 1891	increase or decrease on proport.	% increase or decrease on 1891	increase or decrease on proport.
Class 1	+ 65.52	− 0.54	− 18.62	− 0.16
Class 2	+ 37.64	− 3.78	+ 138.84	+ 1.93
Class 3	+ 118.07	+ 4.29	+ 337.45	+ 4.02
Class 4	+ 76.51	− 0.09	− 10.29	− 11.93
CLass 5	+ 87.52	− 0.77	+ 70.69	+ 0.12
Working population				
Totals	+ 78.58	+ 0.64	+ 38.34	− 6.02
Others	+ 71.24	− 0.64	+ 81.08	+ 6.02
Total	+ 77.15		+ 65.31	

Table 12
Croydon 1861–1911: social classification: changes

	Males		Females	
Class	% increase or decrease on 1861	increase or decrease on proport.	% increase or decrease on 1861	increase or decrease on proport.
Class 1	+ 259.10	− 3.32	− 77.39	− 3.46
Class 2	+ 719.64	+ 4.89	+ 781.43	+ 2.58
Class 3	+ 516.42	+ 3.77	+ 1001.59	+ 3.42
Class 4	+ 182.40	− 19.54	+ 166.65	− 13.43
Class 5	+ 325.31	− 2.89	+ 242.39	− 1.97
Working population				
Totals	+ 3251.15	− 17.09	+ 266.69	− 12.86
Others	+ 5569.07	+ 17.09	+ 538.61	+ 12.86
Total	+ 414.60		+ 419.62	

Church Attendance 1851–1902

Table 1
Church attendance in Croydon in 1851

Denomination	Recorded attendance			Adjusted total	% of popul.
	morning	afternoon	evening		
Church of England	2578	1320	1422	5423*	26.66
Congregationalist	505	–	380	726	3.57
Baptist	370	51	426	695	3.42
Wesleyan Methodist	200	–	185	316	1.55
Primitive Methodist	16	21	10	39	0.19
Society of Friends	357	230	184	633	3.11
Roman Catholic	482	125	205	461 +	2.27
Total	4508	1747	2812	8293	40.77

* All Saints, Norwood, failed to fill in returns for attendances; to provide an estimate for the adjusted total, therefore, the average of adjusted attendances per sittings for other Anglican churches was calculated, and an estimate of 1061 entered for All Saints based upon its available sittings of 972.

+ Since the Community of Sisters of the Chapel of Our Lady at Norwood was also entered, attendances here for the afternoon and evening were ignored on the assumption that the Sisters attended their chapel thrice during the day.

The adjusted totals have been calculated by use of the Mudie Smith 1902 estimate that in Greater London some 36% of attendances were due to 'twicers'; consequently totals are reduced by 18%. This cannot take into account possible changes in the frequency of churchgoing amongst attenders, but it can at least make direct comparisons between the 1851 and 1902 Censuses more consistent.

Source: 1851 Returns of Census of Public Worship, at the Public Record Office (H.O. 129).

Table 2
Church attendance in the Surrey Unions: 1851

Denomination	Epsom Union Adjusted Total	% Popul.	Chertsey Union Adjusted Total	% Popul.
Church of England	6832	35.88	5278	32.68
Congregationalist	801	4.21	225	1.39
Baptist	70	0.37	796	4.93
Wesleyan Methodist	467	2.45	653	4.04
Primitive Methodist	–	–	–	–
Society of Friends	–	–	–	–
Roman Catholic	–	–	50	0.31
Others	85	0.45	95	0.59
Total	8255	43.36	7097	43.94

Denomination	Guildford Union Adjusted Total	% Popul.	Farnham Union Adjusted Total	% Popul.
Church of England	8163	32.56	3309	28.18
Congregationalist	1445	5.76	528	4.50
Baptist	565	2.25	342	2.91
Wesleyan Methodist	375	1.50	78	0.66
Primitive Methodist	–	–	–	–
Society of Friends	32	0.13	–	–
Roman Catholic	84	0.34	–	–
Others	233	0.39	424	3.61
Total	10897	43.47	4681	39.86

Denomination	Farnborough Union Adjusted Total	% Popul.	Hambledon Union Adjusted Total	% Popul.
Church of England	3482	44.42	5063	37.36
Congregationalist	17	0.22	633	4.67
Baptist	132	1.68	129	0.95
Wesleyan Methodist	88	1.12	137	1.01
Primitive Methodist	–	–	–	–
Society of Friends	–	–	–	–
Roman Catholic	–	–	–	–
Others	522	6.66	50	0.37
Total	4241	54.10	6012	44.36

Denomination	Dorking Union Adjusted Total	% Popul.	Reigate Union Adjusted Total	% Popul.
Church of England	2582	22.74	3187	22.24
Congregationalist	613	5.40	984	6.87
Baptist	–	–	569	3.97
Wesleyan Methodist	246	2.17	–	–
Primitive Methodist	–	–	–	–
Society of Friends	49	0.43	28	0.19
Roman Catholic	–	–	–	–
Others	322	2.84	40	0.28
Total	3812	33.58	4808	33.55

Denomination	Godstone Union Adjusted Total	% Popul.	Croydon Union Adjusted Total	% Popul.
Church of England	3197	36.05	8764	27.48
Congregationalist	94	1.06	1644	5.15
Baptist	482	5.43	846	2.65
Wesleyan Methodist	231	2.60	388	1.22
Primitive Methodist	–	–	42	0.13
Society of Friends	–	–	533	1.67
Roman Catholic	–	–	512	1.61
Others	–	–	110	0.34
Total	4004	45.14	12839	40.25

APPENDIX 3

Denomination	Kingston Union Adjusted Total	% Popul.	Richmond Union Adjusted Total	% Popul.
Church of England	8722	32.56	4767	29.97
Congregationalist	952	3.55	440	2.77
Baptist	483	1.80	95	0.60
Wesleyan Methodist	342	1.28	233	1.46
Primitive Methodist	–	–	–	–
Society of Friends	43	0.16	–	–
Roman Catholic	106	0.40	473	2.97
Others	34	0.13	–	–
Total	10682	39.88	6008	37.77

Source: Census of Religious Worship, Parliamentary Papers 1852–3, LXXXIX.

N.B. The adjusted figure for Anglicans and Quakers for this table has been calculated using Horace Mann's 1852 method of eliminating 'twicers', by ordered assuming that a half of those who attended in the afternoon had already attended on the same day, and two-thirds of those who attended in the evening had already attended; to accommodate Nonconformist complaints that this method prejudiced their returns because it failed to account for the widespread practice of attending parish church in the morning and chapel in the evening, for Nonconformists the afternoon attendances have been added directly to the morning, and only half of the evening attendances assumed to be 'twicers'. Horace Mann's method has been used here because the point of the table is not the possibility of comparisons between rural Surrey in 1851 and metropolitan London in 1902, but comparisons between the Surrey Unions themselves.

Table 3
Church attendance in Croydon: 1902

Denomination	Recorded attendance morning	evening	Adjusted total	% of Population
Church of England	11555	12790	19963	14.89
Congregational Church	2931	2799	4699	3.50
Baptist Church	2847	3252	5001	3.73
Wesleyan Methodist	1759	2354	3373	2.52
United Free Methodists	184	244	351	0.26
Primitive Methodists	391	433	676	0.50
Presbyterians	708	739	1187	0.89
Unitarian Church	100	195	242	0.18
Society of Friends	159	50	171	0.13
Salvation Army	471	1200	1370	1.02
Brethren	878	1217	1718	1.28
Roman Catholic	2165	1109	2685	2.00
Others	456	1976	1994	1.49
Total	24604	28358	43430	32.39

Adjusted totals for all denominations were calculated using Mudie Smith's estimate that in Greater London on average 36% of total attendances were taken up by 'twicers'; consequently the totals of attendances are reduced by 18% to eliminate them. This produces a slightly higher estimate for Nonconformists (+ 3.5% original total attendances) and a definitely higher one for Anglicans (+ 6.13% original total attendances) than the method of calculation employed by Horace Mann for the 1851 figures. To some extent the difference between the percentages for 1902 and 1851 may therefore have been higher in fact than the figures here appear to show, but against this must be balanced changes in churchgoing habits and services (described in Chapter 3), changes which are impossible to quantify.

Source: Mudie Smith, *Religious Life*.

The Governing Elite 1829–89

Table 1
Religious affiliations of Croydon's governing elite 1829–89

Board or Council	Total members	Anglican	Non-conformist	Unknown
1829 – Improvement Commissioners	20	13	–	7
1839 – Improvement Commisisioners	20	9	1	10
1849 – Local Board of Health	12	11	1	–
1859 – Local Board of Health	12	9	2	1
1869 – Local Board of Health	12	8	2	6
1879 – Local Board of Health	18	8	4	6
1883 – Croydon Borough Council	48	12	11	25
1889 – Croydon County Council	48	14	11	23

N.B. No entries have been inserted for later than 1889, because the difficulty of identifying religous and political affiliations from the early 1890s becomes acute as the local press ceased to publish lists of supporting committees for general election candidates and sources of information about religious beliefs (lists of interments in Croydon Cemeteries and details of church offices held) also cease to be useful; consequently the number of councillors whose religious and political identity it would be possible to establish from the 1890s onwards would be too small for useful purposes.

Sources for this and for the following tables are local newspapers, street directories, minutes of the Improvement Commissioners for 1829–49, Anon. *Old and New Croydon* and Ward, *Croydon in the Past*.

Table 2
Political affiliations of Croydon's governing elite 1829–89

Board or Council	Total members	Conser-vative	Liberal	Unknown
1829 – Improvement Commissioners	20	2	1	17
1839 – Improvement Commisisioners	20	5	1	14
1849 – Local Board of Health	12	7	2	3
1859 – Local Board of Health	12	7	4	1
1869 – Local Board of Health	12	5	3	4
1879 – Local Board of Health	18	7	8	3
1883 – Croydon Borough Council	48	10	22	16
1889 – Croydon County Council	48	8	21	19

N.B. The difficulty of tracing political affiliations for the first half of the nineteenth century undermines the overall value of the table, though reference to the high proportion of Anglicans and landowners (and the agricultural interest) amongst the Improvement Commissioners would imply an easy majority of Conservatives.

Table 3
Known interest groups of Croydon's governing elite 1829–89

Board or Council	Total members	Interest Groups				
		A	B	C	D	E
1829 – Improvement Commissioners	20	12	5	2	–	–
1839 – Improvement Commisisioners	20	6	8	1	2	–
1849 – Local Board of Health	12	2	2	2	4	1
1859 – Local Board of Health	12	2	3	2	2	1
1869 – Local Board of Health	12	2	3	2	2	1
1879 – Local Board of Health	10	1	4	–	5	1
1883 – Croydon Borough Council	48	–	15	1	5	3
1889 – Croydon County Council	48	–	14	1	7	2

N.B. Interest group is defined by occupation as follows:
A Landed and agricultural
B Retailers, craft businesses and manufacturers based in Croydon
C Drink trade
D Professional men based in Croydon
E Commuters or retired professionals, merchants, etc.

Bibliography

Primary Sources

Brighton Road Baptist Church, South Croydon
Minutes of Church Meetings 1894–1915
Minutes of Deacons' Meetings 1908–1914
'A Brief Sketch of the Origin and Progress of the South Croydon
Baptist Church' by Walter Schwind, London City Missionary in
South Croydon, handwritten, dated 1927
Sunday School Teachers' Meetings minutes 1891–1917

Croydon Reference Library
Anon., 'Alderman John Pelton: memoir', typescript, c. 1920
Anon., 'Francis Moses Coldwells 1827–1895', typescript, c. 1920
Croydon Board of Guardians minutes 1842–92 (incomplete)
Croydon Burial Board minutes 1859–90
Croydon Domestic Mission (Denett Road):
    Rules
    Papers and correspondence
    Minute books 1886–9
    Women's Benefit Society papers
Croydon Local Board of Health
    Ledgers 1844–81
    Rough minutes 1849–53
    Minutes 1849–83
Croydon Manor
    Homage Jury Minute Book 1582–1868 (transcripts)
    Leet Jury Records 1830–55
Croydon Parish
    Churchwardens' accounts 1842–68
    Vestry minutes 1741–1899
    Select Vestry minutes 1819–37
    Poll in the election of a beadle, 1865
    Church rate polls for 1853 and 1861
    Board of Surveyors of Highways minutes 1836–49
    Improvement Commissioners minutes 1829–49
    Waste Land Trustees account book 1803–49
    Waste Land Trustees rough minutes 1801–68

Croydon Primitive Methodist Circuit
  Lind Road Chapel Collection journal 1913–24
  Quarterly accounts for Croydon 1849–69
  Roll books
  Minutes of Quarterly Meeting 1849–1946
  Secretary's minutes, Laud Street Chapel 1876–91
  Sunday School minutes 1869–1914
  Circuit Sunday School Council minutes 1876–96
  Treasurers' books, Princess Road Chapel 1876–99
  Cherry Orchard Road Chapel accounts 1865–1904
  Cherry Orchard Road Chapel stewards' accounts 1876
  Thornton Heath Chapel accounts 1892–1914
  Portland Road treasurers' accounts 1891–1922
Croydon School Board minute books 1871–1903
Croydon Wesleyan Chapel (North End)
  Register of baptisms 1829–38 (transcripts)
  Register of burials 1837–48 (transcripts)
Folder of papers relating to Grange Wood
Notebooks of Cuthbert Johnson
Page, W., 'My Recollections of Croydon Sixty Years Since',
  typescript, 17 Aug. 1880
Paget, C. G., 'The Parish Church of Croydon', typescript, c. 1930
Papers of George Clinch

Greater London Record Office
Trinity Congregational Church (Dingwall Road)
  Minutes of Church Meetings 1864–1918
  Minutes of Deacons' Meetings 1872–1918

Lambeth Palace Library
  Papers of C. T. Longley
  Papers of Archibald Tait
  Papers of E. W. Benson
  Papers of Frederick Temple
  Visitation returns, 1864–1912

Public Record Office
Returns 1851 Religious Census: Ecclesiastical Returns, 1851, H.O.
  129

St Augustine's, South Croydon
  Minutes of vestry meetings 1885–1956
  Register of offertories 1884–1889
  Minute book of the church building committee 1880–1904

Minute book of the church completion fund committee 1898–1904
Minutes of the Guild of St Augustine's 1885–91
Box file of papers, letters, deeds, etc., relating to the establishment
of the new district

St John the Evangelist, Upper Norwood
  Minutes of Churchwardens 1845–1914
  Minutes of Church Council 1906–14

South Norwood Congregational Church, Enmore Road
  Minutes of Church Meetings 1870–1928
  Minutes of Deacons' Meetings 1881–1921
  Sunday School Teachers' Meetings minutes 1869–1918
  Choir Secretary's letter book 1902–5
  Ledger, pastor's Stipend and Building Fund 1898–1900
  Cash book 1891–1900
  Minutes of New Building Committee 1899–1909
  Trustee minutes 1904–7
  Church Management Committee minutes 1901–5
  Sale of work committee minutes 1901

Surrey County Record Office
Christ Church, Croydon
  Church Council minutes 1909–24
Croydon Parish Church
  Preachers' book 1778–1839
  Register of services 1882–1903
  Offertory register 1906–14
St James' Church, Croydon Common
  Register of preachers 1863–99
  Minutes of vestry meetings 1866–1957
  Churchwardens' account books 1906–17
  Dartnell Road Mission, service register 1901–15
St Paul's Church, Thornton Heath
  Preachers' book 1873–1907
  Register of services 1907–14
  Spa Road Mission Church, preachers' book 1901–35
  Mission of St Oswald, register of services 1909–44
St Peter's Church, Croydon
  Preachers' book 1851–94
  Register of services 1902–15

Woodside Baptist Church, Spring Lane
Minutes of Church Meetings 1899–1928
Building Committee minute book 1905–12
Minutes of Deacons' Meetings 1904–13
Minutes of sale of work executive committee 1913–28

Primary Printed Sources

Miscellaneous

Croydon publications, unless otherwise stated

Alexander, H. G., *J.G. Alexander: Quaker missionary* (London c.1920)
Anderson, J. C., *Croydon Church Past and Present* (1871)
—— *A Short Chronicle Concerning the Parish of Croydon* (1882)
—— (ed.), *The Enclosure Award of 1801 for the Parish of Croydon* (1889)
Anon., (The Croydon Advertiser), *Croydon Crayons* (1873)
—— *History of the Whitgift Grammar School* (1909)
—— *Interesting Croydon and Surroundings* (1909)
—— *Life of R.R. Suffield* (Reading 1893)
—— *A Memoir of Edward Foster Brady, Late Superintendent of Croydon School* (n.d.)
—— ('By his daughter'), *A Memoir of John Finch Marsh of Croydon* (1873)
—— *Memoir of John Sharp, Late Superintendant of Croydon School* (n.d.)
—— *A Brief Memoir of Samuel Dale of Croydon* (1916)
—— *The New Wesleyan Church, Addiscombe* (1881)
—— *Old and New Croydon Illustrated* (1894)
—— *St. Andrew's, Croydon: a church for the poor* (1858)
—— (The Surrey Standard), *A Tribute to the Memory of the Late Mr. John Blake of Croydon* (c. 1851)
—— *Memorials and Correspondence respecting the Recent Appointing of an Incumbent for St. Saviour's Church, Croydon* (1869)
—— *Where to buy at Croydon: an illustrated local review* (1891)
Arnott, N., and Page, T., *Report on an Inquiry ordered by the Secretary of State relative to the Prevalence of Disease at Croydon and to the Plan of Sewerage* (1853)
Austin, H., *Further Report from the Consulting Engineer to the General Board of Health, on the Croydon Drainage* (1853)
Bagehot, W., *The English Constitution* (1867; World's Classics edn. London 1955)
Bailey, G., *A Memorial: 'She hath done what she could'* (1882)
Beck, W. and Ball, T. F., *The London Friends' Meetings* (London 1869)

Benson, E. W. and Benham, Canon, *Sermons on the Death of the Rev J. M. Braithwaite* (1889)

Brindley, R. B., *The Darkness Where God Is, and other sermons* (1904)

Buchanan, Dr, *Report on an Epidemic of Enteric Fever at Croydon in 1875* (1876)

Carpenter, A., *The History of Sanitary Progress in Croydon* (1859)

Charity Commissioners, *Reports relating to Croydon Charities* (London 1825 and 1837)

—— *Return of Endowed Charities* (London 1861)

—— *Scheme for the Administration of the Whitgift Foundation* (London 1881)

—— *Scheme for the Administration of the Croydon Charities of Henry Smith and others* (London 1892)

—— *Amended Scheme for the Administration of the Croydon Charities of Henry Smith and others* (London 1893)

—— *Scheme for the Administration of the Almshouse Charity of Elis David* (London 1893)

Cleal, E. E. and Crippen, T. G., *The Story of Congregationalism in Surrey* (London 1908)

Coleridge, S. T., *On the Constitution of Church and State* (London 1830; Dent edn, 1972)

Congregational Year Book (London 1846–1914)

Covell, F., *Sermon preached at Providence Chapel on completion of his 70th year* (1896)

—— *Sermons* (5 vols., 1872–82)

Covell, W. G., *A Brief Account of the Lord's Dealings with the Late Mr. F. Covell, Minister of Providence Chapel, Croydon* (London 1880)

Cox, T., *Report to the Local Board of Health of Croydon relative to Drainage and Water Supply* (1849)

Davies, C. M., *Unorthodox London* (London 1875)

Easter, A. J. T., *God's Light Upon Earth's Problems: six sermons* (1911)

—— *Memoir of Arthur Joseph Easter* (1919)

Elborough, C. M., *Croydon, a Borough* (1882)

Fleming, S. H., *Fire from Heaven* (1892)

—— *The Resurrection Body A Present Germ of the Natural Body* (1893)

Frost, T., *Forty Years' Recollections; Literary and Political* (London 1880)

—— *The Old Showmen and the London Fairs* (London 1881)

—— *Reminiscences of a Country Journalist* (London 1886)

Garrow, D. W., *The History and Antiquities of Croydon* (1818)

Gawthorp, W. E., *Trinity Congregational Church: a record of fifty years 1864–1914* (1914)

Geldart, E. M., *The Brazen Serpent* (1878)

—— *Christmas Day Sermon* (1881)

—— (as Nitram Tradleg), *A Son of Belial; autobiographical sketches* (London 1882)

—— *Last Words to Mr. Moody* (1884)

—— *Let There Be Light* (1884)

Genge, E. H., *Sermon preached on Founder's Day, Whitgift Foundation* (1892)

Godfrey, W. S., *Hazarded Lives* (1893)

Hoare, R. W., *Confirmation* (1891)

—— *Some Practices of our Devotional Life: four sermons* (1891)

—— *The Law of Marriage* (1907)

Hodgson, J. G., *Sermon on the Day of General Humiliation and Prayer* (1854)

—— *Voices from the East! or, The Christian's Condition, Course, and Crown, illustrated by our Soldiers* (1854)

James, W., *The Former Corrupt Government of the Parish of Croydon* (1823)

Jephson, A. W., *My Work in London* (London 1910)

—— *Municipal Work from a Christian Standpoint* (London 1912)

Jupp, W. J., *The Nobility of Service* (1907)

—— *Wayfarings: A Record of Adventure and Liberation in the Life of the Spirit* (London c. 1919)

Latham, B., *Report on the Permanent Sanitary Works and their Cost executed in the Parish of Croydon under the Authority of the Local Board of Health* (1868)

—— *A Chapter in the History of Croydon* (1909)

La Trobe-Bateman, W. F., *Memories Grave and Gay* (London 1927)

Lee, C., *Citizenship* (1893)

Major Scott, W., *The Consecration of Life* (1912)

—— *The Ejectment of 1662* (1912)

—— *The Everlasting Mercy* (1912)

—— *The Lordship of Christ* (1912)

—— *Man's Mystical Masonry* (1912)

—— *The Ordeal of Faith* (1912)

—— *The Soul's Certainty* (1912)

—— *Spiritual Renewals* (1912)

—— *The Winds of the Spirit* (1912)

—— *Christianity and War* (1914)

Mudie Smith, R. (ed.), *The Religious Life of London* (London 1904)

Marsh, T. W., *Early Friends in Surrey and Sussex* (London 1886)

Oakley Coles, J., *The Soul's Earth Life: seven Lent lectures* (1889)

Pelton, J. O., *Relics of Old Croydon* (1891)

Pereira, H. H. and Easter, A. J. T., *Sermons preached before the Mayor and Corporation* (1898)

—— *Intemperance* (London 1905)

Pike, G. H., *James Archer Spurgeon* (London 1894)

Pocock, W. W., *Sketch of the History of Wesleyan Methodism in some of the Southern Counties of England* (London 1885)

Raffe, W., *Guide to Croydon and Surrounding Neighbourhood* (1877)

Ranger, W., *Report to the General Board of Health on a Preliminary Inquiry into the Sewerage, Drainage and Supply of Water and the Sanitary Conditions of the Inhabitants of Croydon* (1849)

Rooker, J., *Seven Sermons preached at St. Matthew's, Croydon 1884* (1885)

Rule, W. H., *Recollections of my Life* (London 1886)

Sandison, A., *Alexander Sandison 1854–1912: minister of the King's Weigh House* (London 1967)

Simon, J., *Report to the Local Board of Health with regard to the Causes of Illness recently prevailing in Croydon* (1853)

Smith, S. and Sutherland, J., *Statement of the Preliminary Inquiry on the Epidemic at Croydon, together with reports by R.D. Grainger, Esq., and Henry Austin Esq., to the General Board of Health on the circumstances connected with the Epidemic attack of fever at Croydon* (1853)

Solly, H., *These Eighty Years* (London 1893)

Steinman, G. S., *A History of Croydon* (London 1834)

Stephens, W. R. W., *Life and Letters of W. F. Hook* (London 1878)

Sterry, R., *Letter to the Landowners and Ratepayers of the Parish of Croydon, 24th August 1849* (1849)

Stockwell, A. H., *The Baptist Churches of Surrey* (London c. 1912)

Suter, A. B., An Ordination Sermon (1874)

Taylor, G., *The Fall of Sebastopol* (1855)

Toulmin-Smith, J., *The Parish* (London 1854)

Trezise, W. A., *Sermon on the occasion of the attendance of the Mayor and Corporation at South Norwood Wesleyan Church* (1913)

Tyrwhitt, M. L., *Outlines of Church History connected with the Parish of St. Mark's, South Norwood* (1892)

Waddington, J., *Surrey Congregational History* (London 1866)

Walker, E. M. and Hawker, J. H., *Two Sermons in Memory of Catherine Byers* (1891)

Ward, J. W., *Croydon in the Past* (1883)

Webb, A. P., *Henry Crombie, Minister of St. Paul's Presbyterian Church* (c. 1917)

Westall, E., *On the Advantages to be derived from the adoption of the 'Local Government Act' as exemplified in Croydon* (address to South-Eastern Branch of the British Medical Association, 1865)

White, J. H., *A Short History of St. Augustine's* (1919)

White-Thompson, *Citizenship* (1909)

Wicksteed, T., *Report on the State of the Works of Drainage and Sewerage in the Town of Croydon, and on Measures proposed to remedy its Defects* (1853)

Wills, J., *The Glory of the Commonplace* (1903)

The British Library
The Croydon Citizen 1904–9
The Croydon Daily Argus 1905–8

Croydon Reference Library
Borough of Croydon Minutes and Agenda 1883–89
Church Magazines: Christ Church 1899–1914; St John's, Parish
  Church 1874–1914; St Mary Magdalene 1900–14; St Michael and
  All Angels 1884–1914; St Augustine's 1913–14; St Andrew's
  1879–1914; St James' 1889–1914; St Matthew's 1898–1914; St
  Stephen's, Norbury 1908–14; St Peter's 1878–1914; St Paul's,
  Thornton Heath 1913–14; St Paul's Presbyterian Church
  1904–14; South Norwood Holmesdale Baptist Church 1912–14;
  West Croydon Baptist Church 1903–14; Woodside Baptist Church
  1914
County Borough of Croydon Minutes and Agenda 1889–1914
Croydon Charitable Society, Annual Reports 1896–1914
Croydon General Hospital, Annual Reports 1861–1910
Croydon Gordon Boys' Home, Annual Reports 1889–1910; 'A Short
  Account of the Early Beginnings'; G. J. Murdoch, *The Reasons for
  the Transfer of the Croydon Gordon Boys' Home to the Church of England
  Society for Providing Homes for Waifs and Strays*
Croydon Guild of Help, leaflets 1908; magazine 1910–14; constitu-
  tion and rules
Croydon Rescue and Preventive Association, Annual Reports
  1883–1913
Croydon Templar Herald 1912
Croydon Union Board of Guardians Minutes 1896–1930
Croydon YMCA, Annual and Weekly Programmes 1903–13
Gray's Commercial and General Directory for Croydon 1851–61
Newspapers and Journals: *Croydon Chronicle* 1855–1912; *Croydon
  Advertiser* 1869–1914; *Norwood News* 1868–1914; *Croydon Review*
  1879–90; *Croydon Guardian* 1883–1914; *Croydon Times* 1890–1914;
  Surrey Standard 1849–55 (cuttings only)
Pigot's Directory of Surrey 1821–23
Seedtime, The Organ of the New Fellowship 1889–98
Statement of the Rents of the Charity called the Hospital of the Holy
  Trinity at Croydon, for the year ending 31st December 1867
Ward's Commercial and General Directory for Croydon 1874–1914
Warren's Commercial and General Directory for Croydon 1865–69

Parliamentary Papers
Census Reports of the Population of England and Wales – 1851,
  1861, 1871, 1881, 1891, 1901, 1911.

St Augustine's, South Croydon
Parish Magazine 1892–1913 (incomplete)

St John the Evangelist, Upper Norwood
Parochial Reports 1903–14
Parish Magazines 1877–1914 (incomplete)

St Paul's Presbyterian Church (United Reformed), South Croydon
Annual Reports 1901–14

Secondary Sources

London publications, unless otherwise stated

Agulhon, M., *Pénitents et Francs-Maçons de l'ancienne Provence* (Paris 1984)
Anon., *Boston Road Mission: the first hundred years* (Croydon 1971)
—— *Crusading for Christ: the centenary brochure of Christ Church, West Croydon 1852–1952* (Croydon 1952)
—— *Historical notes on St. Stephen's Church, Norbury and Thornton Heath* (Croydon 1949)
—— 'H. T. B. Muggeridge', *Dictionary of Labour Biography*, v (1979)
—— *South Norwood Congregational Church Centennial Brochure 1870–1970* (South Norwood 1970)
Baddeley, C. E., *The Tramways of Croydon* (Croydon 1983)
Bailey, P., *Leisure and Class in Victorian England: rational recreation and the contest for control 1830–1885* (1978)
Bailey, V., 'Salvation Army riots, the "Skeleton Army" and local authority in the provincial town', in A. P. Donajgrodski (ed.), *Social Control in Nineteenth Century Britain* (1977)
Bannerman, R., *Forgotten Croydon* (Croydon 1927)
—— *Royal Croydon* (Croydon 1934)
Bateman, H. W., *A Short History of the Church of St. John the Evangelist, Upper Norwood 1871–1937* (Croydon 1937)
Bayliss, D. A., *Retracing the First Public Railway* (Croydon 1981)
Benians, W. A., 'The Trade and Industrial Development of Croydon', *Proc CNHSS*, xiii (1962)
Berwick Sayers, W. C., *Henry Keatley Moore: a brief memoir* (Croydon 1937)
Binfield, C., *George Williams and the Y.M.C.A.* (1973)
Binfield, R., *A History of St. Phillip's Church, Norbury* (Croydon 1977)
Brandon, P., *A History of Surrey* (Chichester 1977)
Briggs, A., *Victorian Cities* (1963)

Brown, C. G., 'Did urbanization secularize Britain?', *Urban History Yearbook* (1988)

Brown, K. D., *A Social History of the Nonconformist Ministry in England and Wales 1800–1930* (Oxford 1988)

Cannadine, D., *Lords and Landlords: the aristocracy and the towns* (Leicester 1979)

—— 'The transformation of civic ritual in modern Britain: the Colchester oyster feast', *Past and Present* (1982)

Chadwick, W. O., *The Secularisation of the European Mind in the Nineteenth Century* (Cambridge 1975)

—— *The Victorian Church* (2 vols., 1966–70)

Chambers, R. F., *Strict Baptist Chapels of England, I: the chapels of Surrey and Hampshire* (Thornton Heath 1952)

Coleman, B. I., *The Church of England in the Mid-Nineteenth Century* (1980)

—— 'Southern England in the census of religious worship, 1851', *Southern History*, iii (1981)

Cox, J., *The Churches in a Secular Society: Lambeth 1870–1930* (Oxford 1982)

Cox, R. C. W., 'The old centre of Croydon: Victorian decay and redevelopment', in A. M. Everitt (ed.), *Perspectives in English Urban History* (1973)

Crossick, G., *An Artisan Elite in Kentish London* (1977)

—— (ed.), *The Lower Middle Class in Britain* (1977)

Croydon Natural History and Scientific Society, *Regional Survey* (Croydon c. 1936)

Cunningham, H., 'The metropolitan fairs; a case-study in the social control of leisure', in A. P. Donajgrodski (ed.), *Social Control in Nineteenth Century Britain* (1977)

Currie, R., *Methodism Divided: a study in the sociology of ecumenicalism* (1968)

—— A. D. Gilbert and L. Horsley, *Churches and Churchgoers: patterns of church growth in the British Isles since 1700* (Oxford 1977)

Dawe, D., 'The Smiths of Selsdon Park', *Bourne Society Local History Records*, xix (1980)

Dixon, J. (ed.), *The Church in the Community: a record of the life and work of Croydon Parish Church* (Croydon 1971)

Donajgrodski, A. P. (ed.), *Social Control in Nineteenth Century Britain* (1977)

Dyos, H. J., *Camberwell: the growth of a suburb* (Leicester 1961)

Everitt, A. M., *The Pattern of Rural Dissent: the nineteenth century* (Leicester 1972)

—— (ed.), *Perspectives in English Urban History* (1973)

Foster, E. N., *The Growth of a Parish: Shirley* (Croydon 1983)

Fraser, D., *Urban Politics in Victorian England* (Leicester 1976)

Gay, J. D., *The Geography of Religion in England* (1971)

Gent, J. B. (ed.), *Croydon: the story of a hundred years* (Croydon 1970)

Gilbert, A. D., *Religion and Society in Industrial England* (1976)

Gill, R., *Competing Convictions* (1989)

Gray, R. Q., *The Labour Aristocracy in Victorian Edinburgh* (1978)

—— 'Religion, culture and social class in late nineteenth and early twentieth century Edinburgh', in G. Crossick (ed.) *The Lower Middle Class in Britain* (1977)

Haig, A., *The Victorian Clergy* (1984)

Harrison, B. H. and Trinder, B., *Drink and Sobriety in an Early Victorian County Town: Banbury 1830–1860, English Historical Review Special Supplement*, iv (1969)

—— *Drink and the Victorians: the temperance question in England 1815–1872* (1971)

—— 'Religion and recreation in nineteenth century England', *Past and Present*, xxxviii (1967)

Heazell, F. N., *The History of St. Michael's, Croydon: a chapter in the Oxford Movement* (Croydon 1934)

Heeney, B., *A Different Kind of Gentleman: parish clergy as professional men in early and mid-Victorian England* (Hamden, Connecticut 1976)

—— *The Women's Movement in the Church of England 1850–1930* (Oxford 1988)

Hobsbawm, E. and Rudé, G., *Captain Swing* (1969)

Hobbs, D. C. H., 'The Croydon Police 1829–1840', *Proc CNHSS*, xvii (1983)

Inglis, K. S., *Churches and the Working Classes in Victorian England* (1963)

—— 'Patterns of religious worship in 1851', *Journal of Ecclesiastical History*, xi (1960)

Iremonger, F. A., *William Temple* (1948)

Isichei, E., *Victorian Quakers* (Oxford 1970)

James, T. M., 'The Inns of Croydon 1640–1840', *Collections of the Surrey Archaelological Society*, lxviii (1974)

Jones, G. Stedman, *Outcast London* (Oxford 1971)

Keith-Lucas, B., *The Unreformed Local Government System* (1980)

Kent, J. H. S., *Holding the Fort: studies in Victorian revivalism* (1978)

—— 'The role of religion in the cultural structure of the Late Victorian City', *Transactions of the Royal Historical Society*, xxiii (1973)

—— *The Unacceptable Face: the modern church in the eyes of the historian* (1987)

Lloyd, R., *The Church of England in the Twentieth Century* (2 vols, 1946–50)

Maggs, K. and D'Athe, P., *South Norwood and the Croydon Canal* (Croydon 1984)

Malcolmson, R. W., *Popular Recreations in English Society 1700–1850* (Cambridge 1972)

Marsh, P. T., *The Victorian Church in Decline: Archbishop Tait and the Church of England, 1868–1882* (1969)

Martin, J. E., *Greater London: an industrial geography* (1966)

McLaughlin, W. H., *The Foundation of St. Mary's, Croydon* (Croydon 1938)

McLeod, D. H., 'Building the "Catholic Ghetto": Catholic organisations 1870–1914', *Studies in Church History*, xxiii (1986)

—— 'Class, community and religion: the religious geography of nineteenth century England', *Sociological Yearbook of Religion in Britain*, vi (1973)

—— *Class and Religion in the Late Victorian City* (1974)

—— 'New perspectives on Victorian class religion: the oral evidence', *Oral History*, xiv (1986)

—— *Religion and the People of Western Europe, 1789–1970* (Oxford 1981)

—— *Religion and the Working Class in Nineteenth-Century Britain* (1984)

—— 'White collar values and the role of religion', in G. Crossick ed.), *The Lower Middle Class in Britain* (1977)

McMinn, R. S., *These Twenty-Five Years: St. Paul's Presbyterian Church, South Croydon* (Croydon 1926)

Meacham, S., 'The Church in the Victorian city', *Victorian Studies*, xii (1968)

Mole, D. E. H., 'The Victorian town parish: rural vision and urban mission', *Studies in Church History*, xvi (1977)

Moore, H. K. and Berwick Sayers, W. C. (eds), *Croydon and the Great War* (Croydon 1920)

Moore, R. S., *Pitmen, Preachers and Politics: Methodism in a Durham mining community* (Cambridge 1974)

Morris, J. N., 'Church and people thirty-three years on: a historical critique', *Theology*, xciv (1991)

—— 'A disappearing crowd? Collective action in late nineteenth century Croydon', *Southern History*, xi (1989)

—— 'The temperance movement in Victorian Croydon', *Proc CNHSS*, xvii (1984)

Norman, E. R., *Anti-Catholicism in Victorian England* (1968)

—— *Church and Society in England 1770–1970* (Oxford 1978)

Obelkevich, J., *Religion and Rural Society in South Lindsey 1825–1875* (Oxford 1976)

Olsen, D. J., *The Growth of Victorian London* (1976)

Paget, C. G., *Croydon Homes in the Past* (Croydon 1937)

—— *Seventy-Five Years of Progress: St. Andrew's Church, Croydon 1857–1932* (Croydon 1932)

Parsons, G. and Moore, J. R. (eds.), *Religion in Victorian Britain* (4 vols., Manchester 1988)

Percy, F. H. G., *A History of Whitgift School* (Croydon 1976)

Pevsner, N. and Cherry, B., *The Buildings of England: London II: The South* (3rd edn, Harmondsworth 1973)

Phillips, P. T., *The Sectarian Spirit: sectarianism, society and politics in Victorian cotton towns* (Toronto 1982)

Pickering, W. S. F. (ed.), *A Social History of the Diocese of Newcastle* (Stocksfield 1981)

Prest, J. M., *Liberty and Locality: Parliament, permissive legislation, and ratepayers' democracies in the mid-nineteenth century* (Oxford 1990)

Rawlins, G. C., *The Story of a Parish: the history of the parish church of St. John the Evangelist, Shirley, 1834–1956* (Croydon 1956)

Raymer, R. A., *The Congregational Church at George Street, Croydon: a history 1672–1964* (Croydon 1964)

Redlich, J. and Hirst, F. W., *The History of Local Government in England* (1903, reissued 1958)

Robson, R. S., 'St. George's Presbyterian Church, Croydon', *Journal of the Presbyterian Historical Society of England*, xxii (1920)

Roebuck, J., *Urban Development in Nineteenth Century London: Lambeth, Battersea and Wandsworth 1838–1888* (Chichester 1979)

Rowell, D. G., *Hell and the Victorians* (Oxford 1974)

Rush, R. H., *St. James Church, Croydon 1829–1933* (Croydon 1934)

Salmon, G. B., *A Centenary History of the South Norwood Methodist Church 1875–1975* (Croydon 1975)

Saunders, P., *Urban Politics: a sociological interpretation* (1979)

Sellers, I., *Nineteenth Century Nonconformity* (1974)

Shaw, N., *Whiteway: a colony in the Cotswolds* (c. 1934)

Smellie, K. B., *A History of Local Government* (3rd edn, 1957)

Sparrow, G., *The Great Swindlers* (1959)

Thompson, D. M. (ed.), *Nonconformity in the Nineteenth Century* (1972)

Thompson, F. M. L., *Hampstead: building a borough* (1974)

Thompson, P., *Socialists, Liberals and Labour: the struggle for London 1885–1914* (1967)

Thornhill, L., 'From palace to washhouse: a study of the Old Palace, Croydon, from 1780 to 1887', *Proc CNHSS*, xvii (1987)

Tönnies, F., *Community and Association* (1888, trans. 1955)

Troeltsch, E., *The Social Teaching of the Christian Churches* (1931)

Tripp, B. H., *The Story of Sanderstead* (Croydon 1922)

Turner, J. T. H., *The London, Brighton and South Coast Railway I: origins and formation* (1977)

Twilley, R. and Wilks, M., *The River Wandle* (Croydon 1974)

Vincent, J. R., *The Formation of the British Liberal Party 1857–1868* (1966)

Wald, K. D., *Crosses on the Ballot: patterns of British voter alignment since 1885* (Princeton 1983)

Waller, P. J., *Town, City and Nation: England 1850–1914* (Oxford 1983)

Ward, W. R., *Religion and Society in England 1790–1850* (1972)

Warren, H. A., 'A history of technical education, with special reference to the borough of Croydon', *Proc CNHSS*, xv (1976)

Warwick, A., *The Phoenix Suburb: a south London suburb* (Richmond 1972)

Webb, B. and S., *English Local Government: the parish and the county* (1906)

Weber, M., *The Sociology of Religion*, ed. T. Parsons (1965)

Wickham, E. R., *Church and People in an Industrial City* (1957)

Wilson, B. R., *Religion in Secular Society* (1966)

Wright, J., *Addiscombe Parish Church: its history and jubilee* (Croydon 1927)

Yates, W. N., 'The major Kentish towns in the religious census of 1851', *Archaeologica Cantiana*, ciii (1986)

Yeo, C. S., *Religion and Voluntary Organisations in Crisis* (1976)

Unpublished theses

Cox, R. C. W., 'The Urban Development of Croydon 1870–1940', unpubl. MA thesis, Leicester 1967

—— 'The Urban Development and Redevelopment of Croydon 1835–1940', unpubl. PhD thesis, Leicester 1970

Finlow, D., 'A Study of the Religious Society of Friends at Croydon 1825–1875', unpubl. thesis, Coloma College 1974

Hobbs, D. C. H., 'Nineteenth Century Addiscombe', unpubl. diploma thesis, Portsmouth Polytechnic 1985

Lancaster, B., 'The Croydon Local Board of Health and the "Croydon Case" 1849–1853', unpubl. MA thesis, Leicester 1981

Lister, R. J. M., 'The Electoral History of the Croydon School Board 1870–1903', unpubl. BA thesis, Leicester 1972

McLeod, D. H., 'Membership and Influence of the Churches in Metropolitan London, 1885–1914', unpubl. PhD thesis, Cambridge 1971

Morris, J. N., 'Religion and Urban Change in Victorian England: a case study of the borough of Croydon 1840–1914', unpubl. DPhil thesis, Oxford 1985

Tichelar, M., 'Labour Politics in Croydon 1880 to 1914', unpubl. BA thesis, Thames Polytechnic 1975

Yeo, C. S., 'Religion in Society: a view from a provincial town in the late-nineteenth and early-twentieth centuries', unpubl. DPhil thesis, Sussex 1971

Index

Liberalism, political, 90–1, 93,
106–7, 114–23, 125–6, 147,
149–50, 153–4, 165–6; and
Liberal Association, 120, 150
Liberalism, religious, 53, 82
Liberator Building Society, 150
libraries, 35–6, 155, 160–1; and
Free Libraries campaign, 156,
160–1, 170
Licensed Victuallers' and Beer-
sellers' Protection Society,
138
Lister, R. J. M., 80n
Literary and Scientific
Institution, 145–6
liturgical reform, 50, 54–6
Lloyd, R., 49
Lloyd, T., 116n, 145
Local Board of Health, 25, 29,
33, 88, 111–14, 123–6, 159;
and criticism of, 30, 34, 130,
148–54, 156
local government, 30–6, 105–23,
130–1, 147–71. *See also*
Council, incorporation, Local
Board of Health, parochial
system
London, 2, 8, 17, 135
London Chapel Building
Society, 143
London City Mission, 75,
79–80, 129, 142
London County Council, 134,
174
Longley, C. T., 62
lower middle class, 2, 19, 22,
27–8, 49; and religion, 8–9,
48, 96–7, 102

Maberley, J., 124
Mackray, A. N., 76
McLeod, D. H., 7–10, 13, 70,
174, 182
Malleson, W. T., 119, 160

Manchester, 10, 12, 21
manor of Croydon, 37; and
manorial courts, 30
Marsh, P. T., 4, 59
mayor of Croydon, 89, 140, 184
Mearns, A., 45
membership, church, 6
Merton, 17
Messent, C., 145
Methodism, 6, 48, 78. *See also*
Primitive Methodists, United
Methodist Free Church,
Wesleyan Methodists
Miall, E., 85, 115
middle classes, 27, 134, 137,
165–6, 168; and migration,
23; and religion, 7–10, 12–13,
44, 48, 70, 97–8, 142; and
urban growth, 2, 19, 22, 26
Middlesbrough, 21
Middlesex, 42
migration, 23–4, 192–4
Miller, D. B., 26n, 150, 152n
ministers, Nonconformist, role
and status, 74, 76–7, 84, 94,
129
missionary activity, 59–60,
78–80; and predestinarian
theology, 7
mission churches, 59–60, 80,
133
missions, parish, 60, 80
Mitcham, 17
Mitchiner, J. H., 98, 150
Mole, D. E. H., 69
Moore, F. W., 98–9
Moore, H., 119
Moore, H. K., 166
Moore, R. S., 6
Morden, 17
Morland, C. C., 125
Morland, J., 48, 76n
Morley, S., 144
Mormons, 99